JN417294

NEW
GOVERNANCE
ISSUES AND CHALLENGES

New Governance
Issues and Challenges

Park Jai-Chang

HU:iNE

Contents

Introduction

The South Korean government's inability to rescue the victims and properly respond to the tragic accident of *Sewol* ferry, capsized at the West coast in April of 2014, led the people to see the naked face of contemporary governing system in Korea. The corruption and rampant malpractices in the shipping industry stemming from dubious connections to bureaucrats led to the uploading of cargo far beyond its maximum capacity. The ship drained its ballast water, which sailors often call "lifesaving water," to carry more freight without any proper supervision by relevant checking authorities.

The responsible bureaucrats have been captured by the built-in connections and subsequent lobbying power established through the tradition, as in the other fields of the Korean society, in which retired government officials are hired by either private or public organizations related to their previous jobs, being guaranteed high positions and massive salaries. For instance, most of the previous chairmen of the Korea Shipping Association, a supervisory body for coastal shipping companies and safe sailing of their ships, were former officials from the Ministry of Oceans and Fisheries (Shin & Seo, 2014.04.24.).

It was also released that more than two dozen lawmakers from both the ruling and opposition parties received financial sponsorship from the Korea Ship Owners' Association for five overseas trips in the past five years (Seo, 2014.05.02.). Revelations concerning a series of sponsorships have raised suspicions as to whether the association was lobbying the legislators to have the resolution passed, which was eventually introduced and urged "policy-wise support for the marine industry to boost competitiveness for national economic development" by providing financial subsidies (Seo, 2014.05.02).

The government had crises management manuals for disaster situations, but they were useless at the actual scene of the tragedy. It was so because they were drawn up by bureaucrats lacking first-hand experiences without the knowledge of on-the-spot reguirements. The rescue teams were not trained well enough to respond properly to the rapid upsurge of needs and demands at the disaster scene. In addition to that, the extreme form of departmental egotism pertinent to government bureaucracy blocked smooth horizontal collaborations among the relevant agencies such as Coastal Guards, Marines, Navy Forces, private companies, and volunteers.

It was beyond expectation to the eyes of general public that the prime rescuers were neither the coastal guards nor the navy forces but the contracted-out private company divers even at such a critical situation, where we need dedication and commitment instead of efficiency and economy. It is also unbelievable that they stopped divers and advised them to greet high ranking government officials at such an imminent situation where they compete for a second to salvage the drowned.

Our experience with such government bureaucrats in responding to *Sewol* ferry accident has made it clear that the modern bureaucracy in Korea is no longer a source of solution but only the cause of problems. Even if we accept the general explanation that the disaster scene requires very special correspondence techniques among the relevant stake-holders and makes it very difficult to succeed, it still becomes evident that we cannot trust government and enjoy the luxury of entrusting the protection of our lives and properties to the incompetent government officials any more.

Recognizing such a sentiment widely spread among the people, the president Park Geun-Hye announced that they would like to exercise a large scale clean-up drive of the government and a remodeling of the nation. Such an announcement, however, reminds us that they still believe in the supra-rational decision-making capability of the modern bureaucracy, which could not be realized in such a rapidly changing and highly inter-connected society. Mechanistic structure of modern bureaucracy is not consistent with fluidity, flexibility, and complexity of the information society any longer.

My journey as an academic in the field of public administration has started by questioning about such institutional viability, relevance and accountability of a government. I felt dubious as to whether the government would work as a goodwill spirited problem solver of the contemporary society without being compelled by the external control of the legislature, which has been counted as a source of governmental legitimacy and people's support for democratic governance.

That is why my research focus of interests, at the initial stage, has hovered around the issue of reforming the National Assembly and after a while political parties in a perusal to promote their institutional capability to closely observe, oversee and supervise the executive (Chapter 2, 3, 4 and 5). It does not take a long time to realize, however, that it is helpless as long as the legislators do not adopt reform suggestions and stipulate relevant measures even if many ideal reform suggestions are produced. Reforming the legislature and political parties is not a matter of ideas but that of a power struggle between the established power holders as like the elected officials and the general public yearning for them to reflect their aspirations.

It is very natural for me to move my academic interest, in such a context, to find ways to empower the people vis-á-vis the government. I began to conduct researches on NGOs in the expectation that NGOs would promote, mobilize, and organize people's participation to the governing process and thus upgrade external pressure to the government including the legislature and political parties (Chapter 6, 7, 8 and 9). I also started to work at the forefront of NGO movements in Korea in an attempt to strengthen countervailing power of the people against the government. During 1990s and 2000s, there sprang many NGOs, and the magnitude of their voices in Korean society was upgraded very rapidly. It was the heydays of NGO movements in Korea.

NGOs were counted as if they were replacing even the representation role of political parties. They enjoyed a high rate of people's support and trust. It did not take long a time to realize, however, that NGOs are not the ultimate solution to our governing problem and the "NGOs' failure," in fact, is built in being based on the same logic and rationale with "government failure." As long as NGOs are operated and managed by standing staff as a voluntary delegate of the people, the same negative effects of running the government by bureaucrats take place. There arises a very serious reason that the people should govern by themselves instead of delegating their suffrage to the others.

Technological advancement also made it available to open up participatory conduits of the people owing much to the advent of information society, which provides a completely different social and political environment conducive for the wider and substantive participation of the people. It becomes very natural that they began to talk about co-producing system of government replacing indirect governing system with semi-direct democracy. Citizens are now considered as a partner in governing process being released from the passive position of being consumers of government services. The idea of new governance has become to receive wide supports. In such a context, it becomes very much important to have the people with self-reflexive power for the successful operation of the partnership government since the franchise is going to be returned back to the people in such a system of semi-direct governance. That is why I began to emphasize the importance of civic education (Chapter 1). Such shifts of research focus reflect well of my academic pilgrimage searching for solutions to better governance under the social frame of the relationship between government and citizen or state and civil society.

During my journey of searching for better governance, social environment, in which governance takes place, has changed drastically from industrial to information society and further to globalization of the world. Such a contextual change is also reflected in my researches for better governance mechanism. Globalization has brought in the emergence of global civil society by instigating and consolidating interconnectedness of the people and NGOs of the world. There were several tides of globalization in the human history. But the contemporary one is different from the previous ones in the sense that a globalizing phenomenon takes place anywhere and everywhere and thus omnipresent and holistic as well. It is so especially in the arena of civil society creating, for the first time, global civil society as a counter veiling and/or complementary force against state oriented international community of the world. We see sprouts of co-partnership between government and NGOs at global level. It is a high time to explore possibilities of global governance system and examine pending thrusts arising in the process of establishing global civil society networks. Naturally my academic focus of interests has been expanded to such topics (Chapter 7, 8, 9 and 10).

All through such a journey of my academic research, I become to learn the importance of a comparative approach and have tried to maintain a contextual understanding of political phenomena. Comparison between state and civil society, that between industrial society and information society, and that between nation state and globalizing world are the major bases of my intellectual scheme and tools leading me to read configurative maps of contemporary world. At the extension of such an endeavor, a longitudinal evaluation of the political development in Korea was ventured during the conversation with the editor of Le Banquet from France as an effort to sum up my understanding of contemporary Korean politics (Chapter 11).

This book is a collection of such articles that I produced in English alongside of my journey in searching for better governance. At the extension of such a journey to search for the alternative to contemporary governing system in Korea, I was motivated strongly to publicize this book especially when I came across with the news that Park regime was trying to remodel the nation. In other word, they were interested in reforming the inside structure of the state, which is a fruitless venture, I believe, in this informatized world. We have to adjust the vertical relationship between state and civil society itself and not simply the horizontal relationship between and among the components inside of state.

It is my humble aspiration to contribute to the pending discussion about the alternative to the current governing system in Korea by the publication of this book by sharing ideas, stimulating semi-direct democracy which I believe a temporal solution to our pending thrusts, providing rationale for the reform minded social movements to expand citizen's participation. I trust wisdom and sincerity of people instead of their political and administrative delegates especially in this era of informatization and subsequent globalization.

I seized the wake-up call triggered by the tragic accident of *Sewol* ferry in the sense that it produced every reason to withhold our centuries-old confidence in the government and remind the weight and importance of general public in our governing process. I tribute my heartfelt condolences to the victims of the sunken ship and the sunken rationale mobilized to legitimize the monopoly of governing opportunity by the state as well. I would like to take this opportunity to express my sincere gratitude to Simon Kim of the Texas State Alliance of YMCAs for his proofreading. I also would like to acknowledge the financial support from the Research Institute for Korea Future Governance. My special thanks go to Hankuk University of Foreign Studies Knowledge Center, for venturing to publish this book as a token of support, I believe, for the ideas and suggestions shared in this book.

Park Jai-Chang

Part One

Reforming Politics in Korean Society

Chapter 01

Deepening of Democracy and Civic Education

I. Current State of Democracy in Korea

Korea is unique in the sense that it has achieved both economic and political developments since World War II. It makes us assume unconsciously that democracy and economic development advance side by side. Indeed there are many empirical research outputs arguing economic development is a precondition for democracy, or at least works as an intermediary variable, and Korea has been cited frequently as a representative example. However, it cannot be denied such understanding has stimulated us to assume that economic development and democracy keep continue to grow in a smooth and gradual manner, which is likely to lead us to believe that democracy will be strengthened as long as economy flourishes.

The current state of Korea, as the 9th largest country in the world in terms of international trade volume, however, implies that there are different sorts of democracy in terms of its quality and makes us realize that there are a certain point where economic development doesn't guarantee development of democracy any more. Korean society has expected that democracy in Korea would mature with constant economic development, as the natural extension of the achievement of procedural democracy that has been counted as such after 1987. Deepening of democracy was perceived as the obvious route. But there are rising concerns for the growth of democracy, which appears to be less successful than expected and even concerns for the democratic deficits or declining democracy.

Though we achieved the procedural democracy, the citizens' trust for the government is not high as we can see in recent incident of the Navy corvette *Cheonan*[1], and there is prevalent cynicism toward politics and politicians, and the level of distrust for the current political system is critical as candlelight vigils[2] have shown. A sense of political efficacy is questioned both in individual level, as the sense of confidence that one can have an impact on public affairs by participating in the political process, and in institutional level, as the measure of efficiency that one conceives how much government is efficient in solving social problems.

---

1) The **Cheonan sinking** occurred on 26 March 2010, when the Korea Navy ship carrying 104 personnel, sank off the country's west coast near Baengnyeong Island in the Yellow Sea, killing 46 seamen. A South Korean-led official investigation carried out by a team of international experts concluded that the warship had been sunk by a North Korean torpedo fired by a midget submarine.

2) Roughly speaking, South Koreans have started a candlelight vigil in May 2008. The protest has started against the US beef import and anxiety on mad cow disease to ask the government and president Lee Myung-Bak to reconsider the details of US beef import agreement. 70% of people who joined the protest were teenage girls and their parents, and lots of teachers, children, businessmen and students went to speak out their opinions (CNN Report, 2008.05.25).

Citizenship and political freedom in terms of legal structure and institutionalization of governing process surely have grown through the democratization process, but in social-structural level, democratic practice has not been internalized enough to be a part of everyday life in every corner of social activities (Frame & Khan, 2007: 1). We need more fairness in the process of political competition like the elections, the expansion of political freedom of free press, assembly and association, openings of more opportunities for civic participation in governmental process, the more responsiveness of representatives for their constituencies, and the expansion of the political, economic equality. Some might say that the level of democracy in our society stays at elementary. There would be numerous factors contributing to such democratic deficits or stalemate in Korea. I will discuss endogenous and exogenous factors, which can be found when we search the reasons inside of the society or outside.

II. Stalemate of Democracy in Korea: Exogenous Factors

If we try to find the reasons from outside of our society that democracy in Korea fails to consolidate further and keeps to stale, one of them would be the global characteristics of our times. The globalization of market order or the expansion of social networks, which occurs beyond the borders of nation states, brings interference effects on the domestic political process of any nation state that has worked only within a national boundary. The difference in negotiation power between the capital and the labor, which results from the fact that the capital can move freely beyond the borders of nations while the labor can't in time of the globalization, and the recognition of this difference causes the labor to realize how unrealistic it is to conciliate and/or compromise through the current pluralistic political system. It was natural for the labor to doubt the usefulness of constitutional order that promises democracy based on pluralism. And they are likely to be tempted by a hard-line position that seeks the group interest through conflicts and fights rather than conversation and compromise within establishments.

This is the other side of our present situation that liberal democratic system has been hollowed out by being captured by multinational corporations and interest groups. It also means that the policy making process dominated by the professional experts transcending national boundaries, not by the citizens who are distanced from the process geographically, cannot be a bastion of democracy. Such phenomenon reminds us theory of the managerial revolution in global level. The neo-liberalism, in accompany with globalization, degenerates citizens, the main agent of participation, into consumers who obsessed with narrow interest and, thus, citizens have been driven to make choices among the limited alternatives provided by the government. Downsizing democracy is unavoidable as long as citizens communicate with their representatives through online survey or market research. Though a survey collects citizen opinion, it is still a unilateral accumulation of information on the side of political leaders, not bilateral one. We are all aware that this has caused the world to suffer from political distrust and hatred.

The story does not end here. Owing much to the advent of global government, functions of nation states based on national boundaries are constrained by interventions and mediations of the global government. Regional collaborative organizations, like NAFTA, ASEM and EU, and global collaborative organizations, like UN, WTO, and G20, are empowering and are aggressively intervening and influencing in policies that had been made by individual nation states independently. The opportunities for participation in the policy making process in these organizations, however, are not fairly or freely distributed to the general citizens. As a result, the advent of global government is practically causing distortion and downsizing of the representativeness of citizens.

Korea is not an exception. It is facing the limitation where the established theory of liberal democracy works just as prospective reality, not as retrospective reality. This diagnosis goes well with in parallel perspectives that in case of Korea, the imitation development theory (or catch up theory) is not useful anymore. The imitation development theory explains that the economic and political growth was possible in spite of its constraints as an "impaired nation" because it has imitated and promoted development policies of developed nations and that this imitation development strategy is useful only when external and international environment is supportive and favorable. The problem is that current international environment is hard to satisfy the conditions as the past and so that it's hard to promote economic and political development as they did.

These perspectives are named as so called "the development trap theory of semi-developed country" and are related to "uselessness of pro-American inertia" or to the argument that we need to get out of the "confinement to American imagination," because the object of imitation was mainly U.S.A. They reconsider the usefulness of the strategy from "flying geese model" where a nation becomes a member of a formation flight which is led by America and seeks the development by harvesting crumbs from the formation. And they argue that we need to rigorously question whether to stay in the formation when the collision of globalization and nationalism becomes tense.

The more fundamental problem is that it is becoming harder to vitalize national economy using the global expansion of free market systems or to realize the dream of constructing a nation based on global standard adjusted to our needs and demands. And if we foster mercantilism while emphasizing the opening of market and cooperation unilaterally, it will obviously stimulate nationalistic response and resistance from the other side. It is also true that we need strong solidarity in our nation more than ever to endure the push from the massive outside capital to force the global standard and the pressure of maintaining one-centricism led by U.S.A.

However, if we overstress the closed nationalism as North Korea does, it will only bring self-destruction to us as repeating isolation and decline. It seems obvious that we need to nurture the republican patriotism and loyalty based on civic solidarity and communality, not the nationalism constrained by historical and cultural boundary like language, geography, race and religion. We need to modify the concept of nationalism so that it can accept multicultural families and immigrant workers as members of our society and they can participate in political process without discrimination and have affection and loyalty for the community they belong to.

This demand for the open nationalism is also brought up by the perspectives that the reason that we see democracy in Korea has been staled and have pessimistic view is because we have judged by American standard locked in American imagination. They suggest that we need to reflect on misunderstanding or error resulting from a lack of effort to evaluate the current state of democracy in Korea using Korean standards. It's natural for them to address that it is the time to establish Korean standards, which leads us to consider the endogenous factors that cause the stalemate of democracy in Korea.

III. Stalemate of Democracy in Korea: Endogenous Factors

After 1987 system, there has been a rapid transition to information society in Korea. Though it causes the explosion of the factors for social conflicts, there was lack of concerns about the modification or reform of conflict management institution or about designing new alternatives. Korea has made rapid transition from industrial society to information society even before transition from agrarian society to industrial society could be completed. Because of that, we have threefold overlapping structure where agrarian society, industrial society and information society coexist. Naturally factors for social conflicts have increased and it was hard to pursue and build common interest. It is a characteristic of information society that fosters expansive reproduction of social conflicts, as well as that helps to drive the social consensus.

The mobility of information has increased interchanges and interdependence between public and private areas and made the line between public and private interest ambiguous, and this is making it hard for us to reach public consensus. Meanwhile, the narrowness of preferred information circulation promotes fragmentation, specialization, and individualization of social relationship, causing the trouble in finding communal denominators. Social relations are becoming more and more complex, professional, and technical. Now it is hard to chase a causal relationship and to reach a policy consensus based on it. Even if we happen to succeed in developing alternative policies, its utility might be reduced by the interference effect that can occur when we intervene with policies into the society to make social relationships better in a way. Democracy is suffering from such retrogressive phenomena.

Moreover, utilities of the traditional political institutions cannot be guaranteed with the advent of the information society. Political parties have monopolized the role as windows for public inputs in the process of the public's political participation. However, in information society that transcends the limit of time and space, it's not easy anymore to keep their utility as a device to make mediation and agreement through staged, gradual, and consecutive process. Even before a political party can articulate the meaning of a specific phenomenon, collect preferences and opinions of the interested and make a decision, the information will spread fast to all over the country through information communication technologies and members of society will be already divided into supporters and objectors about this issue. The time and the space for mediation and agreement vanished.

As the government's overload theory that is based on transition cost theory or exchange failure theory suggests, there is a rapidly increasing need for direct connections between the government and the public based on the consideration of the high speed of information circulation and the volatility of social relationship, but it is not being followed by the efforts to make the alternative. The result is a gap or a cleavage between the institutional capability of the government and the public's increased desire for the political participation, as was seen in the site of recurrent candlelight vigils. Despite that social structures and relationships are already on the cutting edge of digital age, corresponding political institutions and governmental organizations are still staying in analog age. Korean society failed in systematic response and adjustment to time differences between the civil society and the representative government or the modern administrative state because it had the misfortune to be swallowed by the giant typhoon from the dimension of cultural anthropology, that is, information society.

We can easily find the explanation that political development can be languished or even regressive when there is an unfilled gap between the institutional capability of the government and the public's aspiration for political participation in the theoretical framework of Huntington (Huntington, 1991). According to researchers following Huntington's theory, democracy in Korea is experiencing recurrent recessions because there are outbursts of participation that established political institutions and process cannot cope with and it can be explained as "excessive democracy" or "compressive growth stress" (Kim, 2010) in that these outbursts became possible by virtue of democratization and economic development. These perspectives lead to the conclusion that to protect the rationality of democratic political system from excessive political participations of the unprepared public, we need to give attention to the rational role and professional judgment of democratic elites instead of reducing the public's political participation. It would be more favorable and rational for the public with common knowledge if they focus on the selection of elite with professional knowledge and education to delegate the government administration rather than on the direct participation in the policy-making process.

In that sense, the election has important meaning as a process to select democratic elites. The election makes it possible for the public to politically control, watch, and replace elected officials and to call them accountable to the promises they made. Generally, the election consists of two elements: one is the broad area where the various factors constraining electoral process interact and another one is the narrow area where the transformation from the votes that each party and candidate win to the seats is made after an election. Election campaigns and the voting systems as methods used to assign seats are the examples of the latter. In case of the former, the electoral system with many regulations causes voter's apathy and the retrogressive environment of elections such as the party system based on regional hegemony, candidates nomination by central party and the aggravation of intra-party conflicts is restricting the space for the public's participation and the motives, which calls for the efforts to improve the predictability, accessibility, policy-oriented approach, fairness, and spontaneity.

If the electoral system, especially the constituency system, does not promise the fair and open representativeness, democratization process set off by outburst of desire for political participations will not guarantee democratic soft landing however elections go well. Thus, the constituency system should allow significantly the freedom of political expression and electoral campaign and, more importantly, by adhering to the principle of the representativeness, it should contribute to the realization of democratic values. In that sense, it is important to search the alternatives for the regionalism which is the most regressive factor of practices in Korean elections, but it is more important to thoroughly look for a way to maximize citizen participation.

From these perspectives, we come to wonder if democratic soft landing will be possible just with the redesign of government organizations or institutional reform. Increasing adequacy of systems, like the constituency system, is on the supply dimension in terms of deepening of democracy and a question of how citizen will correspond to such systems is on the demand dimension, which is never less important than anything. So we need to work on both downward and upward reform, which suggest that in terms of electoral process, we need to consider more fundamental problem of the civil society development as well as the constituency system reform.

With regard to the delay in deepening of democracy, there have been assertions that one of the reasons is a gap that is made because the speed of the civil society development couldn't keep up with the speed of political democratization. However, the suffrage expands and the freedom of political participation is guaranteed, it's hard to expect democratic soft landing without the vitalization of civil society which functions as a leverage of making a balance with government power. As we have seen, the general characteristics of perspectives emphasizing the civil society development is that it focuses more on independent supervision or surveillance in order to secure the government responsibility, rather than on the quantitative and qualitative improvement of the citizen participation in the political process.

It seems to be natural that these demands for associational democracy pay attention to sudden rise of NGOs and the social reform movement of civic organizations. And this is why Korean society was so enthusiastic for the rise of NGOs. The perspectives that see NGOs or civic organizations as a panacea solving all social problems, however, have lost their persuasive power when distrust about civic organizations without citizens spread and the conflict between supporters for "the alliance of reform forces" and "strengthening of checks for powers" arise inside civil society movement organizations. Naturally, there are rising doubts in the strategy of approaching democratic consolidation after democratization through the civil society development, due to its monism and its idealistic imagination about democracy. The one of the more fatal flaws of the democratic consolidation strategy through the civil society development is that it lacks the positive verification whether the civil society development will automatically promote the democratization of state power. So the more fundamental job is in discovering why and how civil society works as checks and balances for state power, not in a civil society development itself.

This awareness of issues and reality has asked for the demand for participatory democracy. When we see excessive democracy or the outbursts of desire for political participations in the perspective of participatory democracy, the problem is not in the outbursts of desire for political participations itself but in the fact that institutional devices to embrace these outbursts are not enough or not working properly. That is because the key factor in solving this problem is not growing the ability to keep watch on and resist the government, as the civil society development theory sees, but reflecting or investing the potentials and energy of civil society into the deliberation process of current issues. It is that we need to vitalize a state, which is downsizing itself falling into a trap of neo-liberalism, through the expansion of political participation and to reflect the citizens' voice, erupting irregular participations into the regular and established participation process.

This includes various forms of governance system emphasizing civic participation in the extension of the government failure theory: participating in government committees or appointing a civil representative as a surveillant or partner in the government administration like the citizen participatory budgeting system. This kind of participatory democracy, however, bears the possibility of being misused as a kind of mobilization mechanism by political elites and, as the result of that, dangerousness of promoting the appearance of "new tyranny." And, above all things, participatory democracy theory has a limitation that its understanding of political power is very naïve. It sees the expansion of civil participation as a key factor but ignores the explanation about power struggles and political process. So, questions about people who are participating in participatory democracy, specifically who they are, will be easily raised.

This awareness promotes the discussion about deliberative democracy. The key point of the problem is not expanding range and space of political participation but securing qualitative deliberations and communication between the government and society through political participation. It suggests various forms of consensus-building decision-making mechanism aiming collaborative democracy. Civil jury system, town hall meeting systems, and Dynamic planning Charrette are the examples. Some of them have adopted, but most of them are still in the proposition state. This has brought the awareness that crucial factors for deepening of democracy are ultimately in securing civil leadership, and this works as an opportunity to give attention to political and social meaning of volunteers.

IV. Existential Citizen and Civic Education

After all, the deepening of democracy after initial democratization depends on whether we can effectively transform from the elite-oriented to citizen-centered political culture. It is because democracy dynamically evolves or develops through the interaction between political institutions or designs and citizens' correspondence to them. The problem is that before deepening of democracy, there are only teleological citizens, making it hard to find existential citizens. Liberal democracy by normatively formed citizens, not by real citizens, must lack substances and simply encourages false consciousness. This has been clearly shown by civil society movement without citizen. In this circumstance, control for government organizations would not be effective, resulting in the increase of political costs such as corruption or an abuse of power.

The problem is that existential citizens cannot be cultivated overnight. Existential citizens, unlike teleological citizens, are not formed by status given by the legal and institutional authority of the government, but grow with the accumulation of citizenship that can be achieved by continuous effort of members of society in the historical and social context of a given society. Thus, the effort for deepening of democracy cannot be achieved by the tactic action determined overnight because of the pressure of reform demand. We need to predict the reform demand beforehand and deal with it in the long term. But if we don't interfere in the matter of accumulation of citizenship or depend on historical trends of it, it will be harder to achieve effectively what we expect.

So there is no need to reiterate the need for dealing with the matter of accumulation of citizenship more aggressively by systematic ways. And the one of the alternatives trying strategic approach is the civic education. Citizenship is one of the cultural characteristics, which is developed and is made possible to accumulate with the knowledge of democracy, democratic values, and the practices of techniques or skills necessary for the operation of democracy. This does not close the possibility for different opinions about the claims that democratic civic education will grow the citizenship of a society and, moreover, work as a key factor to change political culture. There have been debates among negative view, eclectic view, and positive view.

According to negative viewers, civic culture of a society changes gradually and progressively over a long period of time and works with political, economic, and social factors such as economic modernization, shifts in generations, long-term experience and exposure to democratic institution, shifts in political power, and activities of responsible opposite parties, thus making it limited to change political culture by democratic civic education. It includes mainly traditional structural determinism which argues that it's hard to attract and change civic culture with short-term motivation because individual political attitudes and cultures, they think, are determined by experiences from childhood. This means that political, social, and economic factors which affect individual childhood, factors like socioeconomic status, are the key components defining political culture, thus making it hard to be changed by factors outside of a system. It can be said that it is based on static view.

Eclectic viewers, on the other hand, argue that first-hand political experiences determine political culture. They think that perception in current economic status, assessment of government competitiveness and experiences of government power define individual tolerance for others, trust in social institutions, and political efficacy. They put emphasis on political experience in adulthood and are different from negative viewers in that childhood experience can be strengthened, modified and transformed by after-childhood experience even if political, social, economic order which defines childhood experience is the key factor determining individual political orientation. There is a reciprocal relationship that political and economic system of a society affects members' political orientation and also this orientation constrains the system (Almond & Verba, 1980), which is mainly argued by researchers who emphasize the life time learning model (Mishler & Rose, 2001).

Positive viewers put emphasis on democratic civic education

for adults, most of all the effect of participating and experiencing NGOs. According to them, democratic civic education directly influences on individual democratic attitudes, values, and behaviors and contributes to the accumulation of civic culture in a society at any time. So it tends to give attention to the role of advocacy NGOs that promote the participatory learning effect. They assert that individual political perception and attitudes determine political behaviors of members of society and the result of these political behaviors is the political order and institution. So if we define political culture as political norms or customs, belief systems, ways of thinking, the attitudes and orientations toward political system that members of a society share, we cannot ignore the importance of civic education effect (Pattie *et al.*, 2004). Democratic civic education is about cultivation of citizenship and without citizenship, it will be hard to achieve the accumulation of social capital or the establishment of practices that favor tolerance and compromise and that approves the difference, which is the key characteristic of democratic political culture.

Korean society, which went through democratization process and is facing the problem of how to enter the stage of deepening of democracy, needs to pay attention to the task of reforming political, social, and economic systems and of improving effectively individual identity that is making new orders by dynamically interacting with political, social, and economic institutions or organizations. If we attribute the cause of democracy stalemate to globalization as exogenous changes and its regressive components, the urgent priority will be the strengthening of individual awareness of these changes in global environment; if we think of the advent of informational society and corresponding radical changes in social structures, as endogenous changes, as problems, the improvement of civic awareness and understanding of these changes will become the important matter. Korean society overwhelmed by new social structural order changing and constructing internally and externally. If we understand and react to the new social order only based on the social order and experience we had in our childhood, this will cause social conflicts and confrontation and make it difficult to open the road to tolerance and cooperation. It is urgent that individual citizen understands new social order through new civic education and develops corresponding and appropriate standards on their own terms.

This does not mean that we do not need any radical changes in political institutions or organizations corresponding to the changes in social structures. We should not ignore the fact that existing political institutions and organizations are too lethargic to react effectively to new social structural demand. And even if new institutions and organizations are formed, we should keep in mind that it is individual citizen that eventually interprets, performs, and corresponds to new ones. The change in a society is the kind of a thing that is dynamically shaped with the interaction between upward and downward reforms. It is also the problem that current Korean society has no immediate alternative that we can seek for deepening of democracy if we agree on negative view. In case of eclectic view, it does not deny the fact that making changes in the frame of individual awareness of democracy is the one of important factors for social and cultural changes. So to cope with the problem of deepening of democracy that Korean society is facing currently, we cannot but agree with positive view that emphasize political-cultural approach and cannot but focus on civic education.

V. Civic Education as Political Process

We need to keep in mind that civic education is itself a highly political process and has the characteristics of power struggle. It raises the question if the effect of democratic civic education can be distributed to all members of a society in a balanced way so to guarantee the equality and the fairness which are the key component of democracy. Unfortunately, it is not easy to answer this question. Civic education itself is related with the accessibility to and the ability of understanding relevant information: socially superior groups are relatively more accessible to this kind of education, and it is highly possible that it works as the basic resource for power. In other words, civic education has the characteristic that fortifies the status of socially superior groups, which means that the degree of the effect of civic education are different among different social groups and that it can cause some groups to become more democratic while other groups not to.

The higher the degree of democratization in a society that is receiving civic education is, the bigger the effect of democratization of political social systems through civic education is. If a society is already democratized, it will make the opportunity for the access to informational resource and participatory learning opportunity for members of that society being distributed more fairly, and this will reduce the difference in citizenship among members of the society, resulted by civic education, and the polarization of the degree of democratization. The lower the social demand or desperate need for civic education is, the larger the effect of civic education enhancing citizenship becomes. In the opposite case, the contribution of civic education to the democratization process will get smaller. In that sense, civic education falls into self-contradiction.

But this is nothing less than a strong suggestion that effect of civic education is greater in a society with a process of deepening of democracy than in a society with a process of democratization, if we compare them. Current Korean society, which is experiencing recurrent stalemate before deepening of democracy, urgently needs civic education. The problem is whether we can measure the civic education effect on an individual or a society. Even if we agree on positive view, the very concept of citizenship is itself vague and many-sided, resulting in the difficulty in concrete evaluation, and, moreover, there are so many factors influencing on the degree of citizenship and political culture of a society where citizen belongs (Dee, 2003: 1). So it is not easy to prove the relationship between input resources and collected effects of civic education and, thus, it will be hard to show tangible accomplishments or benefits of it. This will limit the persuasion for the necessity of democratic civic education, bearing the risk of lowering the support for it.

There is a far more difficult question than problems about conditions of civic education: whether members of society can make consensus about the cause the civic education will provide. When we identify problems the current Korean society is facing, the urgent ones are the understanding and reflection of global citizenship, new concept of open nationalism, electronic democracy, associational democracy, participatory democracy and deliberative democracy. Civic education involves struggles because the concept itself deals with the power relationship and it has characteristics of political process which promote diverse interests. So it is difficult for members of a society to reach consensus or an agreement point about what they need to focus on in civic education out of aforementioned problems, and it also is not easy for civic education to be provided worldwide with systematic forms. As a result, we face the problem that we should not over-evaluate function of civic education pulling political democratization.

Nevertheless, I would like to point out that democratic civic education is an almost only alternative and might be the last resort for deepening of democracy. It means that though we cannot say that civic education is the best alternative for deepening of democracy, it is hard to search for other alternatives other than this. Individual perception and understanding of democracy, and changes in attitudes will be eventually required for deepening of democracy, whatever alternative we look for. This is the reason that makes us obsessed with democratic education.

Chapter 02

Legislative Reform Directions and Issues

I. Introduction

It is very natural for the proponents of legislative reform to conceive political reform as a precondition to overall social reform. And legislative reform, to overall political reform. Any reform suggestions to Korean National Assembly cannot be an exception from such a way of understanding reform strategies. That is, without the reform of the National Assembly, which has long been perceived as one of the fundamental causes of social retrogressions and distortions in Korea, it is impossible to achieve overall social reform at all.

Such a reform strategy is all the more demanding since any reform measures have a tendency to alter present situation (Caiden, 1982: 92-3) by its own nature. It is very natural that any reform measures alter the pre-existing power relations. It also should be reminded that such an altering nature of reform deepens conflicts and confrontations within a society, which becomes inherent in the reform process. Therefore, it is an imperative for any reform suggestions to be concerned of promoting and maintaining, at least, political integration and stability. Judging from a normative standpoint of view, managing such political integration and stability is the institutional raison d'etre of the legislatures (Jewell & Patterson, 1977: 6-11). There is no need to underline that vitalizing such a role of legislatures is the important precondition for any smooth and steady reform process of any society.

In Korea, whose reform measures have mostly been initiated and driven by the chief of the executive, the role of the National Assembly becomes all the more crucial. In such downward-directed reform process, it becomes more important that the will of reform initiators and direction of reform be fully spread down to the general public from the government leadership, which requires an effective information flow or communication mechanism between them. As the legislature is composed of the representatives of the people, it has the relative advantage in functioning as such an information mediator or transmitter between the center of power and the periphery (Bosley, 1977: 3-4).

In this regard, the fact that most of the reform objectives driven by the executive leaders fail to reach to the lower echelon of the governmental hierarchy (Kho, 1993: 12) is an undeniable indicator that the division of labor among the tripartite branches of government has not been maintained properly in the reform process. As a matter of fact, there is a rising criticism that the president seems to be a sole runner in reform process and so much emphasis is laid upon moral objectives of reform as to the extent that such attitude reminds even a tyrannical model of governance. This implies that the executive leadership initiated reform is in the lack of effective control of itself. Being reminded of the fact that the major roles of the National Assembly is to control the executive, such a relative lack of self-control implies that it was not effectively controlled by the National Assembly. Defining reform as an effort or attempt by government leaders to change status quo and to establish new social order (Mosher, 1967: 494), the final step of any reform measure should necessarily be to legislate necessary stipulations through the National Assembly. For the legislation is the most effective mean to establish a new order and to revise social system accordingly, which is possible only through the authorized deliberation process inside of the National Assembly.

In this regard, it is impossible to expect a successful reform without the National Assembly playing a leading role. Nevertheless, due to the authoritarian regimes of the past days in Korea which have caused over-emphasizing implementation capacity rather than consensus building one, resulting in an unbalanced development, the National Assembly could not but function in a distorted way and be hindered from development (Collier, 1979: 41). Therefore without the normalization and revitalization of its functions, the National Assembly will fail to be the driving engine of social reform. To summarize, reform of the National Assembly is the uppermost prerequisite for successful reform of social structure in Korea.

The idea that reform should be launched first within the National Assembly is not conformable to conventional development theories. According to the traditional development theories, only when the reform of overall political system including power structure of government is accomplished can the reform of the legislative system be achieved. Such a theory or perspective makes it difficult to operationalize concrete and practical measures necessary to promote political development. And it falls in a tautological fallacy also. It is very logical and natural for any political reform to include legislative reform since legislative system is a sub-system of the whole political system. In that sense, such a strategy falls in a sort of tautology.

On the other hand, however, when we approach it from a completely opposite perspective as like legislative reform should be taken prior to political reform, it becomes much easier to develop and suggest practical and concrete measures to b taken for legislative reform. Seen from the philosophy from which the legislative institutions are founded, the legislature is created at the extension of social community. It is still true, however, that the routinized working mechanism of the legislature reminds the traditional form of an organization with a managerial dimension. Therefore, the development of legislature acts as an "independent variable" for social development, and accordingly the managerial dimension of the legislature should also be regarded as an "independent variable" for the legislative development. In this sense, the development of legislature's managerial dimension naturally becomes a core determinant for the development of overall social system.

In conclusion, Korean society seen in 2002 is placed at the most crucial juncture of reforming the National Assembly, especially from the managerial perspective.

II. Theories and Strategies of Legislative Reform

It is not an easy task to apply an objective and scientific theory to the real world of legislative reform and find suitable measures. Most of the existing reform measures have an inclination to overemphasize certain values and keep normative elements (Shaw, 1977: 396). It owes much to the fact that most of the reform leaders, consciously or unconsciously, set their goals following an a priori model which they personally prefer, and expect or advise the legislators to follow the same steps to reach to that goal or objective (Shaw, 1977: 396). Moreover, it is equally difficult to reach a consensus among diverse a priori models and to decide upon a certain measure accordingly. Since it is the legislators themselves who implement legislative reform measures at the final last, it is in a sense meaningless that the outsiders as a third party suggest reform directions according to their own preferences or judgments. Therefore, in dealing with legislative reform from a vantage point of third party or objective researcher, it is important that the task be limited only to supporting or advising the legislators after analyzing and evaluating such a priori models or goals and distinguishing their differences and similarities so that it may facilitate the process of decision-making and settlement on the issue of legislative reform.

In this regard, the first step is to settle competing concepts of representation among numerous actors interacting in the legislative process (Manning, 1994: 2-5). Among the same party members, different parties, legislators and constituents, there is no agreement upon the most ideal and normative relationship between legislators and constituents (Manning, 1994: 2). Based on the delegate theory of representation, for instance, legislators' main role is supposed to simply represent policy consensus assuming that the voters have already reached the agreements on policy directions. On the other hand, according to the mandate theory of representation, the legislators are conceived as like debtors, who have the obligation to fulfill the public commitments they have made during their election campaigns. To elaborate, this creates the perception that legislators need to choose only between being a delegate or a trustee according to their own needs and judgments. In other words, following the trustee theory of representation, a legislator should participate in the legislative process following his/her own judgments and choices. For this theory assumes that it is impossible to predict or propose specific policies during the election process, and therefore equally impossible to reach an agreement or settlement beforehand.

At any rate, such diversity among the perceptions about the role of legislators brings difference in opinions regarding resources, decision-making system and modes of conduct required for performing the roles. Accordingly this will be followed by diverse opinions on what particular function or role of the legislature should be enforced through the reform measures (Rieselbach, 1978: 1). For example, due to the diversity of opinions, different priority will be given among the different roles of representation, policy-making, and close observation of the executive. When the emphasis is given to the representation role, more efforts will be put in promoting open, transparent, and direct deliberation of bills by means of enacting a law on information disclosure, improving the appealing and petition system, introducing a new code of ethics or a law on asset disclosure of legislators and etc. In case of emphasizing the policy making role, more consideration will be placed on professional, scientific, and efficient means of deliberating bills, by reorganizing the structures, rules, and procedures within legislatures, which will include measures to reorganize committee system or improve the speaking right of the individual legislators. When the weight is put on controlling the executive, greater emphasis will be put on expanding the supply of information or promoting both the quality and the quantity of the legislative support system. In short, there are many specific measures of reform ranging within a great variety.

On the other hand, this fact also implies that there are diverse perspectives or approaches for a reform. Different opinions challenge each other about which aspect should be reformed first. From a power structural approach, the priority will be insisted on being given to bringing plurality in the power relations within the legislature. For the unified power structure within the legislature will harm individual legislator's freedom and equality, thereby limiting equal discussion or free and individual expression of opinions. Consequently, top priority will be given to promoting plurality within the legislature by such measures as reorganizing the structure or legal measures to reestablish the relationship between the legislature and the political parties, and between the legislature and the executive. However, while such an approach tends to neglect managerial aspects such as procedures, rules, and techniques in running a legislature, the managerial technique-oriented approach emphasizes them as the main agendas of reform. It emphasizes the importance of managerial aspects such as rules and procedures in handling bills, means of collecting information, and arranging legislative bureaucrats and, etc. That is this approach emphasizing the organizational dimension of the legislature and focusing on correcting such problems as like inefficiency and irrelevancy of its management. On the other hand, a cultural approach deals with improving value systems or conventions of the society within which the legislature exists. For example, based on this approach, a society rooted in agriculture is originally homogeneous and lacks plurality in its value system, and therefore easily conforms to uniformity, authoritarianism and accepts unilateral orders from the upper echelon of hierarchy. In this kind of society, people are reluctant to suggest diverse individual opinions, have few opportunities of discussion, and also lack in recognizing the needs of diversity itself. Within the same context, ascriptive values centered on primary groups, military values of overemphasizing the goals and results, formalism being concerned too much to the others, and sentimentalism being detached from reasoning are the exemplary elements estimated as anti-democratic and thus work as hindrances to the smooth flow of legislative works. However, the ultimate goals of these diverse approaches could be classified into two categories: promotion of the legislature's responsiveness and upgrading its managerial rationality (Grumm, 1979: 3). To promote legislature's responsibility, democracy or representation and efficiency is tantamount to, in the end, enhancing its responsiveness to the people. Nevertheless, there are varying opinions regarding which direction the legislatures should respond. When it is conceived important to respond to the needs and demands of individual voters, the focus will be placed on improving and enhancing measures to facilitate communication with the constituents. On the other hand, when they view it more important to respond to the practical public needs of the society, the focus will be put on enhancing the legislature's ability to collect information and investigate materials so as to make an objective analysis and come up with more efficient and relevant alternatives, whereas those who wish to enhance the legislature's own rationality seeks to reorganize the decision-making system on the base of "rational decision-making model" (Etzioni, 1967: 385-6). So that the main focus of reform goes to enhancing mechanical efficiency and frugality through the reorganization of legislative structures and procedures. In general, as for legislatures whose level of institutionalization is relatively low, the first goal will be to establish and stabilize the main bodies of the legislature, in which case enhancement of its responsiveness will be the first priority. As the legislature becomes more and more institutionalized, the focus will be shifted to enhancing the managerial rationality of the institution. In short, achieving openness and transparency of the legislature is prioritized to enhancing efficiency.

However, as for what will be the ultimate goal to achieve by enhancing responsiveness and rationality, still diverse opinions are vying each other (Rieselbach, 1978: 3). Those who emphasize that the legislature is a governmental body composed of elected public officials advocate theory of legislative supremacy, according to which the goal of reform should be laid on recovering the original supremacy of the legislature over the other branches of government including the executive. On the other hand, those who oppose to this theory, in that it is unrealistic and unpractical in the contemporary social structure, promote the theory of legislative subordination. Acknowledging that, in actuality, the executive has greater capability in policy making, they argue that the right of policy making should be entrusted to the executive, while the legislature should put more efforts to improving its service to the public and to enforcing the function of overseeing the executive. Still, those who would like to promote the co-equal relationship between the legislature and the executive argue that, since the legislative reform should be led by legislators themselves, neither of the theories is suitable. That is, while promoting legislative subordination is unpractical, asking for legislative supremacy is also being over-obsessed with normative obligations. Accordingly, the goal of the reform should be sought in reaching equilibrium between the legislature and the executive.

However, in addition to the above-mentioned diverse perspectives, more alternatives could be conceived as to whether reform should be the goal itself or the means to accomplish another goal. In this regard, rather than seeking a single goal or direction of reform being based on a priori model, it would be better to develop and suggest really wide range of goals and objectives reflecting outcomes of the needs assessment of the legislature and let the legislators themselves take one among the alternatives suggested on their preferences.

III. Reestablishing the Functional Locus of the National Assembly

From a managerial point of view, legislature has been counted as an organization and community as well. Therefore, it is very natural that a legislature becomes a part of the environment in which it is placed. Since the major elements of the environment are the people, the parties, and the executive, the functional locus of the legislature is dependent upon the way they interact each other among themselves. It is an imperative, in this context, to enhance responsiveness of the National Assembly as long as we try to upgrade interactions among them. In this respect, reestablishing the locus of the legislature should be directed in a way so that it enhances the responsiveness of the National Assembly.

1. Relationship with the People

For the National Assembly to resume its representation role and to perform the role of integrating political forces, resolving conflicts, and maintaining the political system, the relationship between the National Assembly and the people, who are the root of its authority, should be bound in a more intimate and direct relations. However, not only has the National Assembly been negligent in enlarging such opportunities for the people to participate in the legislative process, it has even blocked the smooth passage of mutual communication by bureaucratizing itself. Therefore, it is one of the uppermost goals to bring the separated relationship between the people and the National Assembly closer and thereby enhancing the National Assembly's political responsiveness further. To achieve this goal, the National Assembly needs to provide enlarged opportunities for the people to contact with it. Among possible measures to achieve this, there are: further disclosure of the bill deliberation, enlargement of measures for people's participation, positive public relations, exchange of ideas and opinions and, etc.

1) Internet & Television Broadcasting of Bill Deliberation Process

One of the reasons enhancing people's distrust to the National Assembly is the lack of information about the National Assembly's activities. So, by disseminating information related to its activities and procedures on the internet, television and radio, voters would be able to obtain more information, which will help in reducing their distrust to the National Assembly (Bosley, 1977: 3). The internet will prevent any addition, omission, filtration or time lag in the information dissemination process of the bill deliberation and deliver the facts directly to the constituents, thereby enhancing the public's comprehension of the legislative system. On the part of the legislative members, being aware of the public, they will be more cautious and serious in making statements and in deliberation, which will contribute to enhancing its bill deliberation function as a whole (Ottawa Citizen, 1977: 6). What is more important, by doing this, it will create, to a certain extent, conditions necessary for more direct democracy. Moreover, the constituent, who has been watching the bill deliberation process on the internet or on television, could even immediately comment on the pending issues through a "public participation portal" site and/or make a telephone call to a legislator and express his/her opinion, which will help to reduce the time gap or indirectness of communication between the two.

Nevertheless, this does not mean this measure is without any negative effects. For, first of all, the legislators, being too aware of the voters, may make unnecessary statements or excessive amendment proposals, which will hinder the normal flow of bill deliberation (Bach, 1981: 148). And, instead of seriously devoting themselves to performing their duties, they might even be excessively attached to gaining popularity through the screen (Rutus, 1978: 48). Moreover, by even showing the crippled operations without any filtration to the voters, it might bring down the National Assembly's image and authority and result in deepening the public's mistrust and indifference (Addison, 1979: 367). Nevertheless, in Korea, where most of political information is not widely available, high level of political distrust and cynicism is widely dispersed and means of communication is relatively blocked, facilitating the distribution of information is undeniably the uppermost task. At present, the homepage of the National Assembly is only for a unilateral communication and there is no internet broadcasting system established[1]. The television broadcasting is limited to the plenary session only, thereby restricting the amount of firsthand information on the legislative deliberation process and the opportunities to participate without a delegate[2]. Therefore, it is also necessary to establish measures to expand the broadcasting to the standing committee as well and to

1) In 2001, for the first time, they introduced a real time internet broadcasting system to plenary session and steering committee. From 2005, they broadcast all of the standing committees through internet.

2) From2010, they broadcast 24 hours through cable TV channel.

develop a bilaterally communicable internet system.

2) Introduction of a Special Statement System

There is a need to guarantee free speech of individual legislator by allowing special remarks even after the adjournment of the plenary session and by broadcasting it. By facilitating the internet and the CATV system in each region, a proper utilization of the special remarks system would contribute to promoting mutual communication between the National Assembly and the public. However, when we broadcast a legislator making a special statement, it is important not to spot empty seats and to spot only the starter since not all legislators would continue to attend the meeting even after the plenary session,.

This system is in a sense an alternative measure to overcome the conflict between the principle of efficiency and the principle of representation or democracy in management of legislatures. When the whole procedure of the legislature is normally broadcasted on the internet and the television, there will be an increased amount of requests for access to the internet and television screens, resulting in increasing the pressure for a fair division of remarking opportunities (Cook, 1986: 25). This, in effect, might infringe upon the principle of equal opportunities for making statements. In the course, it might even reinforce the powers of the party leadership that already possess oligarchic authority in allocating opportunities of making speeches, which runs counter to democracy (National Assembly Steering Committee, 1992: 13).

Even to prevent such possible side effects, however, the special statement system is all the more crucial since the introduction of such system will provide larger opportunities for the legislators to reach their constituents and thus less reliance upon the leadership who holds actual power in allocating such opportunities. And above all, by doing this, the National Assembly will be able to reach closer to the public.

3) Introduction of Compulsory Public Hearings

According to the current National Assembly law (article 64), the committee may hold a public hearing to examine important bills or issues that require professional knowledge (Chung, 2000: 614). However, the actual situation is that such optional public hearings have not been properly or actively utilized up to the present. In this regard, it should be made compulsory so that a public hearing must take place whenever a bill is under deliberation, except when the committee regards it unnecessary and votes against it. Not only is a public hearing a means to provide professional and authorized knowledge into the legislative process, but it also raises the quality of deliberation by highlighting each policy's merits and demerits by listening to the opinions of each related parties. Moreover, it also raises the public interest regarding the subjects under deliberation. It also contributes to reducing social conflicts by promoting the public's comprehension and understanding of certain issues.

What is more important is that public hearings could function as the public's controlling device of the National Assembly. Once the voters elect legislators, there are no effective and direct means to control them in the legislative activities until the end of their tenure. But public hearings can be an effective device for voters to control legislators. For, by reducing coverture of the legislative process and enhancing transparency and openness, public hearings promote the public's observation and political pressure. Moreover, it can also prevent rough-and-ready practices in legislation by dividing the legislative procedure into multi-stages. And the clarification of the pros and cons of the public opinion shown through the hearings will also contribute to reducing confrontation and conflict between the ruling and the opposition party.

In particular, despite the vast and extensive scope of the budget, it has been dealt with by limited members of the special committee on budget and settlement, especially the sub-committee on computation, in a closed and unofficial manner, which cannot but put the propriety of the evaluating process in doubt. Therefore for the transparency or openness of the budget and settlement evaluation process, public hearings of the special committee on budget and settlement are all the more crucial. As constituents will be able to directly observe the evaluation process of budget and settlement and freely express their opinions on it, which will facilitate the distribution of required information and data, conflicts from lack of information and misunderstanding will be reduced and this, in turn, will exalt the quality of the debate. Moreover, since it will become possible to confirm the whereabouts or origins of the public opinion regarding the budget and settlement, it will prevent any forceful pressure of a certain opinion, which will promote debate, reconciliation, and mediation.

2. Relationship with Political Parties

In that a party is a political device aimed to bring unity between the civil society and government, it plays a similar role to that of the legislature. Therefore, how the political parties and the legislature cooperate is a key element in determining the substance of the two entities. In fact, in Korea, the relationship between the legislature and the political parties has been too distanced, and, therefore, there has been much difficulty for the National Assembly to achieve its true entity. In this regard, to normalize the function of the National Assembly, it is one of the most pressing issues to overcome such separation, to unite the two bodies, and to establish a closer relationship between the National Assembly and the political parties.

1) Integration of Leadership between the National Assembly and the Parties

In Korea, there is discordance in the power rankings among the practical leaders of the National Assembly and the political parties. This causes the estrangement between legislative negotiators among the political parties and the decision makers within a party. As a result, not only does this block the normal communication and flow of information among parties and form a rigid bureaucracy, it also makes it difficult to narrow differences and to promote mutual understanding and coordination. Despite the fact that the legislature's main purpose is to mediate conflicts and differences among political parties, that main function is not being performed properly nor effectively at present. Therefore, it is necessary to bring consistency between a party's practical leader and its highest decision maker within the National Assembly as well, by clarifying the actual leadership of the Assembly. This will help to reduce the current managerial inefficiency. In other words, it is most crucial to normalize leadership contour of the National Assembly. In particular, such integration of the parties and the National Assembly should be realized on a physical level as well. That is, the main duty offices of the parties should also be established within the National Assembly building so that more frequent contact and communication could be realized among legislators, thereby bringing unity of the function between the National Assembly and the political parties[3].

2) Introduction of Partisan Committee Professional Staff

At present, the legislative committee staff consist of special counsels, legislative evaluators, legislative investigators, etc. Besides these staffs, there are other staffers such as party policy consultants and outside specialists. Nevertheless, except for the party policy consultants, nominally most of the staffers are supposed to provide a bipartisan and neutral assistance in the process of legislation. However, the actuality is that they are all subject to the circumvent influence of the ruling party. In the case of the party policy consultants, though they are supposed to be loyal to their respective political party, as their reversion to each belonging party is over-emphasized, it even has the side-effect of isolating the party from the National Assembly. In this regard, first these systems should be restructured, and then, a partisan staff for each committee's negotiation group should be established so that they could support the legislative activities of each negotiation group in respective committees. Through this kind of reform or provision of partisan staffers, it will be possible for legislators of both the ruling and the opposition parties to review matters of common interest of the committee, which, in turn will have the effect of creating phantom means of communication and dialogue among parties. This, as a result, will strengthen the relationship between the National Assembly and the parties.

3] From 2005, after abolishing local party offices in each constituency, they began to allocate offices for party leadership in the National Assembly.

3) Management of Legislative District Offices

Up until now, legislator's district offices or a party's local chapter offices could be described as having been managed on a personal base as each member's personal office. However, it is necessary to change its concept so that it can function as a local office of the National Assembly. Such reform is in a sense essential since the legislative district offices could also be one form of a governmental institution aimed to reflect public opinion into the legislative process.

When this kind of reform takes place, once he/she is elected as a legislator, they will be relieved of the financial burden of securing assistant human resources and raising funds for basic expenses. This, in turn, will also help to reduce or eliminate any possibility of illegal fund raising by corrupt and distorted political practices. When each legislator becomes the official manager of the National Assembly's district branch office, instead of managing their district offices on a personal base, its function can be integrated with that of the district party chapter offices that perform a similar role, in that they collect the local public opinion and reflect it in a systematic procedure. That is, through such measures, the integration of the party and the National Assembly district offices can be realized on a local level, which was formerly rare or non-existing in Korea. This, without doubt, will contribute to bringing the parties closer with the National Assembly and thereby integrating the two bodies.

3. Relationship with the Executive

One of the reasons of the malfunctioning of the National

Assembly is that it has been subordinated to the administration. Therefore, to normalize the functional locus of the National Assembly regarding the relationship with the executive, it is necessary to enhance the National Assembly's autonomy against the executive branch. In this regard, one of the greatest priorities is to enforce the National Assembly's function of controlling the executive.

1) Improvement of Interpellation System

The interpellation of the executive is one of the major controlling devices for the legislature to inquire the justness of a certain government policy direction and the current situation of the government's activities (Silk & Walters, 1987: 181). Therefore it is also, in a sense, a means to inform the public of their policy directions on the part of the legislators, while it is a means to advocate its policy justness and to educate and socialize the public on the part of the administration. In this respect, it is natural that it is sensitive to the sensationalism of the media. Nevertheless, Korea's situation is that the interpellation system, having lost its original purpose of tracing and disclosing administrative practices and information, is being used as a means of political propaganda (Kim, 1992: 12). Therefore, it cannot carry out its original function of tracing and inquiring after administrative practices. Moreover, during the interpellation, repetitive questions and unfaithful answers have become a chronic sight. In this respect, the administrative interpellation system no longer performs its original function of promoting political integration, and even contains the danger of aggravating political confrontation.

Therefore, measures to resolve such problems could be suggested as in the following: ⓐ Additional questioning system should be introduced. Though not the original questioner, a legislator who holds interest in or has an opinion regarding the subject should be allowed to make additional inquiries after the primary question and answer between the questioner and the government officials is over. With the current practice where the original questioner and the government officials exchange nothing but formal questions and answers, the original controlling purpose of the system cannot be fully performed. Moreover, the current questioning system makes it needless for other members to attend the interpellation. When, accordingly, a large number of members do not show up at the questionings, it will result in deepening the mistrust of the public regarding the National Assembly (Kim, 1992: 11). Therefore it is necessary to allow additional questions to other members as well, so that it may increase the attendance of members and raise the quality of the question and answers, which will eventually contribute to enforcing the control function of the National Assembly. ⓑ The reduction of the questioning time and the expansion of question opportunities are required. Allowing each member to question for about as long as 15 minutes, the current system allows the members make unnecessarily long-winded and repetitive speeches. This, in turn, makes the questions too formal and showy. To correct this problem and to create an environment for more practical and useful questions and answers, it is necessary to reduce the questioning time to 10 minutes and enlarge opportunities for more members to make questions. The current monopoly of interpellation opportunities by a few members of the legislature not only runs counter to the fundamental spirit of the legislative institution, which guarantees fair statement opportunities and openness, it also weakens the control power of the legislature[4]. ⓒ Under the current system, in which all members should make inquiries for each subject, questions have been limited to too general and all-inclusive ones within each subject. As long as such superficial and general questions on the overall governmental policies are allowed, the essence of the interpellation system cannot be realized. Moreover, it may also increase political propaganda by exploiting the system (Kim, 1992. 04. 02.). Though, in a way, it is not totally meaningless that the system provides opportunities for political propaganda, the fact that the system has lost its essential motive of seeking the truth and has turned into a space of confrontation cannot but be a serious problem that requires immediate correction. ⓓ The system of written questioning should be facilitated. To bring out sincere answers, it is necessary to develop other means of administrative interpellation other than that performed at the plenary session hall. It is necessary to make it official and to record the written questions and the following answers in the Assembly records to serve as a ground for accountability and evaluation afterward. And unless arrangements are made so that the records do not show such big discordance between the spoken questions during the session and the written questions, it will be impossible to prevent congestive requests for questioning opportunities, nor will it be possible to guarantee fair opportunities among members. Expansion of questioning opportunities will no doubt enhance the control function of the National Assembly towards the administration.

4) In 2003, they have increased interpellation time for individual questioner from 15 minutes to 20 minutes, which is completely opposite to the suggestion.

2) Reinforcement of the Information Disclosure Right

It is needless to argue that the disclosure of information and data of the executive is essential to enforce the National Assembly's control capability toward the executive. In Korea, in particular, where the level of plurality within the social structure is still relatively low and most of the weighty information and data are produced and kept by the executive, the disclosure of administrative data is a prerequisite for raising the quality of the legislative deliberation. Nevertheless the current law on the disclosure of government information is too limited, and even when disclosure is legally allowed, in practice the disclosure is hindered during the implementation process in most cases. Practicing the right to require submission of information and data by the legislators holds a great significance in this regard.

The current National Assembly law(article 128) states that, in requiring the submission of data for the deliberation of bills regarding the government, administrative agencies, etc, or for the annual inspection and investigation of the State administration, it be subject to the decision of the plenary session or the committee meeting (Chung, 2000: 626). However, when the individual members' right of requiring information is restricted in such a manner, it becomes difficult to obtain important and useful information within the appropriate time period (Lee & Ahn, 1989: 425). Moreover, considering that bill deliberation or legislative inspections of the administration causes, in effect, controversy and confrontation among individual members or among different political parties, the current law actually puts it in the hands of the actual opponents of opinions and interests to decide whether to disclose the information that is required in settling the conflict. As a matter of fact, no one would be in a better position to judge the necessity of the information than the actual individual who is in need of the information. Therefore, the current law is, in a sense, restricting the functional locus of the National Assembly of its accord within the relationship with the executive. On the other hand, there are concerns that, when the right to require information is not restricted, the right will be abused and paralyze the normal operation of the executive branch. However, once the right is fully guaranteed, such phenomenon is certain to decrease. The present situation of over-requisition of information is rather a side effect due to needless restriction. Therefore, it is necessary to reinforce individual members' right to require the submission of information and data.

3) Innovation of the Inspection and Investigation of the State Administration

(1) Alleviation of Requisites to Carry Out

It is needless to say that increasing the number of inspection and investigation of the administration by the National Assembly would lead to enforcing its control power, which will raise the level of its autonomy in its relation with the executive. Nevertheless according to the current law on inspection and investigation of the State administration (article 3), when a special or a standing committee plans to inspect or investigate certain administrative issues, it must obtain the support of more than 1/4 of registered members of the National Assembly (Chung, 2000: 634). Considering the basic characteristics of the inspection and investigation, to exercise such right is to inspect or investigate the operations of the executive carried out, in fact, by the majority party of the National Assembly. In this regard, the actuality is that the minority party's right to inspect or investigate the conducts of the executive is restricted and thus that of the National Assembly (Lee, 1989: 314). Therefore, it is necessary to alleviate the prerequisites to exercise the right of inspection and investigation so that the right can be operated even by a minority of members.

According to the current system, even when the right is put into action, it cannot be carried out if the inspection or investigation plan prepared by the committee fails to pass the vote of the plenary session (Chung, 2000: 634). That is, unless it gets the approval of more than half of the present members of the plenary session, the right cannot be carried out in the actuality. Therefore, the requirement of the approval of the plenary session should be abolished so as to facilitate the inspection and investigation of the executive. Only through such innovations is it possible to guarantee the original purpose of the right and to enforce the National Assembly's function of controlling the executive.

(2) Establishment of a Program-Evaluation Office

One of the major roles of the National Assembly is to collect information for legislative activities, and to correct possible flaws or disparities that might have occurred during the implementation process of the law by exercising its right of inspection and investigation of the executive. Nevertheless the reality is that this function fails to be carried out properly. The reason for such malfunctioning is because there is no sufficient supporting system for the National Assembly to carry out such right. That is there are no sufficient measures to support the National Assembly with the information or professional expertise required for the inspections, nor are there sufficient legislative staff resources or any kind of system or institution to perform this task.

In this respect, an independent program evaluation office should be established within the National Assembly that is in an equivalent position to the Secretariat. The office should be given the task of evaluating administrative policies and programs in a systematic way, and utilizing the evaluation results in the legislative and inspection activities of the legislators. By doing so, not only will the valuation process itself perform a control function of the executive, but will also systemize and reinforce the control function of the National Assembly by reflecting the results of the evaluation to the bill deliberation process. Moreover, since the evaluation office would be run by a specialist group being in full charge of the analysis and evaluation of administrative policies and programs, it will not only lead to raising the quality of the inspection and investigation itself, but, by continuously evaluating policies and programs, will also enable the inspections and investigation to be carried out at all times. Considering that the purpose of evaluating policies and programs is to discover and correct any possible flaws or disparities between the legislative intent and the implementation of that legislation, it is important that the legislative intent is clarified in the first place.

IV. Reform of the Managerial Dimension of the National Assembly

In the above, it has been stated that, to normalize the function of the National Assembly, it should gain greater independence and autonomy within the relationship with the executive, and that it must form a stronger and closer bond with the public as well as with the political parties. And I have made several recommendations of measures to achieve those goals. Innovating of the functional locus of the National Assembly is eventually directly related with the reform of the managerial dimension of the legislature including the structure, operating system, distribution of information, and utilization of human resources, etc. That is the reestablishment of the National Assembly's external locus is directly connected with its internal locus, which is affected by the managerial dimension of the National Assembly. The main functions of the National Assembly, which could be summarized as representation, conflicts management, and maintenance of the political system, can be enhanced by promoting specialization, openness, morality, and economy of the internal bill deliberation process. In other words, there is a necessity to seek measures to enhance a rationality of the organizational and procedural dimension of the National Assembly.

1. Organizational Management

1) Reorganization of the Committee on Legislation and Judiciary Affairs

The current National Assembly law(article 37) states that the Committee on Legislation and Judiciary Affairs re-evaluate the legal structure and form of the bills after their evaluations of substance by each standing committees (Chung, 2000: 607). However, a piece of legislation is no other than stating the legislative intent within the legal structure, form and terms. In this regard, the evaluation of such elements of a piece of legislation, even though it is limited to technical issues, holds the same meaning of evaluating the legislative intent.

In this respect, the evaluation by the Committee on Legislation and Judiciary Affairs fails not to treat the substance of a piece of legislation. The legislation's substances are put in the hands of the committee that does not possess sufficient knowledge and information of the related field, which consequently institutionalizes the mechanism for the standing committee (on legislation and judiciary affairs) without proper capability and jurisdiction to deal with to influence the legislative intent of each standing committee. As for amendment bills that have been sent back to the related standing committee from the Committee on Legislation and Judiciary Affairs review, instead of asking the whole member of the committee on whether to accept the opinion of the Committee on Legislation and Judiciary Affairs, most of the committees conventionally treat the bill in a limited way based on the opinions of a few members of the committee. Therefore, the legislative intent of each standing committee is not properly expressed nor protected in most cases. Moreover due to this present system, even when a bill is examined and approved at the related standing committee, if the Committee on Legislation and Judiciary affairs delays or ignores its evaluation, it may have to face a delay or even a failure to be presented at the plenary session. Although the Korean National Assembly follows a unicameral system, the current status of the Committee on Legislation and Judiciary Affairs takes a similar position to that of the senate in a bicameral legislature. This not only causes a functional imbalance among standing committees but also runs counter to the basic principle of horizontal division among standing committees.

Therefore, first of all, the Committee on Legislation and Judiciary Affairs should be abolished. Then a new Committee on Judiciary Affairs should be established to perform the tasks currently being carried out by the Committee on Legislation and Judiciary Affairs except for "the evaluation of the structure, form, and terms of legislation and parliamentary rules". As for the technical support for legislation, it should be put in the charge of the bill drafting office of the Secretariat. Only through such reforms can true specialization be enhanced, which is the real intent of establishing standing committees.

2) Utilization of Adhocracy

To establish a democratic system through the division of power within the National Assembly, it is, above all, necessary to pluralize the division of operations to a greater extent. The current managerial leadership of the National Assembly is highly centralized to the integrated authority of the Steering Committee and the floor leaders. Such situation must be improved. It is desirable to enhance flexibility by forming a functional alliance based on a matrix structure or a project-base method. Through this, it will be possible to prevent congestion in the legislative operations due to over-concentration of tasks during a certain period of time, and will also contribute to promoting democracy through the decentralization of powers and disclosure of the alliance.

Moreover, expanding this kind of horizontal and non-permanent structure will prevent the formation of a bureaucracy within the National Assembly, and enhance flexibility, responsiveness, and adaptability of the legislative process. In other words, it is necessary to divide the tasks, which is currently under the full charge of the Steering Committee, and put them under the charge of adhocracy committees. For example, up until now, the floor leaders, which is, in fact, integrated with the Steering Committee, has been responsible for the appointment of members of the standing committee. However, it is desirable for the Steering Committee to function only as a managerial axis, and to establish a separate adhocracy committee for the appointment task. This kind of power division will contribute to bringing equity and openness within the National Assembly.

2. Time Management

1) Improving the Bill Deliberation Procedure

At present, it is a routine practice that, at the end of each session, vast amount of bills are submitted in piles, causing a congestion which results in crippled and rough-and-ready operations of the deliberation process. Therefore, as a means of guaranteeing the quality of deliberation, it is necessary to guarantee a certain period of time so that, once a bill is submitted to the session, its deliberation cannot close until after a certain time limit. Moreover, the true significance of deliberation lies not so much in the result that has certain legislative forms and requirements, as in the process through which emotional refinement and education are obtained while various opinions are expressed and debated to reach a certain level of agreement and consensus. The National Assembly will find itself lowering its status and authority of its own accord if it continues the practice of such rough-and-ready deliberations.

In this respect, all bills submitted during the session should be subject to a mandatory period for evaluation. Only when negotiation groups reach an agreement on the necessity of a speedy deliberation or when they do not hold different opinions should the application of such mandatory period be reserved so as to overcome unnecessary delay. However, to normalize the function of the National Assembly, it is necessary to apply a certain minimum time limit for the deliberation of each legislative procedure including the preparation of the draft bill, submission of the bill, assignment of committees, reporting to the committees, evaluation of the committees and the plenary session, and forwarding to the administration, etc.

2) Stipulating the Evaluation Period of the Settlement Bill by Law

It is natural that the results of the previous year's administration be reflected in the evaluation process of the upcoming year's budget. In this regard, it should be stipulated by law that the settlement bill of the previous year be evaluated during July, previous to the upcoming regular session in September. Such stipulation is essential to prevent any improper evaluation of the settlement bill that may be caused when the budget evaluation and the settlement bill evaluation are performed at the same time (Kang, 1989: 634). In particular it is also important to complete the evaluation of the settlement bill before the annual auditing of the State administration, which is scheduled before the budget evaluation. For the results of the settlement bill, evaluation must be examined and confirmed during the annual auditing of the State administration. In other words, it is necessary to guarantee the appropriate amount of time needed in making a budget and settlement bill evaluation process more systematic and consistent.

Above all, it is important to notice the fact that, up until now, the evaluation process of the settlement bill has been excessively formalized and conventionalized. But, in that the evaluation of the settlement bill serves as the foundation for judging the soundness of the previous year's administration, it is undeniably the most essential material in preparing the upcoming year's budget. When we substantiate the settlement bill evaluation process, it will directly contribute to raising the quality of the budget evaluation. It is, in this regard, inevitable to stipulate the settlement bill evaluation period by law so as to be performed before the opening of the regular session[5].

3. Information Management

1) Expanding Legislative Support System

It is necessary to expand and innovate of the legislative staff system, not only to make the internal workings of the legislature more professional, scientific, and technical, but also to fully utilize the information that they have already possessed (Kim *et al,* 1985: 399). At present, as there are no scientific specialists among the professional staffers supporting the National Assembly, the deliberation of scientific and technical issues cannot, but remain at a formal and ritualistic level. It is most urgent to recruit staffs that can be put in charge of researching on hard science. On the other hand, it is also necessary to develop managerial strategies regarding the scheduling of the deliberation or the opening and closing of sessions etc, so that the legislative process could be performed more efficiently and, thus, the interest conflicts among the legislators could be managed more smoothly. However, the National Assembly has not been introduced even the basic concept of such staffers. It is one of the first priorities to supplement legislative staff to specialize in such bill flow management strategies.

In addition, there is no parliamentarian who can authoritatively

---

5) In 2003, they adopted early settlement bill evaluation system.

settle down parliamentary disputes occurring in the process of bill deliberations. The internal working process of the legislature, in a sense, represents one form of a power struggle based on the standing orders of the legislature. Therefore, the pre-possession of information and better knowledge on the parliamentary rules and orders determines which party or negotiation group has an advantage over the other. Nevertheless the fact that there is no official mechanism to give technical advice on the interpretation and application of parliamentary rules and orders is another proof of the National Assembly's abnormal and crippled operations. In this regard, it is necessary to establish an authoritative office within the National Assembly to take full charge of the parliamentarian's role, which, in turn, requires the supplement of special officials in charge of proceedings.

All of the above-mentioned problems boil down to the fact that the National Assembly lacks the mechanism to supply special and technical information required in the legislative process, which is crucial to enhancing efficiency within the legislature.

2) Refinement of the Information Management System

By refining the proceedings and communication mechanism through the utilization of information & telecommunication tools, it will be possible to systemize the flow of information, which will contribute to enhancing productivity, dividing powers, and to refining knowledge. In this regard, it is necessary to establish an internet network connecting the offices of legislative and committee members and the plenary session hall, so that, during the meetings, members can make easy access to the information that they need from their offices. And this network will be all the more intensified, by being connected to universities, outside specialists, the executive and local governments. When the legislative network is connected with outside sources, the total amount and variety of usable information will be greatly expanded, which, in turn, will bring a higher level of qualification of the bill deliberation process. The establishment of an information distribution network will not only enhance the quality and quantity of information resources but will also decentralize vested interests by incapacitating any exclusive monopoly of information. Those who were formerly in an exclusive position of possessing information will lose its ground of power, which will result in promoting division of power and democracy within the National Assembly. In other words, such measures will increase the total amount or diversity of information, which will improve the quality of legislative outputs. This will eventually enhance the legitimacy of policies, thereby contributing to enhancing social consensus and integration.

4. Personnel Management

1) Intensifying the Education of Legislative Staffs

Considering the diversity, complexity and high-technology of the policy issues in the current society, it is needless to argue that those policy issues should be put in the hands of legislative staffs. Nevertheless the actuality is that it is difficult to recruit staffers with the appropriate qualifications and capabilities for this task. A legislative staff should, besides possessing professional knowledge and expertise within a certain field, also possess political sensitivity and legislative knowledge. They are also required to have a thorough knowledge of the internal organization and situation of the National Assembly. Therefore, when the National Assembly does not make positive efforts to recruit staffers, it will face difficulty in securing qualified human resources to perform the task.

Therefore, the National Assembly should, first of all, make positive efforts to motivate more people to apply for the job. Moreover, it should seek long-term and fundamental means to secure necessary human resources, such as measures to establish and support a department of related studies within the college curriculum. More than anything else, the re-education of the present legislative officials should be preceded. To do this, it is necessary to analyze and evaluate their job and then to stipulate their qualifications in an elaborate way based on the result of the job analysis and evaluation. Long-term measures to reorganize the legislative staff system on the base of the job analysis result are also required, in that social policies are changing rapidly and that the amount of special knowledge required for the legislators is also increasing.

2) Introduction of a Pension System for Legislators

It is necessary to take the retirement problem of legislators into consideration to enable them to be more faithful to their duties during their tenure. This is all the more required not only to inspire the morale of legislators, but also to prevent any possible political corruption or distortion. Under the current system, once a candidate loses an election, no financial support is guaranteed for them. In this situation, legislators are apt to fall into corruption to secure their livelihood after retirement. In this regard, based on the principle of integrity and faithfulness, it is necessary to introduce a pension system for legislators who have faithfully served their duty during their tenure so that they need not worry about retirement.

3) Improving the Annual Expenditure System

According to the present system, all of the expenses of a legislator's office are added up within the individual member's salary, which is the cause for the public criticism that a legislator's salary is unnecessarily high. Though the annual expenditure does not mean a salary in the form of compensation money for the legislator's service, it is true that it may become a political burden by adding the sum up in an overall package. Therefore, when the National Assembly increases its indirect financial support for each legislator's activities, this will accordingly increase the sum of a legislator's total annual expenditure, which will aggravate the public opinion regarding legislators. As a matter of fact, a legislator's salary and their legislative activity expenses are different in their nature and essence. Therefore, the two expenses should be distinguished and paid separately.

In particular, as a legislator's salary has the aspect of the compensation for the labor or service they provide, there is no problem in paying it in a flat sum or by cash. On the other hand, expenses to support legislative activities including transportation, telecommunication, and office management, etc, should be paid in the perspective of the compensation for their actual expenses. Therefore, the current system of a fixed income payment should be changed into a system of compensating for actual expenses when they occur. In this case a voucher system would be more efficient than cash payment.

V. Conclusion

The function of the National Assembly cannot possibly be normalized without enhancing morality, specialty, openness, autonomy, activeness, and etc. Unless its functional locus is normalized, it is needless to say that it would be impossible to reform the society as a whole in Korea.

In this regard, it is a social obligation to reform the managerial dimension of the National Assembly for it to perform its essential roles. That is; the reform of the National Assembly is not an issue limited within the political arena, but a goal that requires the unified efforts and attention of the whole society. As a matter of fact, there is a general perception that the management of the National Assembly is nothing but a sub-divisional matter of political system. It has, in fact, been understood only from a technical and managerial perspective, and therefore, it is true that its significance has been underestimated and overlooked.

Nevertheless since all the activities of the National Assembly eventually need the support of its administrative and managerial functioning, the management of the National Assembly is, in effect, the core of all power relations within the National Assembly. It is also due to this fact that it is not such an easy task to reform and reorganize the managerial dimension of the legislature. For, reform in the management system is sure to bring a change in the power relations, which will lead to change in the power relations of a society as a whole.

On the other hand, it is also true that, due to the fact that all social power and authority is condensed to such a limited space of the managerial dimension of the legislature, the significance of its authoritative status has been neglected. That is why the pervasive social neglect and ignorance of the management of the National

Assembly have long been taken place. However, now this "zone of indifference" could be a new means to bring social reform. In other words, the very neglect or ignorance on its managerial dimension could make it all the more difficult to trace the effects of its reform on the political structure and easier to reform it.

In fact, the reform of the managerial dimension of the legislature could create greater conflict and self-contradictions. This is because reform on one level is apt to enhance specialty on the one hand while on the other it may weaken the level of democracy. Or it may upgrade responsiveness while at the same time weaken rationality. It may even promote cooperation and mediation of conflicts while at the same time may deepen conflicts.

Nevertheless, due to this fact, this approach to reform the National Assembly from a managerial perspective is not based on any argument or belief that these reform measures will bring definite effects or resolve issues pertinent to the legislature. Rather, instead of regarding that these reform measures imply definite effects and resolutions, I would like to suggest that their effects and results may differ according to how they are applied and directed. Considering the fact that, though there is a consensus on the needs of reform, the Korean society has been lacking practical or realistic ideas and measures to carry out, the purpose of this chapter is to make cautious recommendations on practical measures for the reform of the National Assembly.

That is only when the above recommendations be selected and realized can it produce any tangible results in facilitating the function of the National Assembly. Nor does it intend to argue that the above measures are the only means that are needed for reform. Besides those suggested in the above discussion, there would be a vast amount of practical measures regarding organization, personnel, time, operations, information and financial management, and etc, to enhance openness, specialization, autonomy, and democracy of the National Assembly.

In this respect, it is true that this research contains the limits of reductionism in its essence. And, for this reason, this research was not intended to set a ranking of priorities among the suggested measures, which could be marked as another limitation of this research.

At any rate, the purpose of this chapter is to support and provide any possible guidelines for those who are determined to bring in reform within the actual arena of the National Assembly. In this regard, the measures and suggestions in the above discussion should follow continuous social changes, and its soundness should also be judged accordingly.

Through the research, it could be seen that a managerial perspective in dealing with the legislative institution provides us with a more systematic evaluation scheme in assessing the needs and necessities of the legislative reform. Thus, it makes it easier for us to locate the parts of the puzzle in the assessment process of the reform needs and demands. And recollecting that the managerial approach is common in the field of public administration but not in political science, the application of a managerial perspective in the study of legislatures, which has long been treated as an object of political science rather than that of public administration, truthfully extends the scope of the public administration studies to the field of political science.

Chapter 03

Annual Legislative Auditing of the Executive[1]

I. Introduction

Korean's interest in "small and efficient government" has increased remarkably since the imposition of the IMF disciplines. The economic crisis has created wide acceptance of the following: (1) the important causes of government failure, which led to such misfortune, lie in the government's excessive intervention in social relationships and its arbitrary use of power; and (2) these problems have to be corrected. In a society like Korea, where a delegation of legislative power to the executive is too freely permitted, it is very natural that worries about

1) The meaning of "Kookjungkamsa (in Korean)" by the Korean National Assembly could be interpretd either as annual auditing or as annual inspection by the legislature. In this chapter, it is translated as annual auditing by the legislature. But in some other places of this book, it is translated as annual inspection by the legislature as well.

administrative corruption and other administrative shortcomings become more serious. It also goes without saying that shortages resulting from economic difficulties increase the level of criticism of government inefficiency. In other words, Korean society has arrived at the consensus that bureaucratic moral susceptibility has to be minimized.

Such an agreement makes it the first priority of Korean society that governmental intervention in social relationships should be fundamentally reduced and that governmental management processes should be reformed. A decrease in governmental intervention in social relationships, however, can not be accomplished by simply reducing, in scope, the policy tasks of the government. It can be done when the government abandons its existing authoritarian hierarchical position and makes itself a partner with society in solving social issues by co-planning or co-production. To do so, the locus of government power should be changed. This requires external controls over the government to be activated, because it is naturally very difficult for the government to limit its power of its own volition.

Co-operation between government and society is destined to accomplish its objectives when both the economic rationality that the government is pursuing and the political rationality that society desires are taken into account. In other words, views and values outside the government need to be taken into the governmental equation.

It is true that the effective control cannot be expected without internal controls because the objects of control become more professional, more high-tech and more complex in modern society. However, it is undeniable that the internal controls are inherently subjective and closed. Thus, it cannot be fully effective without external control. Among the external controls over the executive in Korea, the control exercised by the National Assembly is most institutionalized. Its methods are diverse; the annual auditing of the executive by the National Assembly being the most active and direct. In Korean society, therefore, its activation has a meaning more than that of simply restoring checks and balances among the three agencies of government.

Nevertheless, it could be claimed that the existing annual auditing by the National Assembly is used as a means to weaken the restraining power of the Assembly over the executive or to legitimate the supremacy of the administration. In the annual auditing by the National Assembly, for example, the ministers have a tendency to propagandize government policies and programs, to publicize their own legitimacy, and to protect themselves from political criticism.[2] It should be a place where the opposition parties could voice their complaints that the government actually overwhelms the National Assembly through the ruling party. Thus, it can be used as a means to diminish the complaints of the opposition parties and to neutralize their political offensives. In the annual auditing, assemblymen commonly put political pressure on solving issues requested by their electorates and on assigning policy-driven programs to their constituencies. The annual auditing could possibly develop a peer group relationship between bureaucrats and assemblymen, makes it possible for corruption and lobbying to occur. If this proves to be the case, the audit fails to function. Therefore, it is a necessary condition of "small and more efficient government" that the functional effectiveness of the audit is systematically reviewed so that its social costs and benefits are comparatively analyzed. It is coming

2) Chosun Daily News Paper(1998.11.12.). For the annual auditing by the National Assembly, these things should be changed first.

to be accepted that a 'mega-audit' of the annual audit is required.

But, most of the existing studies on 'annual auditing' issues are based on legal and institutional approaches (Shin, 1989; Lee, 1989). Some based on behavioral approaches are focused on understanding simply audit processes, and fail to grasp its substantial function (Kim, 1996; Oh, 1990). Even a few studies on the functional locus of the annual auditing are primarily normative (Kim, 1997). They see the annual auditing as a kind of investigation or inspection of the executive, not as a public audit.[3] This means that the mega-audit for the annual audit has been unsystematic and impressionistic. Therefore, it is self-evident that the previous studies are not helpful in upgrading the function of the Korean National Assembly from a control-of-the-executive standpoint.

In this context, this chapter intends to overcome the weakness of existing studies and to discuss practical strategies useful for successful government reform which confronts Korean society. Thus, the study has the primary objective of providing the basic information required to consolidate the control function of annual auditing. In the study, the data for the 1998 annual audit is analyzed.

II. Annual Auditing of the Executive from a Public Auditing Perspective

The objectives of the annual auditing are to obtain the data and information necessary for legislative activities and

3) Kim Hyun-Koo is exceptional from these previous studies in the sense that he tried to understand and conduct researches on the annual auditing from a public auditing perspective and not from an investigation (Kim, 1989; 1996).

deliberation on the budget through precise understanding of the overall realities of national-affairs and to efficiently perform such functions as representation, legislation, deliberation on the budget, and national-affairs control through exposing and correcting mistakes (Secretariat of the National Assembly, 1996: 3). The underlying concept of the above is national action which scrutinizes the actions of the administration, the judiciary and the legislature (Lee, 1989: 302). Thus, from the viewpoint of its relationship with the executive, the annual auditing is an institutional mechanism to make each assemblyman, a people's representative and to evaluate and report on the working attitudes and performance of bureaucrats. The audit can be expected to minimize the information imbalance between the people and their bureaucrats. According to Antle (1982) and Tirole (1986), an auditing activity is a three-tier hierarchy composed of owners, inspectors and agents, and a public auditing is an auditing for public sectors. Therefore, there is no doubt that the annual auditing of the executive by the National Assembly is of the nature of a public auditing since it is composed of the people, the assemblymen, and the bureaucrats forming a three tier hierarchy.

A public auditing is generally divided into three: legality, performance and policy auditing. The objective of legality auditing is the maintenance and improvement of account and administrative orders. It is a mechanism that seeks to check injustice by creating main executors who are honest, law-conforming, account-responsible and law-abiding (Lee, 1994: 25). It emphasizes effective enforcement of administrative regulations, because it sees government as a mechanical bureaucracy (Brazelay, 1996: 18). Therefore, its areas of concern are financial conditions, working behaviors, managerial duties and so on. Its methods are focused on examining whether or not statutes and accounting principles have been violated. Its criteria lie in the domain of legality or morality, and in some cases, its results require punishment, compulsory correction and compensation. The statute, a basis of a legality auditing, normally involves economy, efficiency, validity, rationality and efficacy (Lee, 1994: 27) and values are applied in the same order.

Performance auditing aims at improving public service quality and at using resources efficiently by preventing errors in public policies, programs and services. Because it sees a government as a feedback system in the input-output model, it emphasizes the increase of productivity in a given environment and in the objective-attaining process (Brazelay, 1996: 18). Its interests are in the following aspects: quantity in information and data of administration planners, techniques and expert knowledge, veracity of statistics and data, motivation of managers, pre-examining, cooperation among institutions, understanding of executive branches of plans, and environmental flexibility, etc. (Lee, 1994: 25). Thus, its objects involve budgetary business, administrative behavior, policy implementation and policy impact. Its method is based on policy evaluation. The auditing standards are legality, economy, efficiency, validity, rationality and efficacy (Lee, 1994: 30; Kim, 1996: 30). It may result in corrective recommendations, policy governing suggestions and inducements to improve institutions. Therefore, performance auditing and legality auditing are not mutually exclusive and ideally the former is seen to include the latter (Walsh, 1996: 233).

Policy auditing is useful for attaining policy objectives or for improving group conditions of a society, because it recognizes a government as a kind of public intervention for improving collective conditions of a society (Barzelay, 1996: 18). Its objects cover budgetary businesses and basic policies, including policy implementation, policy impact and policy making in the concrete

(Kim, 1996: 28). Its methods are based on policy analysis and policy evaluation. And its criteria involve legality, economy, efficiency, validity, rationality, efficacy, conformity-to-objectives, equity, consistency, responsiveness and democracy (Kim, 1996: 30). As a result, budget control, policy change and institutional improvement may be required. The attainment of policy objectives can be a center of public auditing, and, at the same time, its standards, such as legality, economy, validity, rationality and efficacy can be standards of performance auditing. In sum, policy auditing is a major concept including most of performance auditing.

Thus, the three auditings can be envisaged as forming a concentric circle relationship. Considering audit areas, they form an overlapped relationship that partly shares financial operation, working behaviors, managerial duties and basic policies. In particular, performance auditing and policy auditing are in a straight line and they include policy implementation, policy impact and policy making. From an auditing criteria standpoint, the three audits are in an interlocked relationship sharing to some extent: legality, economy, efficiency, validity, rationality, efficacy, conformity-to-objectives, equity, consistency, responsiveness and democracy. In respect to methodology, they are in a joint relationship which is concerned with accounting principles, law-application, policy evaluation and policy analysis. In other words, public auditing can be conceptualized as a comprehensive continuum with two extreme points. Legality and economy are at one end of the continuum; responsiveness and democracy are at the other.

Annual auditing is based on representation, in that it is exercised by the National Assembly which is the foundation of representation. Meanwhile, public auditing by the executive is based on professionality and techniques. The power balancing function of the three arms of government is important in the annual auditing, while the supervision of the executive is embodied in the public auditing. Therefore, the auditing of the executive should fulfil a fact verification function and the annual auditing by the National Assembly should have a demonstrative role (Her & Kim, 1998: 39-42). The auditing by the executive focuses on the relationship between policy behaviors and policy objectives and thus its evaluation criteria involve legality, economy, efficiency and effectiveness. The annual auditing by the National Assembly aims at verifying the appropriateness among policy evaluation, social phenomena, cultural system and ideal values. Therefore, its evaluation standards include legality, validity and rationality (Kim, 1989: 41). Summing up, it is emphasized that annual auditing by the National Assembly attaches importance to policy auditing while the public auditing by the executive stresses legality and performance auditing (Kim, 1989: 40).

In fact, the annual auditing by the National Assembly commands goals, objects and criteria of legality, performance, and policy auditing, which is inevitable in that policy auditing is a major concept which encompasses legality and performance auditing. In respect to actual management, the annual auditing by the National Assembly includes all the elements of legality, performance and policy auditing.

Moreover, the annual auditing by the National Assembly does not always attach importance in auditing activities of the executive. It pays attention to expanding assemblymen's cognitive limits and sensitivity to basic collective conditions of society, and thus to improving, qualitatively and quantitatively, legislative and budgetary deliberation. The traditional manner of exercising legislative power is necessary to effectively realize the normative and basic roles of legislatures and to evaluate specific incidents (Lee, 1989: 303), and therefore, it is the investigation of the executive which puts more emphasis on disclosure and sharing of information than on supervision and correction (Shin, 1989: 294). Simply put, the annual audit and investigation overlap. In fact, annual auditing is similar to investigation to the extent that they need not really be distinguished from each other (Kim, 1997: 5). However, they are different in that the annual auditing requires active correction measures or handlings through examining substantive issues closely while the investigation examines it more simply and does not take any further measures. In this respect, the annual auditing could be regarded as a major element of the investigation.

Incidentally, one result of investigation into specific incidents is to expand the understanding of assemblymen about collective conditions of society; this is a prerequisite to reinforcing auditing activities of the executive. Therefore, annual auditing can be a major concept that extends the investigation to include public auditing. The investigation is a supplementary apparatus to fulfill an essential function of the legislature which is to pursue the maximization of political rationality. Thus, efforts are made to improve political rationality through the investigation. On the other hand, all kinds of public auditings see input-economy or productivity-maximization of input-output as one of their important criteria. The pursuit of economic rationality is consequently a common denominator. Therefore, the annual auditing is a general manifestation of a comprehensive concept, which consists of two poles. Public auditing to pursue economic rationality is at one end, while investigation to seek after political rationality is at the other. <Table 1> shows the results to be discussed above.

<Table 1> Comprehensive Concept of Assembly's Annual Auditing of Executive

Types / Components	Legality Auditing	Performance Auditing	Policy Auditing	Investigation to the Executive
Objects	• financial management • working behaviors • managerial duties	• budgetary business • managerial duties • policy implementation • policy impact	• budgetary business • basic policies • policy implementation • policy impact • policy determination	• overall processes of national affairs
Criteria	morality, legality	legality, economy, efficiency, validity, rationality, efficacy	legality, economy, efficiency, validity, rationality, efficacy, conformity-to-objective, equity, consistency, responsiveness, democracy	Morality, legality, economy, efficiency, validity, rationality, efficacy, conformity-to-objective, equity, consistency, responsiveness, democracy
Methods	• accounting principles • law-application	• policy evaluation	• policy evaluation • policy analysis	• fact survey
Measures	• compensation decision • punishment • compulsory correction	• correction recommendation • suggestions to drive policies • inducement of institution improvement	• budgetary control • inducement of institution improvement • demand for policy change	• fact publication

Source: Modified, complemented and reorganized on the basis of Kim (1996: 30).

As outlined, the annual auditing by the National Assembly is a continuum, which has two poles: at the one end is the pursuit of economic rationality and at the other is the search for political rationality. Therefore, it is a concept in which the following four are arranged on a continuum: at one end is legality auditing for economic rationality; at the other is the investigation of the Assembly for political rationality; performance auditing and policy auditing fall between these two extremes. Legality auditing is seen as the smallest category and the scope of other audits is broader. Finally, the investigation of the Assembly includes all of these areas. To sum up, the functional category of the annual audit is composed of the four audits mentioned above. <Figure 1> shows the results discussed .

<Figure 1> Conceptual Scope of the Annual Auditing and Public Auditing

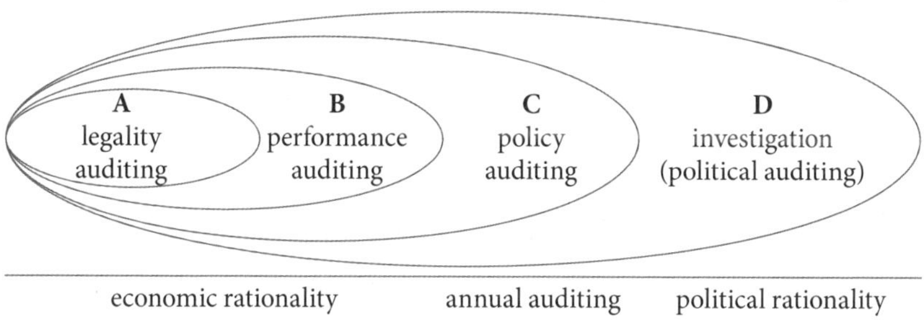

Diverse auditing types and characteristics of the investigation of the Assembly shown in <Table 1> are combined realities of annual auditing cases. Therefore, in order to show up special characteristics inherent in individual auditing types and national-affair investigations, overlapped areas need to be excluded. 'A' shown in <Figure 1> is legality auditing. 'B' excludes legality auditing from performance auditing. The result is that inflexible factors of auditings are excluded from performance auditing. In other words, the parts paying attention to legality and abiding principles are excluded. C is the area that results from the subtraction of performance auditing from policy auditing. Therefore, it corresponds to the political affairs auditing that Kim (1989: 36) detailed. 'D' is the result of the fact that policy auditing is excluded from national affairs investigation and inspection. In other words, it is an area in which public auditing factors are excluded from national affairs investigation. Kim (1996: 30) describes it as political auditing in order to emphasize its politicized intentions. In short, A is referred to here as legality auditing, B as performance auditing, C as policy auditing and D as political auditing. The rate at which they form managerial reality of the annual auditing is a pivotal point in understanding the functional substance of annual auditing.

III. Contents of the Annual Auditing of the Executive by the National Assembly

It is important to identify how many auditing activities take place and for what purpose in order to grasp the totality of the annual auditing. In that review, it is imperative to identify the ratio of parts constituting target agencies, audit issues, time input, and audit types respectively. Information about three former items are expected to supply the basic ideas about the total size of auditing and, finally, the objectives and intentions of annual auditing.

1. Target Agencies

Theoretically speaking, the annual auditing by the National

Assembly is designed to cover the whole spectrum of state affairs since auditing is a type of supplementary apparatus in realizing the normative role of legislatures which are designed to deal with nation-wide affairs by their very nature. In reality, however, the concrete objects of auditing are stipulated by the act relating to the annual auditing and investigation by the National Assembly. According to the act, audit target institutions are divided into two groups: agencies deemed to be selected by the standing committees and those approved by a resolution of the plenary session. The former becomes an auditing target agencies simply by being selected by a committee while the selection of the latter group needs support from members of other committees. In brief, it must be a legislative intention to make it easier for the agencies in the former category to become audit targets and in contrast to make it more difficult for the latter. Because of this characteristic, the former are even dubbed "natural audit committee objects".

In the former category stipulated by the act, there are 1) government agencies established under the Government Organization Act and others, 2) the special city, great-sphere cities and provinces controlled by local governments, 3) authorized government investment organizations such as the Bank of Korea, the Federation of Agricultural Cooperative Associations, the Federation of Fisheries Cooperative Associations, and the Federation of Livestock Industry Cooperative Associations. The latter category includes, 1) local administrative agencies and local government agencies except those in the former category, and 2) agencies subject to inspection under the Board of Audit and Inspection Act, excluding those in the former category- for instance: local government investment agencies, reinvestment agencies, donated agencies, subsidized agencies, resubsidized agencies, debt insured agencies, national treasury agents, agencies with government appointed board members, etc. Generally speaking, most of the agencies in the former category are comprised of central government agencies dealing with national affairs. Those in the latter consist of local administrative agencies dealing with specific regional affairs. However, the categorization is not based on any strict grouping principle. They seem to be categorized simply for a convenience and not on the basis of fixed rules.

Considering such situations, it is intended, here, to make groupings on the basis of more rigorous principles and to categorize the audit targets, prescribed at the auditing and inspection act of the National Assembly, into central administration agencies, local administration agencies and other auxiliary agencies. The former two groups of agencies can be discerned from the latter since they are formal government agencies. The central administration agencies are distinct from local administration agencies as the former deal with national affairs and the latter deal with local or sectoral affairs. Such categorization reflects the fact that central administration agencies play an important role in planning while local administration agencies and other auxiliary agencies are concerned with implementation. The result of grouping audit target agencies into such categories is shown at <Table 2>.

According to <Table 2>, a total number of 327 agencies were audited. It means that 20.4 agencies per committee were audited on average. Among them, the committees auditing more agencies than the average were the finance & economy committee (34), the legislation & judiciary committee (31), the culture & tourism committee (28), the industry & energy committee (27), the government administration & local autonomy committee (26), the agriculture, forestry, maritime affairs & fisheries committee (25) and the national defense committee (22). Meanwhile, the

< Table 2 > Target Agencies by Committees in 1998

Committees \ Agencies	Central ad. agencies	Local ad. agencies	Other aux. agencies	Total
House steering	8(88.9)	0(0.0)	1(11.1)	9(100.0)
Legislation & judiciary	8(25.8)	23(74.2)	0(0.0)	31(100.0)
National policy	9(50.0)	0(0.0)	9(50.0)	18(100.0)
Finance & economy	6(17.6)	15(44.1)	13(38.2)	34(99.9)
Unification, foreign affairs & trade	2(13.3)	9(60.0)	4(26.7)	15(100.0)
National defense	9(40.9)	0(0.0)	13(59.1)	22(100.0)
Government ad & local autonomy	3(11.5)	20(76.9)	3(11.5)	26(99.9)
Education	3(16.7)	9(50.0)	6(33.3)	18(100.0)
Science, technology, information & telecommunication	3(17.6)	3(17.6)	11(64.7)	17(99.9)
Culture & tourism	3(10.7)	0(0.0)	25(89.3)	28(100.0)
Agriculture, forestry, maritime affairs & fisheries	5(20.0)	4(16.0)	16(64.0)	25(100.0)
Commerce, industry & energy	3(11.1)	0(0.0)	24(88.9)	27(100.0)
Health & welfare	2(12.5)	5(31.3)	9(56.3)	16(100.1)
Environment & labor	3(15.8)	9(47.4)	7(36.8)	19(100.0)
Construction & transportation	2(11.1)	7(38.9)	9(50.0)	18(100.0)
Intelligence	2(50.0)	0(0.0)	2(50.0)	4(100.0)
Total	71(21.7)	104(31.8)	152(46.5)	327(100.0)
Average	4.4	6.5	9.5	20.4

Source: Compiled and modified from 1998 Year Annual Audit Related Data Compilation (in Korean) (Secretariat of the Korean National Assembly, 1999: 4-15).

committees auditing below the average were the environment & labor committee (19), the education committee (18), the construction & transportation committee (18), the national policy committee (18), the science, technology, information & telecommunication committee (17), the health & welfare committee (16), the unification, foreign affairs & trade committee (15), the house steering committee (9) and the intelligence committee (2).

When we categorize the agencies from the viewpoint of their nature, approximately one fifth of all the agencies audited are central administration agencies (21.7%), one third are local administration agencies (32.1%) and the rest are other auxiliary agencies including central and local governments investment agencies. It is apparent, therefore, that annual auditing emphasized in order, other auxiliary agencies, local administration agencies and central administration agencies when judged in terms of the number of agencies audited. When we group the target agencies on the basis of the committees under whose jurisdiction they belong, the house steering committee (88.9%), the intelligence committee (50.0%) and the national policy committee (50.0%) laid more emphasis on central administration agencies than the others. The committees with more emphasis on local administration agencies were the government administration & local autonomy committee (76.9%), the legislation & judiciary committee (74.2%), the unification, foreign affairs & trade committee (60.0%), the education committee (50.0%), the environment & labor committee (47.4%) and the finance & economy committee (44.1%), the committees with more stress on other auxiliary agencies were the culture & tourism committee (89.3%), the commerce, industry & energy committee (88.9%), the science, technology, information & communication committee (64.7%), the agriculture, forestry, maritime affairs & fisheries committee (64.0%), the national defense committee (59.1%), the health & welfare committee (56.3%), the construction & transportation committee (50.0%), the intelligence committee (50.0%), and the national policy committee (50.0%). In conclusion, most of the committees did not focus primarily on central administration agencies except for the house steering committee.

2. Target Issues

The result of the analysis on the number of issues reviewed in the process of annual auditing is shown at <Table 3>. According to the table, the annual auditing by the Assembly has reviewed 12,349 issues. It means that each committee audited 771.8 issues on the average. When we regroup them with respect to committees raising issues, the committees which audited more issues than the average were the construction & transportation committee (1,541), the education committee (1,331), the agriculture, forestry, maritime affairs & fisheries committee (1,290), the finance & economy committee (1,229), the legislation & judiciary committee (1,161), the culture & tourism committee (1,061), the national policy committee (884), the government administration & local autonomy committee (879), and the environment & labor committee (862). Meanwhile, those with less than the average were the science, technology, information & telecommunication committee (542), the national defense committee (380), the unification, foreign affairs & trade committee (380), the health & welfare committee (361), the commerce, industry & energy committee (253), the house steering committee (164) and the intelligence committee (30).

Seen from the nature of target agencies, it is demonstrated that the annual auditing by the National Assembly has paid more attention to central administration agencies (36.4%), other auxiliary agencies (34.4%) and local administration agencies (29.2%). However, the differences are very trivial. The committees with more emphasis upon central administration agencies in the process of bringing up audit issues were the house steering committee (97.6%), the national defense committee (84.2%), the intelligence committee (56.7%), the agriculture, forestry, maritime affairs & fisheries committee (50.9%) and the finance & economy committee (46.7%). The committees focusing on local administration agencies were the government administration & local autonomy committee (76.3%), the education committee (75.8%), the legislation and judiciary committee (57.4%), the health

<Table 3> Target Issues by Committees in 1998

Committees \ Agencies	Central ad. agencies	Local ad. agencies	Other aux. agencies	Total
House steering	160(97.6)	0(0.0)	4(2.4)	164(100.0)
Legislation & judiciary	495(42.6)	666(57.4)	0(0.0)	1,161(100.0)
National policy	376(42.5)	0(0.0)	508(57.5)	884(100.0)
Finance & economy	574(46.7)	143(11.6)	512(41.7)	1,229(100.0)
Unification, foreign affairs & trade	112(29.5)	148(38.9)	120(31.6)	380(100.0)
National defense	320(84.2)	0(0.0)	60(15.8)	380(100.0)
Government administration & local autonomy	137(15.6)	671(76.3)	71(8.1)	879(100.0)
Education	160(12.0)	1,010(75.8)	162(12.2)	1,332(100.0)
Science, technology, information & telecommunication	143(26.4)	100(18.4)	299(55.2)	542(100.0)
Culture & tourism	510(48.1)	0(0.0)	551(51.9)	1,061(100.0)
Agriculture, forestry, maritime affairs & fisheries	657(50.9)	94(7.3)	539(41.8)	1,290(100.0)
Commerce, industry & energy	56(22.1)	0(0.0)	197(77.9)	253(100.0)
Health & welfare	86(23.8)	144(39.9)	131(36.3)	361(100.0)
Environment & labor	290(33.6)	248(28.8)	324(37.6)	862(100.0)
Construction & transportation	400(26.0)	378(24.5)	763(49.5)	1,541(100.0)
Intelligence	17(56.7)	0(0.0)	13(43.3)	30(100.0)
Total	4,493(36.4)	3,602(29.2)	4,254(34.4)	12.349(100.0)
Average	280.8	225.1	265.9	771.8

Source: Compiled and modified from Correction & Treatment Requested Items of the 1998 Year Annual Auditing by the National Assembly (in Korean) and Reports of 1998 Year Annual Auditing by the Committees (in Korean).

& welfare committee (39.9%) and the unification, foreign affairs & trade committee (38.9%). The committees with most emphasis on other auxiliary agencies were the commerce, industry & energy committee (77.9%), the national policy committee (57.5%), the science, technology, information & telecommunication committee (55.2%), the culture & tourism committee (51.9%), the construction & transportation committee (49.5%) and the environment & labor committee (37.6%).

3. Time Input

Another way of gathering basic information related to the functional locus of annual auditing is to measure the time involved in the process of auditing. The result of analysis on the input time is shown at <Table 4>. According to the table, they spent 1,834 hours and 24 minutes for the entire auditing in 1998. This means that each committee spent 114 hours and 39 minutes on average, which makes about approximately 5 days. When we re-examine this on the basis of differences between target agencies, they spent 680 hours and 4 minutes on auditing central administration agencies (37.1%), 462 hours and 59 minutes on local administration agencies (25.2%), and 691 hours and 21 minutes on other auxiliary agencies (37.7%). In other words, the bulk of the time went on reviewing central administration agencies and other auxiliary agencies and the least for local administration agencies-judged comparatively .

When we review the time spent on a committee by committee basis, the committees that put in more time than average were the government administration & local autonomy committee (183 hours and 28 minutes), the construction & transportation committee (166 hours and 27 minutes), the agriculture, forestry, maritime affairs & fisheries committee (149 hours and 15 minutes), the commerce, industry & energy committee (145 hours and 13 minutes), the finance & economy committee (143 hours and 20 minutes), the education committee (136 hours), health & welfare committee (128 hours and 39 minutes), the environment & labor committee (127 hours and 9 minutes) and the legislation & judiciary committee (115 hours and 58 minutes). The committees with below-average input times were the agriculture & tourism committee (109 hours and 38 minutes), the science, technology, information & telecommunication committee (106 hours and 28 minutes), the unification, foreign affairs & trade committee (96 hours and 21 minutes), the national defense committee (95 hours and 45 minutes), the intelligence committee (17 hours and 30 minutes) and the house steering committee (8 hours and 47 minutes).

When we analyze the time in view of the nature of target agencies audited, the committees to outlay more time for auditing central administration agencies than for auditing others were the house steering committee (88.8%), the national defense committee (60.7%),the legislation & judiciary committee (57.2%), the national policy committee (50.6%), the health & welfare committee (43.7%), and the environment & labor committee (42.1%). The committees with more time for local administration agencies were the government administration & local autonomy committee (67.6%), the education committee (52.0%) and the unification, foreign affairs & trade committee (44.2%). The committees with more time for other auxiliary agencies were the culture & tourism committee (76.7%), the commerce, industry & energy committee (66.9%), the intelligence committee (66.8%), the science, technology, information & telecommunication committee

(66.3%), the construction & transportation committee (52.5%), the finance & economy committee (45.9%) and the agriculture,

<Table 4> Time Input by Committees in 1998

Agencies / Committees	Central ad. agencies	Local ad. agencies	Other aux. agencies	Total
House steering	7:48(88.8)	0:00(0.0)	0:59(11.2)	8:47(100.0)
Legislation & judiciary	66:18(57.2)	49:40(42.8)	0:00(0.0)	115:58(100.0)
National policy	52:52(50.6)	0:00(0.0)	51:31(49.3)	104:26(99.9)
Finance & economy	52:36(36.7)	24:59(17.4)	65:45(45.9)	143:20(100.0)
Unification, foreign affairs & trade	39:08(40.6)	42:37(44.2)	14:36(15.2)	96:21(100.0)
National defense	58:05(60.7)	0:00(0.0)	37:40(39.3)	95:45(100.0)
Government administration & local autonomy	46:25(25.3)	124:00(67.6)	13:03(7.1)	183:28(100.0)
Education	50:22(37.0)	70:46(52.0)	14:52(10.9)	136:00(99.9)
Science, technology, information & telecommunication	25:25(23.9)	10:26(9.8)	70:37(66.3)	106:28(100.0)
Culture & tourism	25:30(23.3)	0:00(0.0)	84:08(76.7)	109:38(100.0)
Agriculture, forestry, maritime affairs & fisheries	65:16(43.7)	17:23(11.7)	66:36(44.6)	149:15(100.0)
Commerce, industry & energy	48:01(33.1)	0:00(0.0)	97:12(66.9)	145:13(100.0)
Health & welfare	56:15(43.7)	29:27(22.9)	42:57(33.4)	128:39(100.0)
Environment & labor	53:33(42.1)	41:18(32.5)	32:18(25.4)	127:09(100.0)
Construction & transportation	26:39(16.0)	52:23(31.5)	87:25(52.5)	166:27(100.0)
Intelligence	5:48(33.1)	0:00(0.0)	11:42(66.9)	17:30(100.0)
Total	680:04(37.1)	462:59(25.2)	691:21(37.7)	1,834:24(100.0)
Average	42:30	28:56	43:13	114:39

Source: Compiled and modified from 1998 Year Annual Audit Related Data Compilation (in Korean)(Secretariat of the Korean National Assembly, 1999: 4-15).

forestry, maritime affairs & fisheries committee (44.6%). Generally speaking, such distribution of time input among committees and agencies audited reflects and parallels the nature of the target agencies. The committees under whose jurisdiction more agencies dealing with nation-wide affairs were placed more emphasis on central administration agencies. The committees with more agencies dealing with local issues put more emphasis on local administration agencies. And committees with agencies dealing with specific consumer-oriented interests put more stress on other auxiliary agencies. Reviewing the research results from this perspective, the health & welfare committee and the environment & labor committee were exceptional in the sense that they put more emphasis on central administration agencies although they serve the interests of groups with specific interests.

4. Audit Types

It cannot be denied that motives determine auditing objectives and strategies; this, in turn, leads to a certain locus of function. Therefore, it is an imperative to identify motives in order to clarify the functional locus. Since the types of auditing classified previously are mainly based upon motives and intentions of the auditing, we can grasp the thrust of auditing motives when we group the auditing works into legality (A), performance (B), policy (C) and political auditing (D) and classify their composition rate. It is a known fact that the former three types of auditing are completed by requesting corrective measures and by evaluating the executive's responses as with other public audits. The last type, political auditing, is completed simply by raising issues with the public and not reaching up to the level of requiring compulsory corrections and real control of the executive. In other words, the prime objective of political auditing is not to control the executive but only to signal the desired response. Therefore, we can classify audit types into two : 1) public auditing to require correction and

<Table 5> Audit Types by Committees in 1998

Agencies / Committees	Legality (A)	Performance (B)	Policy (C)	Political (D)	Total
House steering	1	64	32	67	164(100.0)
Legislation & judiciary	4	47	10	1,100	1,161(100.0)
National policy	3	42	26	813	884(100.0)
Finance & economy	16	141	48	1,024	1,229(100.0)
Unification, foreign affairs & trade	3	80	15	282	380(100.0)
National defense	5	40	12	323	380(100.0)
Government ad & local autonomy	24	157	18	680	879(100.0)
Education	16	298	12	1,006	1,332(100.0)
Science, technology, information & telecommunication	4	172	25	341	542(100.0)
Culture & tourism	10	416	155	380	1,061(100.0)
Agriculture, forestry, maritime affairs & fisheries	6	88	52	1,144	1,290(100.0)
Commerce, industry & energy	2	82	30	139	253(100.0)
Health & welfare	9	81	19	262	361(100.0)
Environment & labor	49	123	38	652	862(100.0)
Construction & transportation	11	179	66	1,285	1,541(100.0)
Intelligence	0	1	6	23	30(100.0)
Total	163(1.3)	2,001(16.2)	564(4.6)	9,621(77.9)	12.349(100.0)
Average	10.2	125.1	35.3	601.3	771.8

Source: Compiled and modified from Correction & Treatment Requested Items of the 1998 Year Annual Auditing by the National Assembly (in Korean) and Reports of 1998 Year Annual Auditing by the Committees (in Korean)

feedback on responsive measures 2) political auditing to simply raise pertinent issues. Those classified as public auditing could be grouped into legality, performance and policy auditing after analyzing their contents. The result of such classification is shown at <Table 5>.

According to the above table, legality auditing dealt with 163 items (1.3%); performance auditing 2001 items (16.2%); policy auditing 564 items (4.6%) and political auditing 9621 items (77.9%). In other words, three fourths of the entire annual auditing process is political auditing. Performance auditing constitutes the largest portion (16.2%) of the public auditing, policy auditing the second largest (4.6%), and legality auditing the smallest (1.3%). Such findings confirm the fact that the annual auditing does not lay prime emphasis upon sensationalism-oriented legality auditing as they have become used to frequent journalist criticism (Ahn, 1998: 2). On the contrary, the National Assembly's priority is in bringing political issues to the public's attention. Therefore , it is difficult to call this public auditing.

When we review such characteristics from the vantage point of committees, we can see that all of the committees are paying most attention to political auditing with the exception of the culture & tourism committee. And when we restrict our review to legality, performance and policy auditings, all of the committees emphasize performance auditing except for the intelligence committee. In the case of the government administration & local autonomy committee, the education committee and the environment & labor committee, legality auditing receives most attention.

The result of arranging the audit types according to the difference of target agencies' nature is shown at <Table 6>.

<Table 6> Audit Types by Target Agency's Nature

Auditing / Agencies	Legality (A)	Performance (B)	Policy (C)	Political (D)	Total
Central ad.	53(1.2)	751(16.7)	332(7.4)	3,357(74.7)	4,493(100.0)
Local ad.	62(1.7)	507(14.1)	57(1.6)	2,976(82.6)	3,602(100.0)
Other aux.	48(1.1)	743(17.5)	175(4.1)	3,288(77.3)	4,254(100.0)
Total	163(1.3)	2,001(16.2)	564(4.6)	9,621(77.9)	12,349(100.0)

According to the table, it is clear that the emphasis is laid on political, performance, policy and legality auditing in that order all through the process of auditing the central administration agencies, local administration agencies and other auxiliary agencies. When we see the situation from the standpoint of audit types, legality auditing receives more emphasis in the case of local administration agencies, and performance auditing in the case of central administration and other auxiliary agencies. Policy auditing is the emphasis of central administration agencies, and political auditing is the main interest of central administration agencies and local administration agencies.

Seen in totality, more audits are undertaken by the legislation & judiciary committee, the finance & economy committee, the government administration & local autonomy committee, the agriculture, forestry, maritime affairs & fisheries committee, the environment & labor committee and the construction & transportation committee. The auditings of other auxiliary agencies and central administration agencies constitute the main body of the annual auditing process. Generally speaking, the central administration agencies are emphasized more than other agencies by the house steering committee. Local administration agencies are the main interest of the government administration & local autonomy committee and the education committee. Other auxiliary agencies are emphasized by the national policy committee, the science, technology, information & telecommunication committee, the culture & tourism committee, the commerce, industry & energy, and the construction & transportation committees. This indicates that central administration agencies and local administration agencies are dealt with most frequently by the committees to which the agencies with nation-wide constituents belong while other auxiliary agencies are emphasized by the committees to which the agencies dealing with narrower interests belong.

When we evaluate them by objectives, political auditing is most dominant and performance, policy and legality auditing are emphasized in sequence. Policy auditing and legality auditing receive the lightest weighting.

IV. Functional Locus of the Annual Auditing

The functions of the annual auditing will become clear when it is decided what and how much to audit. By the same reasoning, the functional locus of the annual auditing is dependent upon the accomplishment level of the objectives and the intensity of the auditing process; the accomplishment level of the audit, in turn, is dependent upon the intensity and the indepth nature of the entire procedure.

1. Intensity of the Auditing

In order to assess how intensively they have audited, each audit target agency is examined in view of number of issues raised per agency. The result of such examination is shown at <Table 7>.

<Table 7> Audit Issues Per Target Agency

Committees \ Agencies	Central ad.	Local ad.	Other aux.	Average
House steering	20	0	4	18
Legislation & judiciary	62	29	0	38
National policy	42	0	56	49
Finance & economy	96	9	39	36
Unification, foreign affairs & trade	56	16	30	24
National defense	36	0	5	17
Government ad & local autonomy	46	34	24	49
Education	53	112	27	74
Science, technology, information & telecommunication	48	33	27	32
Culture & tourism	170	0	22	38
Agriculture, forestry, maritime affairs & fisheries	131	24	34	52
Commerce, industry & energy	19	0	8	9
Health & welfare	43	29	15	23
Environment & labor	97	28	46	45
Construction & transportation	200	54	85	86
Intelligence	9	0	7	8
Average	63.3	34.6	28.0	37.8

According to the table, the annual audit deals with 42 issues per target agency on average. When we re-examine them on an individual committee basis, the distribution of the culture & tourism (89 issues), the construction & transportation committee (86 issues), the education (74 issues), the agriculture, forestry, maritime affairs & fisheries committee (52 issues), the national policy committee (49 issues), the government administration & local autonomy committee (47 issues) and the environment & labor committee (47 issues) reveal that these committees have dealt with more issues than the average. Committees with below the average figures are the legislation & judiciary committee (38 issues), the finance & economy committee (36 issues), the science, technology, information & telecommunication committee (32 issues), the unification, foreign affairs & trade committee (24 issues), the health & welfare committee (23 issues), the house steering committee (18 issues), the national defense (17 issues), the commerce, industry & energy committee (9 issues) and the intelligence committee (8 issues). In other words, the committees dealing with nationally significant agencies raised relatively fewer issues than those with sectoral or regional interests. Therefore, it is natural to expect that the auditing intensity of the former would be stronger.

When we re-examine in light of the nature of the target agencies, it is shown that the number of issues raised was proportioned as follows: central administration agencies (73.5 issues), local administration agencies (34.6 issues) and other auxiliary agencies (32.8 issues). The committees with an emphasis on auditing central administration agencies were the culture & tourism committee (411), the construction & transportation committee (200), the agriculture, forestry, maritime affairs & fisheries committee (131), the environment & labor committee (97), the finance & economy committee (96), the legislation & judiciary committee (62), the unification, foreign affairs & trade committee (56), the science, technology, information & telecommunication committee (48), the government administration & local autonomy committee (47), the health & welfare committee (43), the national defense committee (36), the house steering committee (20), the commerce, industry committee and energy committee (19) and the intelligence committee (9). The committee with an emphasis on local administration agency was the education committee

(12) and that which focused on other auxiliary agencies was the national policy committee (56). In other words, almost all of the committees lay emphasis upon central administration agencies.

2. Indepth of the Auditing

The time input indicates the auditing intensity per issue. Therefore, it is imperative to measure time input in order to learn

<Table 8> Time Input Per Issue

Agencies / Committees	Central ad.	Local ad.	Other aux.	Average
House steering	3	0	15	3.2
Legislation & judiciary	8	5	0	6.0
National policy	8	0	6	7.1
Finance & economy	6	11	8	7.0
Unification, foreign affairs & trade	21	23	7	15.2
National defense	11	0	38	15.1
Government administration & local autonomy	20	11	11	12.5
Education	19	4	6	6.1
Science, technology, information & telecommunication	11	6	14	11.8
Culture & tourism	3	0	6	6.2
Agriculture, forestry, maritime affairs & fisheries	6	11	7	6.9
Commerce, industry & energy	51	0	30	34.3
Health & welfare	39	12	20	21.4
Environment & welfare	11	10	6	8.9
Construction & transportation	4	8	7	6.5
Intelligence	21	0	54	35.0
Average	9.1	7.7	9.8	8.9

about the intensity of the auditing process. The result of such measurement is shown at <Table 8>.

According to the table, time input per issue is 8.9 minutes on average. Such time input includes time for reporting the current situation of each agency by the executive and for adjournment. When we subtract such time from the total auditing time, it becomes apparent that the real audit time is too short to conduct any indepth auditing. When we review the input time by committee, the committees with above-average audit time are the intelligence committee (35.0 minutes), the commerce, industry & energy committee (12.5 minutes), the health & welfare committee (21.4 minutes), the unification, foreign affairs and trade committee (15.2 minutes), the national defense committee (15.1 minutes), the government administration & local autonomy committee (12.5 minutes), the science, technology, information & telecommunication committee (11.8 minutes) and the environment & labor committee (8.9 minutes). Those with below-average input time included the national policy committee (6.5 minutes), the finance & economy committee (7.0 minutes), the agriculture, forestry, maritime affairs & fisheries committee (6.9 minutes), the construction & transportation committee (6.5 minutes), the culture & tourism committee (6.2 minutes), the education committee (6.1 minutes), the legislation & judiciary committee (6.0 minutes) and the house steering committee (3.2 minutes).

When we re-examine in view of the nature of the agencies, issues of central administration agencies were audited for about 9.1 minutes per unit on average, those of local administration agencies for 7.7 minutes, and those of other auxiliary agencies for 9.8 minutes. In other words, auxiliary agencies, central administration agencies and local administration agencies were audited more intensely in sequence. The committees with more audit time on each issue for central administration agencies were the commerce, industry & energy committee (51 minutes), the health & welfare committee (39 minutes), the government administration & local autonomy committee (20 minutes), the education committee (19 minutes), the environment & labor committee (11 minutes), the legislation & judiciary committee (8 minutes) and the national policy committee (8 minutes). Those with more audit time per issue for local administration agencies included the unification, foreign affairs & trade committee (23 minutes), the finance & economy committee (11 minutes) and the construction & transportation committee (8 minutes). Those with more audit time per issue for other auxiliary agencies were the intelligence committee (54 minutes), the national defense committee (38 minutes), the house steering committee (15 minutes), the science, technology, information & telecommunication committee (14 minutes), the agriculture, forestry, maritime affairs & fisheries committee (7 minutes) and the culture & tourism committee (6 minutes).

3. Fidelity of the Auditing

The annual auditing by the National Assembly requires the agencies to take corrective measures and report their responses in some cases. It is clear that one of the major objectives of public auditing is to remedy the mistakes and misconceptions of the executive; this is a precondition of successful public auditing. Thus, it is required to identify which portion of the issues in the annual auditing process require corrective measure requests. It would tell us which portion of the annual auditing reached the final level of correcting errors by the executive and, thereby, satisfy the general qualifications of a genuine public auditing. The ratio between the entire number of issues raised and remedial request issues is shown at <Table 9>.

According to the table, the objective accomplishment rate in the annual auditing process reaches 22.1%. In other words, 77.9% of the annual auditing is political-auditing-oriented. Evaluating this on a committee basis those with higher accomplishment rates than average are the house steering committee (59.2%),

<Table 9> Ratio of Issues for Corrections and Treatments

Issues / Committees	Target issues (a)	Issues requested corrections & treatments(b)	Ratio(b/a)
House steering	164	97	59.2
Legislation & judiciary	1,161	61	5.3
National policy	884	71	8.0
Finance & economy	1,229	205	16.7
Unification, foreign affairs & trade	380	98	25.8
National defense	380	57	15.0
Government administration & local autonomy	879	199	22.6
Education	1,332	326	24.5
Science, technology, information & telecommunication	542	201	37.1
Culture & tourism	1,061	581	54.8
Agriculture, forestry, maritime affairs & fisheries	1,290	146	11.3
Commerce, industry & energy	253	114	44.5
Health & welfare	361	109	30.2
Environment & labor	862	210	24.4
Construction & transportation	1,541	256	16.6
Intelligence	30	7	23.3
Total	12,349	2,728	22.1

the culture & tourism committee (54.8%), the commerce, industry & energy committee (44.5%), the science, technology, information & telecommunication committee (37.1%), the health & welfare committee (30.2%), the unification, foreign affairs & trade committee (25.8%), the education committee (24.5), the environment & labor committee (24.4%) and the intelligence committee (23.3%). Those with a lower rate than the average are the finance & economy committee (16.7%), the construction & transportation committee (16.6%), the national defense committee (15.0%), the agriculture, forestry, maritime affairs & fisheries committee (11.3%), the national policy committee (8.0%) and the legislation & judiciary (5.3%). Generally speaking, the committees dealing with the national agencies show a lower rate in realizing the basic objectives of the annual audit. In other words, they approach the process from a more politics-oriented perspective.

When we reexamine according to the nature of the agencies audited, the results are shown at <Table 10>.

<Table 10> Issues Requested Corrections and Treatments Per Audited Issue and Agency Type

Issues / Agencies	Target issues(a)	Issues requested corrections & treatments(b)	Ratio(b/a)
Central ad. agencies	4,493	1,136	25.3
Local ad. agencies	3,602	626	17.4
Other aux. agencies	4,254	966	22.7
Total	12,349	2,728	22.1

According to the table, the objective-accomplishment rate on central administration agencies is 25.3%, that on local administration agencies 17.4% and that on other auxiliary agencies 22.1%. The nature of the annual auditing as a public matter is reflected most in the auditing of central administration agencies.

Political auditing is typical in the process of local administration agencies. Summing up these findings, the government administration & local autonomy committee and the environment & labor committee show high objective-accomplishment rates in both intensity and scope. They audited more issues using more time. The higher rate of accomplishment is shown in the committees dealing with agencies serving particular interests. In these committees, more emphasis is laid upon public auditing in general and upon performance auditing in particular and less upon political auditing. However, seen from an overall vantage point, the annual auditing is so highly biased toward political auditing that we may call it politicized auditing rather than public auditing. Studying this in view of the nature of agencies audited, the annual auditing of central administration agencies reviews more issues and shows a relatively stronger public auditing element. In the annual auditing of local administration agencies, the least time per issue is allocated and the political nature of the process is most apparent. In the auditing of other auxiliary agencies, most time is allocated per issue and a relatively smaller number of issues is involved. The auditing nature - political and public - of other auxiliary agencies lies in between those of central and local administration agencies.

V. Conclusion

The annual auditing is one of the control mechanisms of the National Assembly on the executive. It comes into effect in the following order: central administration agencies, local administration agencies and other auxiliary agencies. When the evaluation criterion is the number of target agencies, however, more institutions are actually audited in the following order: other auxiliary agencies, local administration agencies and central administration agencies. When it comes to the number of target issues, more issues are audit-targeted in central administration agencies, other auxiliary agencies and local administration agencies. In the case of time input into auditing process, time is outlayed in the following order: other auxiliary agencies, central administration agencies and local administration agencies. In other words, the main target institutions of the annual auditing are other auxiliary agencies and more time is spent on auditing them than on any others. The number of their target issues is placed in the middle of the three agencies. In the case of central administration agencies, the number of audit target agencies is smallest, the number of audit target issues is the highest and time input on the audit process is positioned midway. In the case of local administration agencies, audit target issues and time spent are least significant and the number of agencies targeted is in a central position. Therefore, the totality of the annual audit analysis reveals that the relative importance of other auxiliary agencies is highest and the attention given to local administration agencies is the lowest of the three.

Re-examined in view of audit intensity per unit, the number of target issues audited per agency appear in the following order: central administration agencies, local administration agencies and other auxiliary agencies. But, time input per audit target issue reveals a different order: auxiliary agencies, central administration and local administration agencies. The ratio of target issues requiring corrective action is highest in the following order: central administration agencies, other auxiliary agencies and local administration agencies. In other words, more audit target issues are brought up in the audit process for central administration agencies than in any other audit process and more time is input when individual audit target institutions are precisely reviewed. As a result, audit target issues of central administration agencies lead to correction of the executive more often than those of any other type. That is, audit fidelity is the highest in the auditing of central administration agencies. With respect to local administration agencies, relatively moderate audit target issues are brought up and the least time is input; this results in the lowest ratio of audit target issues requiring correction and treatments vs. total audit target issues. It means that the audit of local administration agencies is relatively formal, ritualistic and political. In the audit of other auxiliary agencies, the number of audit target issues is the smallest and most time is involved. However, the ratio leading to requests for correction is in the middle. It means that the audit investigation of other auxiliary agencies is the most concentrated but its accomplishment degree of audit objectives is in the middle. Therefore, when the annual auditing is reviewed from the viewpoint of audit fidelity, the relative importance of central administration agencies audit is the highest and the weight of local administration agencies audit is the lowest.

When audit contents are taken into consideration, the annual auditing is overwhelmingly politically orientated. The others are composed mainly of performance auditing and the relative importance of policy auditing and legality auditing is very low.

Let me summarize these findings. Among the three types, other auxiliary agencies are the main type in terms of volume of audit issues, and audit process to central administration agencies is the most sincere. But, the relative importance of local administration agencies audit is the lowest in terms of targets and process fidelity. When objectives and intentions of auditing are considered, the annual auditing is political-audit-oriented.

The annual auditing is one of the control mechanisms on the executive. Therefore, it should emphasize more the control duties of national policy-planning agencies. This means that the emphasis on central administration agencies takes priority, the audit of local administration agencies is in second place, and the audit of other auxiliary agencies for assisting implementation is in third place. The contents of the annual auditing require it to center around policy auditing because it is a type of public auditing and an external control mechanism on the executive not an internal one. The findings show that there is a remarkable difference between the original intent of the annual auditing and the actual setting of its targets and objectives. It means that it does not function as a control mechanism.

The critique against the locus of the annual auditing does not simply inform us of its substantial function. It is more meaningful in that it informs us of the relationship between the Assembly and the executive. According to conventional theories of political science and public administration, the fundamental philosophy of a representative democracy required that there should be a division of duty between the National Assembly and the executive. That is, it was suggested that the National Assembly had to embody people's political demands and make policies while the executive had to implement them. Therefore, the National Assembly should confirm whether or not legislative intentions are distorted and damaged in the implementation processes. It should continuously investigate, direct and supervise administrative processes in order to achieve these aims. The annual auditing is one of the means to implement these functional tasks.

The basis of the existence of the National Assembly is on the pursuit of political rationality while that of the executive is on pursuing economic rationality. Therefore, the annual auditing can be seen as a process inputting the political rationality of the Assembly into the economic rationality of the executive. Until now, however, public administration and political science explain simply the functional contact-point between the executive and the legislature from a normative standpoint or discuss it only in a mandatory respect. It comes short of empirical and concrete studies on the interactive process between the two. Therefore, the study on the functional locus of the annual auditing contributes to reducing such shortage of its empirical information.

In this context, it is necessary that the annual auditing creates a hybrid of political auditing for political rationality and public auditing for economic rationality. However, substantial controls should be in force in order for political auditing to be effective. To do so, it is the first task in a reform process to convert political auditing to policy auditing. This is because policies are actual alternatives both for controlling the executive and for achieving tangible performance. But, the empirical studies on the annual auditing show that the ratio of policy auditing in annual auditing is less than 5 percent. It means that the annual auditing does not function as a control mechanism but is simply an extension of the political activities of the legislature.

Chapter 04

Confirmation Hearings for Cabinet Members

I. Introduction

One of the popular political commentators in Korea made a very unusual remark recently asserting that the Park Geun-Hye regime, whose term has eclipsed one and half years only out of 5 years, is already over in terms of its governability as a real power broker(Lee, 2014.08.01.). Popularity rate of the president, which stood near 60 percent in March, is hovering around 40 percent in July 2014(Digital News Team, 2014.08.01.), the lowest ever since she took office in 2013. Such a serious plunging of her popularity owes much to a series of failures in obtaining approval of her political nominees from the confirmation hearings of the National Assembly in addition to the regime's inability and inadequacy as well shown in the process of responding to the April ferry drowning accident.

Up to now, 3 out of 4 prime minister nominees, designated by her ever since the commencement of the regime, have withdrawn in the whirl of controversies raised either by corruption, violation of administrative rules or inadequate remarks made by the nominees, before reaching to the confirmation hearings of the National Assembly. And in case of the incumbent prime minister, she accepted the resignation submitted by him as a token of apologies to the public in the wake of the ferry accident but reaffirmed him as prime minister after two months later from the date of accepting the resignation. Such an unusual retainment was understood widely as an indicator of her fear about possible failure in obtaining approval from the confirmation hearings when she designates a replacement. In addition to that, for the second cabinet formation process only, 3 out of 8 secretarial nominees were either recalled by the president herself, failed in obtaining confirmations from the National Assembly, or self withdrawn by the nominee himself even before reaching to the confirmation hearings, which is interpreted, in fact, as an outcome of covert advice from the president to withdraw.

As an aftermath of such president's successive failures in appointing cabinet members, the president's leadership has been crippled seriously, which is required urgently in the efforts to push through legislation aimed at spurring economic recovery, overhauling government systems and stamping out social ills accumulated through the industrialization process (Ji, 2014.06.30). President Park's plan was to give a fresh impetus to her reform drive by shaking up her cabinet, but she ran into problems being halted by the political hurdles placed in the confirmation hearings of the National Assembly (Ji, 2014.06.29.).

At the extension of the president's strenuous efforts, in such a context, to regain political supports and popularity, at a senior secretaries' meeting held at the presidential office, she asked the political parties to seek ways to improve the confirmation hearings process(Shin, 2014.06.30) implying strongly that her failures in obtaining confirmation of the cabinet member nominees owes much to the inadequacies pertinent to the current hearing system of the National Assembly. Reform needs of the contemporary confirmation hearings system were also raised by the Speaker of the National Assembly(Ha, 2014.06.26.). Touching on mounting criticism that confirmation hearings have been mainly used by legislators to pry into nominees' private lives in an attempt to humiliate them, the Speaker drew attention to the issue of reforming the confirmation hearings system as one of the prioritized reform agendas of the National Assembly (Ha & Kang, 2014.06.27.).

It has become evident that the current confirmation hearings system does not guarantee the professed or expected outcomes of the system but brings in more controversial impacts than positive ones to the contemporary politics in Korea.

II. Why Did We Adopt the Confirmation Hearings System?

The confirmation hearings system is one of the American political inventions. It is designed to verify the competence of high-ranking officials of the executive to carry out their jobs, their personal backgrounds, their political positions and their perceptiveness for grasping social trends and changes, as well as the degree of popular support for their appointments. It reflects American society's deep suspicion about political power and a strong desire to restrain the power. All power, when concentrated, is bound to become corrupt and misused. So the idea of holding confirmation hearings is based on the belief that a collective verification process could reduce the chances of making mistakes and misusing of such power in the selection of government officials.

In the case of career bureaucrats, they have performance evaluation system that can be used to measure their ability and project their future potentials. But in the case of political appointees, it is a challenging task to weigh their capability to response to the constantly changing needs and demands of the people and make flexible collaboration with diverse ideas and aspirations. Confirmation hearings are based on the belief that the best possible way of meeting such challenge is to have a cross-checking mechanism mobilizing multiple examiners in evaluating the ability of appointees in a public session.

Spoils system is unavoidable to guarantee political loyalty and share common political ideologies binding a group of people who are politically accountable for reigning any regimes. But it should not become conduits for the incompetent or the corrupt to gain high ranking positions of the government. In fact, the legislature is conferred various ways to restrain the power of the executive. Among them, the control of human resources management power is considered perhaps the most decisive and effective way of scrutinizing the executive. That is why confirmation hearings have been so vigorous in the United States.

Confirmation hearings are expected to raise effectively the prestige of government officeholders and the public trust in their offices. Obviously, those who have come through confirmation hearings successfully deserve public confidence in their abilities and experiences. And the fact that the elected representatives of the people confirmed their appointments added to their prestige. Knowing the nominees must face the hearings, the president is forced to select nominees with deliberate care. This is another factor that boosts the acceptability of the nominees in the eyes of the public. If cabinet members knew that they were selected through a confirmation committee's assessment and verification rather than because of the personal preference of one individual, it would facilitate the emergence of true leadership from the ranks of public officials. In such an event, it would also become easier for the appointees to administer the ministries they lead.

Confirmation hearings will also boost the prestige of the legislature as well. Wielding many nearly unlimited powers, the president is sometimes called a modern-day emperor. The hearings will confer to the legislature the capacity to effectively restrict, control and supplement the power of the president. Furthermore, during confirmation hearings, nominees are usually forced to reveal the thrust of the policies they will pursue and the kind of approaches they will take for solving pending social problems. This offers the legislature a solid, concrete basis for exercising control over the process of policy implementation by the executive. The hearings will allow the legislature to share the power of appointing high ranking officials, which otherwise would be monopolized by the president. Moreover, they will get the legislature involved in the process of administrative actions.

As long as the prospect of confirmation hearings will be a burden to the president, they will serve as a restraint on the tendency of presidents to quickly dismiss cabinet ministers, making them sacrificial lambs so that the president can escape political responsibility for difficult situations. This will mean that cabinet ministers will serve for relatively longer periods, which will enhance stability in the administration and allow ministers more time to gain a good command of their jobs and to pursue long-term policy goals.

Once the thrust of the administration's policies is spelled out at confirmation hearings, the nominees after becoming cabinet members have to feel obliged and entitled to stick to the policies. This will accordingly generate a certain amount of political pressure onto the ministers as they run their offices. Since administration policies in effect have been endorsed by the legislature through the hearings, the ministries will implement them with greater confidence. The overall effect would be to make national politics more policy-oriented.

Since the hearings are conducted publicly, they provide the nominees with an opportunity to publicize and sell policies to the public. Consequently, the system promotes the political socialization of citizens. Hopefully, it would promote the resolution of political conflict and expedite social integration further. Since the hearings are conducted by legislators, the tendency would be to emphasize political sensibility and responsiveness of the nominees. Administrative processes, which tend to be swayed by objective and scientific rationality, will be exposed through the hearings to accommodate political demands. Cabinet members will be expected to play a greater role as a political bridge between the traditional bureaucracy and the polity. This will encourage the appointment of those with a superior political sensitivity.

With the advent of the information society, one-dimensional hierarchies and unilateral governing system from up to down have become passé. Unless the government promotes joint responsibility and collaborative partnership with the civil society organizations, it will not be able to handle its tasks effectively. Therefore, cabinet members and other high-ranking officeholders need to gain the approval of the people more than ever before. Political rationality rather than bureaucratic rationality should be the base for appointing qualified officials to serve in a future-oriented society. The legislature would be a better judge of such persons than the executive. There is a structural need to institutionalize the legislature's involvement in the task of filling high positions of the executive.

III. Issues Raised in the Operation of Confirmation Hearings in Korea

As we have witnessed in the recent cases of cabinet member nominees confirmation hearings, too much emphasis is laid upon the evaluation of ethical dimension of the nominees and less on professional expertise, policy directions and leadership capacity. The confirmation hearings have been diverted into the bivouac of bloc confrontations between ruling party and opposition ones attempting a sort of character assassination by delving into the private lives of nominees or by making an issue out of affairs not directly related to the nominees' qualifications for fulfilling the tasks at hand. Meanwhile, the legislators from the ruling party are prone to defend the nominees with blind eyes without providing many appealing grounds. Under such circumstances, it becomes evident that the confirmation hearings serve less as a checking mechanism of policy directions that the nominees would like to pursue once they become cabinet members. And thus, less as a promoter of political socialization among the people with diverse focus of interests and perspectives. Instead, the confirmation hearings aggravate further political cleavages existing already among the political parties and the people as well. They bring in political confrontation instead of political integration, which is expected to be promoted by design.

In addition to that, in such situations, few people becomes

to dare in stepping forward to work for the government in the fear of being disclosed of one's own private affairs and penalized as an immoral figure destroying one's own whole life and that of all family members as well. It is very natural, as like the president Park retained current prime minister, that the president becomes hesitant in replacing even improper or incompetent cabinet members in the fear of failing in locating and soliciting competent replacements, who have higher possibility in obtaining confirmations from the National Assembly, and thus maintain mediocre government. It also is possible that damage inflicted on the character of nominees during the hearings could injure their future ability and the trust they will need after the confirmations to lead the ministries.

And there also takes an inclination to designate members of the National Assembly as cabinet member nominees in the expectation that they could be confirmed with more ease than others from out of the National Assembly. There is an unproven belief that the members of National Assembly are relatively more ethical since they have been screened by a series of election competitions and thus less plausible to be accused of ethically unsoundness and/or irregularities committed through one's lives. In fact, personal networks established in the works of National Assembly contribute in relieving the nominees from very challenging scrutiny of their personal lives in the process of confirmation hearings by their colleagues. Aspirations of the legislators to be picked up by the president as members of cabinet also add to such tendency of not attempting hard in character assassination of the nominees designated among the legislators since they would like to induce the president's favoritism for the legislators in the process of nomination. No one from the National Assembly designated as cabinet member nominees has failed in obtaining confirmation from the National Assembly up till now ever since the adoption of the system.

As a natural outcome of such practices, more weight becomes to be placed upon cabinet members holding concurrent job of legislators in spite of the presidential system under which Korean governance system is supposed to work. It is a very unusual phenomenon that the cabinet members have concurrent job of legislators, which is one of the basic institutional quintessence of a cabinet system (Kwon, 2014.07.07). The cabinet system is built on the base of power integration principle. Meanwhile, the presidential system is built on the principle of "check and balance" and " separation of powers" between the executive and the legislature. However, at present, all of the two deputy prime ministers are filled by concurrently legislators. Even if we accept the rationale that the Korean constitutional framework is built on the theoretical base of mixture between presidential system and cabinet system and not of a presidential system in a sure sense and, therefore, there is no problem of constitutional violation or controversies, still it is tilted too much toward the practices of cabinet system. It is especially so when we are reminded of the constant social claims and arguments raised by the leaders in academia(Choi, 2014.07.21) and civil society movements(Citizen's Coalition for Economic Justice, 2013.06.25) as well that the National Assembly law permitting legislators concurrent job with cabinet members has to be changed and declared unconstitutional.

At the extent of such an argument, it is true that the National Assembly could not delve into character assassination of the nominees even if they would like to make use of confirmation hearings as a tool to penalize the political foes as long as the president designates more ethically sound nominees by maintaining an extended pool of talented candidates and keeping further track of their verification records with more in-depth research and considerate investigation. In that sense, the presidential office has to bear some portion of responsibility for such derailed manner of running the confirmation hearings. Amidst of such arguments about which one is more responsible for the "politically intrigued manner" of running the confirmation hearings between the presidential office and the National Assembly, there also arises the issue of pushing the nominees to withdraw even before reaching to the actual forum of confirmation hearings.

As soon as the president designates someone for a cabinet position, not only the political arena but also the public and the media as well start scrutiny over the nominee's personal affairs and threaten candidates' right to privacy. As they escalate in their discussion and denounce about the personal lives of nominees, the public's uproar reaches to a certain point of intolerance, explodes like steam coming out of exit and condemns the nominees to withdraw from candidacy. Obviously the media play a critical role in drawing the people's attention to such personal lives of the nominees and driving the nominees to back off. The media reports in Korea in regards to political nominees are usually very harsh, relentless, and even acrimonious owing much to their political alignment. It is very common in Korea that they side with political blocs, and their reports are, generally speaking, affected by their ideological alliance. They sometimes act like an extension of individual political parties. Such a tendency is fostered by the wide-spread use of internet and SNS as well. Especially SNS plays a key role nowadays in channeling wide-spread rumors and politically motivated messages to the public. Thus, once a nominee is judged by the public as unqualified or unsuitable for the cabinet, then, they begin to ask for self-withdrawal from candidacy even before reaching the confirmation hearings. The rationale for such a demand is that since it has been judged already by the people, there is no need to be evaluated by the delegates of the very people again. They assert that it is a misuse or waste of government resources to hold confirmation hearings for such already judged candidates.

The case of Moon Chang-Keuk, who was nominated for prime minister but voluntarily withdrew his candidacy in 2014, shows us a very clear example of such a working mechanism in Korean society. Conservative bloc including several key leaders of the ruling Saenuri party asserted that he must have been granted the right of reply regarding controversies raised against him through a confirmation hearing. However, the progressive bloc insisted that he should have withdrawn far earlier.

IV. Reform Proposals to Current Working System of Confirmation Hearings

For any cabinet member nominees, whether ethically suitable for the position or not is a pre-condition that has to be cleared, in fact, by the president before being designated. In that sense, the presidential office should revise its personnel appointment system. They shouldn't pin the blame on the confirmation hearings of the National Assembly. However, we also have to pay attention to the assertions that the ethical standards applied by the confirmation hearings are unrealistically too high to locate suitable candidates for the cabinet. It is particularly so when we are reminded of the very fact that the Korean society has gone through a very turbulent time of disorder and confusion for the past several decades of compact development. In such a social and historical context, few people could be free from the allegations of dishonesty as like tax evasion, fake resident registration, and plagiarism which are very frequently accused of in the confirmation hearings. More than anything else, there is no universal standard of ethics being applied to the nominees. Sometimes faking resident registration just one time has been counted as a critical point of unsuitability for passing the confirmation and other times they did not pin it seriously. Sometimes they extend confirmation to the nominees with serious plagiarism and other times not. In other words, they are in the serious needs of detailed rules of operation stating clearly ethical standards uniformly applicable and agreed upon among the stakeholders of the hearings

Even if they come out with such detailed rules of operation, they still could be accused of being too much biased toward the examination of ethical suitability and too less on professional ability and leadership of the nominees. They might be so either because of their political intention to give a hard time to the president or their unpreparedness in discussing policy-oriented issues against the nominees. For the former case, as long as the current political contour in Korea built basically upon political rivalism, confrontation and ideological division leading up to hatred between ruling and opposition blocs is not cured and more freedom is given to individual legislators, there is no way to change such a practice voluntarily by the legislators themselves. In order to drive them to focus more on the evaluation of the candidates' professional suitability in handling the offices, in such a context, it could be recommended to mandate them to hold two separate whole days of hearings for professional suitability only out of three days allocated at the present confirmation hearings law(Park, 2014: 188). And in that case, hearing days should be extended to four days adding one more day to the current practice since not enough time is permitted to the candidates to defend themselves in the question and answer sessions of the hearings and there could be an accusation that such a mandatory measure pre-exempts enough time to review ethical suitability of the nominees, which is not the real intention of proposing such a reform measure.

On the other hand, according to the current system, the president is bound by the outcome of confirmation hearings in appointing prime ministers but not in the case of cabinet members. It is ridiculous, however, to appoint nominees to the cabinet after seriously being inflicted by character assassination of the confirmation hearings and judged even by the public as unsuitable for the cabinet positions. When the president appoints the candidates who failed in obtaining confirmations from the National Assembly, each stake-holders involved in the confirmation hearings lose their legitimacy and leadership basis as well including the president, the members of the confirmation hearings, and the nominees themselves. There is no reason not to bind the president from appointing the nominees to the cabinet when they fail in obtaining confirmations from the National Assembly. It is better to change current confirmation hearings law and bind the president as like the case of prime minister nominees.

It is also advisable not to appoint legislators to the cabinet as long as we adopt and hold the presidential system as a base of the constitutional frame. It should be suggested to change the National Assembly law permitting concurrent job of legislators with the cabinet of the executive and not to allow such a practice anymore (Park, 2014: 178). It also should be reminded that there is no reason to bind withdrawal of the nominees from the candidacy even before reaching the confirmation hearings. There are two perspectives vying each other on this issue. From the standpoint of interests group theory, it is very natural and agreeable to withdraw from the candidacy once a nominee is judged by the public as unsuitable for the office. And hence, either the president or the nominee oneself could decide to withdraw affirming to such political judgment of the public. However from the vintage point of legality and formality, anyone designated as the nominee should be brought to the open forum of confirmation hearings and judged officially by the legislators whether to be confirmed or not. However, it should be reminded that the confirmation hearings are designed not simply for deciding whether to confirm or not but also for other political objectives such as the promotion of political socialization and integration by spreading and sharing information and policy directions as well. In that sense, there is no reason to bind the candidates not to resign before reaching to the official forum of confirmation hearings since all of the political processes related to the hearings are to work for checking acceptability of the nominees by the public at the final last.

On the other hand, in a perusal to promote institutional memory and professionalism of confirmation hearings committee members and thus to make them focus more on professional suitability of the nominees, it could also be suggested to unify current two-track systems of organizing committees. At present, the cabinet member nominees are reviewed by individual standing committees whose jurisdiction covers the ministries for which the nominees are supposed to work. Meanwhile they organize separate special committees to review prime minister nominees, which allows, in fact, leeway for the party leadership to deploy political snipers and thus to make them easy to make use of the hearings as a tool to assassinate personal fame of the nominees and politically assault the president. Such a practice of changing committee membership at the pleasure of party leadership, on the other side, makes it difficult to keep continuity of the committee membership and, thus, to promote committee member's professionalism about the subjects related to the office. It brings in a relatively low level of professionalism of the hearing committee members and makes them hesitant in touching on policy issues instead of an ethical dimension of the nominees.

V. Conclusion

It is not arguable anymore that the confirmation hearings system was adopted from the Unites States without serious consideration of the contextual difference in which they are supposed to operate. The current working mechanism of the system proves that they should have been warned enough to be further cautious in their preparation of the system implantation process in order to guarantee professed outcome of the system in the Korean political context. Any political design does not produce social impacts by itself but by encountering with social energies in which the design operates. Likewise, any reform proposals suggested here could not satisfy all the necessary and sufficient conditions to bring in and thus actualize professed impacts to Korean politics. They should only be counted as a part of the necessary condition for the political reform in Korea. In other word, without changing the bloc confrontation nature and the wide-spread hatred among political blocs in Korea, there is no way to guarantee reform effects expected to be produced in the operation of Korean governance.

On the other hand, it should be noted also that one of the major objectives of the confirmation hearings is to reduce such distrust and tension pending among the political blocs and between the government branches as well, which is required more urgently in Korean politics. In that sense, there is no royal road to make the confirmation hearings produce professed outcomes and thus reform them but to take a zigzag strategy approaching the ideal situation step by step. The reform proposals suggested here would contribute in reshaping the nature of Korean political context a little and such changed context at the next step would contribute for revising further appealing rules and thus better working mechanism.

In this context, the reform proposals suggested here should not be considered as the whole of reform suggestions nor as the only alternative to each reform agendas. There could be a lot of other ways to approach for the similar objectives and to respond to the reform needs and demands of the contemporary working mechanism of the confirmation hearings in Korea. Even if we all agree that the reform suggestions proposed here are more appealing than others, still there remains the issue of whether the National Assembly would accept them and really work on changing the statutes related to the proposals. Anyway, it is true that the reform proposals suggested here are designed with the intention to minimize the undesirable side effects of the confirmation hearings in the context of Korean politics.

The confirmation hearings in Korea examine not only cabinet member nominees but also many other high-ranking officials nominees of the executive and the judiciary as well: as like the Chairman of the Board of Audit and Inspection, the Director of the National Intelligence Service, the Director of the National Tax Service, the Chief Justice of the Supreme Court, and Chief of the Constitutional Court of Korea, and etc. But only the confirmation hearings about the cabinet member nominees are discussed here this time since they have been operated in the most controversial manner in comparison with other cases up till now and have been held very recently making us easier in collecting relevant information and tracing vivid reflections.

Chapter 05

Baseline Assessment of Political Parties

I. Determinants of Korean Party Politics

1. Resilient Regional Antagonism[1)]

There is a long tradition of regional antagonism in Korea. During the Japanese occupation, Japan opened the Korean peninsula to the international community and initiated a series of manipulation programs to the then traditional society of Korea. Under such context, capitalism was introduced to the Youngnam (southeast) region for the first time meanwhile the other parts of

---

* It was assessed in 1997.

1) At the by-election held in July 2014, for the first time ever since 23 years of political regional antagonism, Lee Jung-Hyun from ruling Saenuri party symbolizing Youngnam region was elected as a member of the National Assembly from Honam region. It is counted as a thawing indicator of regional sentiment in Korean politics. The intensity of regional antagonism is loosening after the melting down of the political cartel established among *the three Kims*.

the nation remained dormant since the region was the nearest tip of the Korean peninsula to Japan. In other words, owing to the Japanese manipulation policy to exploit the Youngnam region as a beachhead to make an economic inroad into Korea, the region was exposed to the capital economy system earlier than the other parts of the nation and this continued to bring a regionally unbalanced development of the nation. The region accumulated and produced stronger and larger capital than the other parts of the nation and was able to provide their off-springs with better and higher education opportunities. Those with better opportunities in education and wealth have become hegemonic power holders and remained as such almost all through the modernization process of the nation. And even during the industrialization process of the nation, most of the industrial projects and sites were concentrated in this area partially due to the political favoritism exercised by the hegemonic power holders of the government from the region and partially to the geoeconomic reason of providing better shipping facilities, industrial water, and manpower. This, again, aggrandized imbalance and widened the economic and social gap between the Youngnam region and the other parts of the nation in general and the Honam (southwest) region in particular.

Meanwhile, the Honam region has been the main provider of agricultural products including rice to the nation. It had been the richest area in the nation during the traditional society. However, since rice was a major commodity Japan preferred with a prime interest to exploit, the economy of the region was devastated more than the other parts of the nation during the Japanese occupation. And even after the independence, owing to the unexpected and full-fledged land reform policy launched under the leadership of the first president of the Republic, the economic infrastructure of the area was toppled down even though such measure was an inevitable one to maintain capitalistic system against plausible infiltration of communism from the North. The region became poorer than the other parts of the nation and was provided with lesser opportunity to educate their off springs.

Due to such an imbalance in socioeconomic power of the regions and other coincidental reasons, the Youngnam region has produced a series of regime holders and maintained their hegemonic power in recent years in Korean politics. Such a tilted power balance has brought a regional antagonism between the two areas and politicians manipulated such rivalry sentiments pertinent in these areas for the mobilization of political supports from the people of the regions respectively. It is very obvious that such political manipulation of the regional sentiments has dramatized regional antagonism further. And there takes a new phenomenon in recent days that such a regionalism has spread into Choongchung (midwest) region where has stood aloof from such regional and sentimental confrontation for long time. The regionalism newly found in Choonchung region seems to owe much to political reasons. Those in Choongchung region have evaluated themselves undercounted by the government in comparison with other regions of the country and such negative perception to the central government burst into a local sensibility when they found a political leader who could symbolize such regional sensibility among the people of the region.

2. Politicized Bureaucrats and Depoliticized Legislators

The normative relationship between the executive and the legislature is tension oriented in Korea since they are intentionally designed to share equal and direct representation from the people.

The president, who is the single most important leadership of the executive, is elected directly by the people from the nation at large meanwhile the members of the legislature are also elected by the people this time on the base of individual districts. Even though they are supposed to collaborate with each other in producing policies and programs harmoniously, they also are expected to compete for the protection of the people's interest. Especially political parties interlinking the two branches of government are designed to cooperate and/or scrutinize each other. But in Korea, in fact, political parties are dominated and controlled indirectly and sometimes even directly by the executive.

For instance, the ruling party is tantamount to an assistant to the executive. Such a locus is established and maintained by the president, who holds both headships of the executive and that of the ruling party as well. Due to these double hats, there arises an important result that the head of the executive could nominate the leadership of the ruling party and recommend candidates for the membership of the legislature. By this way the internal working mechanism of the legislature is bureaucratized and controlled by the bureaucrats who exercise their influence via the president's office and the bureaucrats are highly politicized in the sense that they become major agents of the power games among national political leaders.

In the case of opposition parties, they seem to be free from the dominance by the executive at the first glance. But in fact, since the information kept by the executive are not shared with them, they cannot effectively oversee and scrutinize government operation. In other words, the institutional capability of opposition parties is not sufficient enough to control the executive. And furthermore, sometimes, they cannot help but compromise with the executive behind the scene in order to invite government programs and projects to their constituencies, look after grievances of their constituents, and raise funds and donations from business circles who, in fact, are under the influence of the bureaucrats. They are reluctant to scrutinize the executive closely. However, they also try to overcome such shortcomings of not aggressively scrutinizing the executive by aggrandizing political gestures of opposing against the projects and programs submitted by the executive. They fear to be shown to the eyes of the general public as if they cooperate with the ruling party and the executive as well. Once they collaborate with the ruling party and the executive, they believe, their political base of legitimacy as an opposition party would be damaged seriously. Such a perception owes much to the past experiences of the iron rule under the authoritarian military regimes. During that period, any cooperation with the ruling regime was taken as a betrayal to the hopes and aspirations of the people.

Such historical inheritances limit the optional boundaries of alternatives that the opposition parties could take. They almost all the time oppose ideas and suggestions raised by the ruling party and the executive as well, and are prone to be against collaboration with them. Therefore, it becomes very difficult to bargain and compromise among the parties in Korea. Such an attitude is also re-enforced by the lack of experience in regime change in the modern political history of Korea[2]. They are not provided with opportunities to share perspectives and experiences of the other parties. In other words, opposition parties in Korea are not alternative parties to ruling party but supplementary

2) There took two regime changes after 1997 when the assessment was written. Kim Young-Sam regime of the conservative party was succeeded by Kim Dae-Jung regime of the progressive party and No Moo-Hyun regime of the progressive party to Lee Myung-Bak regime of the conservative party.

ones in a broad sense since they assist government legitimacy by their own existence of symbolizing opposition and not by sharing substantive suggestions and accountability. Instead of compromising and collaborating openly with the ruling regime, the opposition parties legitimize the political party system by their existence and participation.

3. Single-member Electoral System

Nearly almost all of political parties in Korea are electoral machine. The prime purpose of organizing political parties is to mobilize voters particularly during the election cycles. In addition to this, since they have adopted a single member district system, election campaigns managed by the political parties are very much severe and competitive. They are enforced to play a zero-sum game since only a single seat is allocated for the district and therefore only one candidate is designed to become a member of the National Assembly. And since the election campaign is so severe, it becomes inevitable to organize and maintain very strong local party networks in each district to mobilize voters. And thus in order to maintain such a large local party chapter, it becomes necessary to raise and dispense a large sum of illegal political funds. Because of this, some radical reformers assert that single member district system should be abolished and medium and large sized district system be adopted since single member district system itself is the prime source of "expensive politics" mandating politicians to solicit slush funds and fall into bribery and other political malfeasances.

And as you might well know single member district system is prone to over-represent majority voters and underestimate political weight of minority voters. Thus, there is an inclination to produce larger and dominant parties and to lessen the possibility of minor parties' entrance to legislature. In such situation, regionalism, as we have discussed above, is enjoyed by dominant parties of each region of Youngnam, Honam and Choonchung. A single dominant party of each region enjoys over-representation of the area respectively.

II. Political Party System in Korea

1. Personalized Party System

There are three major parties currently in Korea in 1997. The ruling New Korea Party(NKP) is a successor of the former ruling Democratic Liberal Party, which was renamed to a party formed by a merger among the then three major parties : the ruling Democratic Justice Party, the first opposition Unification Democratic Party and the second opposition New Democratic Republican Party. The merger was taken place in an attempt to rescue the then ruling Democratic Justice Party from possible defeat of the 14th presidential election. Owing to this merger, the incumbent president Kim Young-Sam was elected to the 14th presidential position. However, he ran for the position not as a candidate of the Democratic Justice Party but as that of the Democratic Liberal Party since he changed name of the merged party from the Democratic Justice Party to the Democratic Liberal Party after he was nominated as a presidential candidate of the Democratic Justice Party.

In fact, the Democratic Justice Party was organized in 1980 when then general turned politician Chun Doo-Hwan climbed up for the position of the 11th president via indirect election. General Chun was elected to the position by the presidential electorate which was consisted with 5,278 delegates. These delegates were elected all across the nation through 2 or 5 member districts. And when he nears to the end of the term of his office as the 12th president, he nominated his close friend and coupde'ta partner Roh Tae-Woo as the 13th presidential candidate of the then ruling Democratic Justice Party. Due to the July Citizen's uprising in 1987 that stood against the president Chun's intention to maintain indirect presidential election system, however, the ruling party was obliged to change the constitution and to adopt direct presidential election system.

Roh Tae-Woo was elected the 13th president by direct election but he suffered from decreasing political support all through his term of office particularly due to his poor leadership and legacy of illegitimate behavior of leading military coupde'ta which toppled down the 10th president Choi Kyu-Ha. When he realized that there was few chance of winning next presidential election for ruling party and of guaranteeing his political safety after stepping down from his presidential officialdom, he tried to merge with minor opposition parties to win the election. Kim Young-Sam, then president of second opposition party, agreed to merge with the ruling Democratic Justice Party on the condition that he becomes the presidential candidate of the newly merged party. Obviously a very gloomy projection over his being elected as the 14th president as long as he remains as a candidate of the second largest opposition party pushed him to agree with the merger suggestion extended by the then president Roh Tae-Woo. But right after the merge, he preferred to change the name of the Democratic Justice Party to the Democratic Liberal Party in order to differentiate political identity of himself from the two former presidents who founded and nurtured the party. The two former presidents, however, were very notorious of their dictatorial control of the nation. They were backed by brutal coercion and political censorship. It was understood that without erasing the image of those two former presidents out from the party, it was not easy to win the presidential election for the ruling party. Such a judgment drove him to change the name of the party.

However, in the middle of the presidential term of office, Kim Young-Sam faced strong political pressure from the general public to purge the two former dictators and put them before the courts. President Kim Young-Sam put the two former presidents into trial and sent them to jail. In an attempt to change the general image of the ruling party, he, then again, changed name of the ruling party from the Democratic Liberal Party to the New Korea Party. Such a change of the party name is a kind of the symbolic gestures to cut out the hovering image of past ownership of the party.

The largest opposition party is the National Congress for New Politics (NCNP), which was organized under the leadership of Kim Dae-Jung. After a defeat from the 14th presidential election campaign, he publicly announced that he would like to retire from political front and to remain as a rank and file member of the Democratic Party (DP), from whose presidential candidate he ran for the election. But he, in fact, never gave up strings to control the Democratic Party indirectly. When the 15th presidential election date comes to near, he returned to politics reversing his pledge of not running for the presidential election again and tried to regain political hegemonic power and leadership of the Democratic Party but in vain. Due to this failure, he departed from the Democratic Party with his followers and created a new party, whose name is the National Congress for New Politics. The party, however, won second largest seats next to the KNP from the general election of the 15th National Assembly, which was held in 1996.

The second opposition party is the United Liberal Democrats (ULD). The party was organized under the leadership of Kim Jong-Pil when he left from the New Korea Party after being purged by the president Kim Young-Sam and his close followers. He made a good use of non-existence of any political party representing regional sentiments of Choongchung region and growing antagonism against the New Korea Party among the people of that region.

The third opposition party is the Democratic Party, which was organized during the 15th general election. The party declared to clean out old-fashioned politics of pork barreling, bribery and cohesive interlocking between capitalists and politicians and to bring generation change in politics but in vain. They won only 9 seats out from 253 seats allocated for direct election from local districts. And there are two more minor parties in addition to these parties that have produced no single seat in the general election for the 15th National Assembly. They are, however, registered to the Central Election Management Commission and met basic qualifications required by the Commission to organize political parties.

As such, the political parties in Korea are organized to decorate hegemonic power of political leaders who have already established power base before the creation of political parties. In other words, the political parties in Korea are created to serve for the personal political interests of the political leaders. That is why political parties in Korea are called as "aristocrats' clubs" and understood as windows to exercise power broking or power contests among leading politicians aloof from the general interests of the people. The political parties in Korea could be described as an end result of "palace intrigues" run by the nobles of higher echelon of the society and not as a political device to facilitate political participation and cohesion of the people. The single most important source of power that holds the political parties together is the personal cult of political leaders in each political party.

The seat distribution among such political parties in the 15th Korean National Assembly is shown at <Table 1>.

<Table 1> Seat Distribution among Political Parties of the 15th National Assembly

Party / Constituency	NKP	NCNP	ULD	DP & Others	Total
Local Districts	121(47.8)	66(26.1)	41(16.2)	25(9.9)	253(100.0)
Proportional Representation	18(39.1)	13(28.3)	9(16.6)	6(13.0)	46(100.0)
Total	139(46.5)	79(26.4)	50(16.7)	31(10.4)	299(100.0)

Source: Data compiled from Central Election Management Commission (1996: 140).

2. Regional Party System

When we classify political parties in Korea into national party and regional parties, it is shown that almost all of the political parties are national parties by name but, in fact, they are regional parties. Such a phenomenon owes much to the nature of political parties, which are highly privatized to the interests of few party leaders. Due to such characteristics, political parties in Korea signify personal leadership of national politicians. And then, national political leaders are usually produced from outside of the political arena and move into politics after making themselves as established national figures. They are grown in military, civil service, academia, anti-government civic movements and politics as well. However, it is very seldom to see politicians grown inside of the political arena[3]. Therefore, it is more important to focus on who leads the political party instead of what the leader insists as one's platforms or programs when we evaluate political parties in Korea. It is very important to learn about the prime group relations of party leaders — as like where he or she comes from, which school he or she has graduated, or which family group he or she is from — for the identification of political parties.

The current leaders of the national political parties are from different regions. In fact, they are identified by the people as representing their home-town pride and sentiments since the three most influential politicians, so-called *the three Kims*, have their own political parties organized on the base of political popularities in their own home towns respectively. Kim Young-Sam, president of the ruling NKP, has his strong power hold in Youngnam region. Kim Dae-Jung, president of the NCNP, enjoys strong popularity across Honam region. And Kim Jong-Pil, president of the ULD, symbolizes political wishes of the people living in Choongchung region. In other words, they are the symbolic figures of regional interests respectively, and a sort of political cartel system has been composed by them monopolizing Korean party politics for the last 30 years or so. They have established a very strong entry barrier into the Korean politics and enjoyed oligopolistic dominance of the Korean party politics. And such a towering position of them in their political parties respectively has brought in the formation of a sort of political syndicate among them.

Such a nature of the Korean political parties is more clearly shown at the elections. Almost all of the national elections have shown that the most dominant factor determining voting behavior

---

3) In December, 1992, Kim Young-Sam was elected as 14th president of the nation. He was the first national leader who has grown up inside of the political arena and became the president.

in Korea is regionalism. The magnitude of such a factor gradually increases as it comes near to the recent elections. Such a factor is clearly traceable at the 1996 general election also, which is the most recent national election undertaken. The result of the election is presented at <Table 2> below.

<Table 2> Seat Distribution among Regions in the 1996 Year General Election

Party / Region	NKP	NCNP	ULD	DP & INDEPENDENTS	Total
Seoul	27(57.4)	18(38.3)	0(0)	2(4.3)	47(100.0)
Kyunggi (Incheon, Kyunggi)	27(55.1)	12(24.5)	5(10.2)	5(10.2)	49(100.0)
Kangwon	9(69.2)	0(0)	2(15.4)	2(15.4)	13(100.0)
Youngnam (Pusan, Taegu, Kyungpuk, Kyungnam)	51(67.1)	0(0)	10(13.2)	15(19.7)	76(100.0)
Honam (Kwangju, Chunpuk, Chunnam)	1(2.7)	36(97.3)	0(0)	0(0)	37(100.0)
Choongchung (Taejun, Choongpuk, Choongnam)	3(10.7)	0(0)	24(85.7)	1(3.6)	28(100.0)
Cheju	3(100.0)	0(0)	0(0)	0(0)	3(100.0)
Total	121(47.8)	66(26.1)	41(16.2)	25(9.9)	253(100.0)

Source: Data compiled from Central Election Management Commission (1996: 142).

As it is shown at <Table 2>, in the Metropolitan city of Seoul, the NKP won 57.4% of the seats allocated for the region, while the NCNP 38.3%. In case of Kyunggi province, the NKP won 55.1% of the seats. In Kangwon province, the NKP won 69.2% of the seats. In Youngnam province, the NKP won 67.1%. However, in Honam province, the NCNP won 97.5% of the seats. In the case of Choongchung province, the ULD won 85.7% of the seats. And in Cheju province, the NKP won 100% of the seats. In other words, the NKP enjoyed dominant political supports from Seoul Metropolitan City, Kyunggi province, Kangwon province, Youngnam province and Cheju province. In the case of the NCNP, they got almost absolute supports from Honam province and comparatively strong supports from Seoul only. And the ULD was very strong in Choongchung province. Such a regional distribution of political supports among political parties is the most dominant and prevailing factor determining political party system in Korea

And, owing to this social heritage, there is no party, in fact, which enjoys nation-wide popularity, but they do only in a certain region. Due to such a political segregation among regions, the parties cannot play the role of political integrator of the nation successfully. In fact, they rather contribute to accelerating political disintegrations and cleavages among the regions and the people. Party functions as a dramatizer of the already grown regional rivalry sentiments and even emotional antagonism which are critically disfunctional to any political entity.

Although the reality of party politics in Korea is as such, the current law dealing with political parties has an intention to decentralize political parties all across the nation. The political party act stipulates that local chapters be dispersed to more than five of the Metropolitan City of Seoul, direct control cities and provinces and the number of local chapters that a political party establishes in any of the Metropolitan City of Seoul, direct control cities and provinces should not exceed a quarter of the total number of local chapters. In other words, the legal framework dealing with political parties in Korea assumes that only national parties contribute to the political needs and so legitimize them as a political tool for the betterment of politics. It seems to have an intention to promote a creation of national parties in an assumption that only such parties better serve for the political integration of the nation. Due to this disparity existing between legal intention and political reality, however, almost all of the political parties in Korea seem to be national parties when we evaluate them from a facade but in fact they are regional parties.

And because of this, the political parties in Korea are impotent in interest articulation cutting across the nation and representing national sovereignty. They function primarily for sentimental catharsis and as a kind of conduit to exit political discomforts and intolerance of respective regions.

3. Ideological Spectrum

When a raison d'etre of political party system is to realize or concretize policy objectives, voters will be more satisfied when they are provided with more policy options and choices. But in Korea almost all of the party platforms are right wing oriented in terms of ideological stance, and there are only slight differences among them. Such an ideological locus of parties owes much to the Korean experience with the communist regime in the North. Because of the Korean War provoked by the North in an intention to spread leftist ideology all across the peninsular, Koreans are very much sensitive and even allergic to leftist ideology and such a political attitude has long been nurtured even by the power holders of the government too. They even used McCarthyism from time to time as a tool to oppress freedom of the society in general and that of the political opponents. In addition to such ideological spectrum, which is so limited as to develop narrow differences among party platforms due to these historical and political reasons, they even copy each other's programs and present almost similar policy options. In other words, all of the political parties in Korea have an intention to employ strategies of catching voters from almost all segments of the society. Thus, voters in Korea are furnished with very narrow spectrum of policy choices. In this way, the needs of the people are not furnished with accuracy and diversity even from the starting point of interest representation system. Such a narrow and almost none difference to be exaggerated naturally requires less necessity of competition in policy development and results in low level of institutional capacity to develop policy programs among the political parties. And party's responsiveness and accountability to the needs and demands of the people naturally become low. In fact, generally speaking, party platforms and political programs are not developed from the bottom of political parties to up but coined by the party bureaucrats in general.

III. Internal Structure of Political Parties

1. Organizational Structure

Generally speaking, parties in Korea are very much hierarchical in their structure and thus highly bureaucratized. The main focus of organizational structure is laid upon administrative supporting system and voter mobilization affairs. And less upon policy making affairs. For instance, the central party organizational structure of the ruling NKP could be grouped into two categories - party decision-making structure and administrative supporting structure. And the administrative supporting structure could be grouped further into 4 categories: party affairs implementation, coordination works with the executive, coordination works with the legislature, and conduits to the general public.

For policy making, the national convention is the highest deliberation platform. The ordinary national convention is held once an every two years, and the extraordinary national convention can be called upon if necessary. As such, it is a ceremonial organ rather than a real deliberation template to build consensus among the party members.

The central executive council is the highest standing deliberation organ of the party. The council is mandated to deliberate and decide important party policy directions and others entrusted by the national convention when the national convention is in recess. These are the main body for party policy decision making. And the day to day operation of this council is entrusted further into the party office holders meeting, which holds meetings on daily bases and run a party. These are the representative apparatus of the party designed to make party policy directions.

For the implementation of party policies, the secretariat of the NKP is the main body to run the daily affairs of the party. The secretariat carries out party affairs by assisting activities of other party agencies and managing the party organizations. At the forefront of party affairs implementation process are the planning and coordination bureau, the general affairs bureau, the organizing affairs bureau, the youth affairs bureau, the functional affairs bureau, the public relations bureau, and the women's affairs bureau. At the early stages of the party institutionalization process, more emphasis was laid upon voter mobilization affairs and thus upon offices like the organizing affairs bureau, the youth affairs bureau, the women's affairs bureau, and the functional affairs bureau. However, nowadays, they come to realize that it becomes hard to mobilize voters simply by maintaining personal linkage with them and try to reach them through mass media and other information and communication technologies. They come to emphasize public relations affairs more than before. They are still, however, far behind laying emphasis upon policy development affairs.

For collaboration with the executive, the policy coordination committees are organized. The committees are mandated to study, deliberate, and shape major party policies. The committees also are expected to work for casework petitioned to the party. They are designed to coordinate with the high echelon bureaucrats responsible for respective social issues. Under the committees, there are the policy affairs bureau, the professional advisors and the casework bureau. The committees are staffed with professional advisors. They assist policy making activities of the party and bill drafting works for the legislators. In fact, the professional advisors are recruited from the executive. They resign from the executive at the requests of the party to join the committees and return to the higher positions of the executive after serving the committees for a certain period. Therefore, it is very natural that they are prone to be more loyal to the executive rather than to the party. Owing to this, the party's policy deliberation has its limits and is confined to the boundary of not directly opposing to the interests of the executive. The executive dominates the committees in terms of advising and guiding policy directions of their deliberations.

For the coordination with the legislature, the members' caucus is set up. The caucus is supervised by the floor leader. The floor leader is responsible for managing legislative deliberation process in and out of the legislature representing the interests of the party. The floor planning committee under the control of the floor leader is designed to provide template for the party legislators to discuss and coordinate major floor strategies and countermeasures necessary to promote and protect party interests inside of the legislature. In fact, however, it is not unusual that major policy directions and strategies are developed by party bureaucrats and leaders and sent to the individual legislators unilaterally. To support administrative needs and demands of the floor planning committee, they have organized the policy support office.

And for outreaching to the general public, the central standing affairs commission is organized. It is designed to provide conduits for functional representation of the people covering 15,000 opinion leaders from all walks of life. They are from about 100 social organizations. The commission is in charge of bridging the party with almost all of the functional segments of the society. The commission is consisted with 24 ad hoc committees in addition to 15 standing committees organized in accordance with the standing committees of the National Assembly. The ad hoc committees include such ones as like international affairs committee, economy revitalization movement committee, women's right promotion committee, rural area development and planning committee, and national unification committee. Each committee consists of about 600 members and holds a meeting about 4 times a year. A steering office is mandated to act on behalf of the central standing affairs commission. As such, the legal facade of the commission is to transform and communicate upward information and demands raised by the rank and file members of the party and the general public at large but, in fact, is to disperse and pass down opinions and thoughts of party leadership to the rank and file members of the party and to the general public.

The globalization promotion commission is also for opinion mobilization and mandated to shape policies necessary to promote globalization. And it receives assistance from the international affairs bureau.

The national advisory affairs commission is an advisory apparatus for the party president for the management of party and state affairs. The commission is consisted with the sate elders who have accumulated high level experiences in the executive branch of the government and/or professional fields as like former ministers, vice ministers, legislators, university presidents and etc. The commission is supported by policy evaluation committee.

The central training institute is mainly for training and educating members of the local chapters. The institute is assisted by the training evaluation committee and the training bureau.

Special committees could be set up in accordance with the provisions of the party constitution depending upon party leaders' requests as like the central ethics committee, the finance committee, the peaceful unification committee, the anti calamity measures committee, and the North Korea residents committee. The Yoido research institute is a party think-tank assigned to develop medium and long term policies. Such organizational structure of the NKP central party is shown at <Chart 1>.

Summing up, the party has many organs with different works and objectives. However, it has a strong reliance upon the works provided by the secretariat. In other words, the party is highly bureaucratized and run mainly by party bureaucrats. Party bureaucrats are recruited through open and competitive examination on the merit basis. They are paid on the salary base comparable to the representative business group employees. This is a little bit different from the cases of the opposition parties. Almost all of the party bureaucrats of the opposition parties are not paid

<Chart 1> Organizational Chart of the NKP Central Party

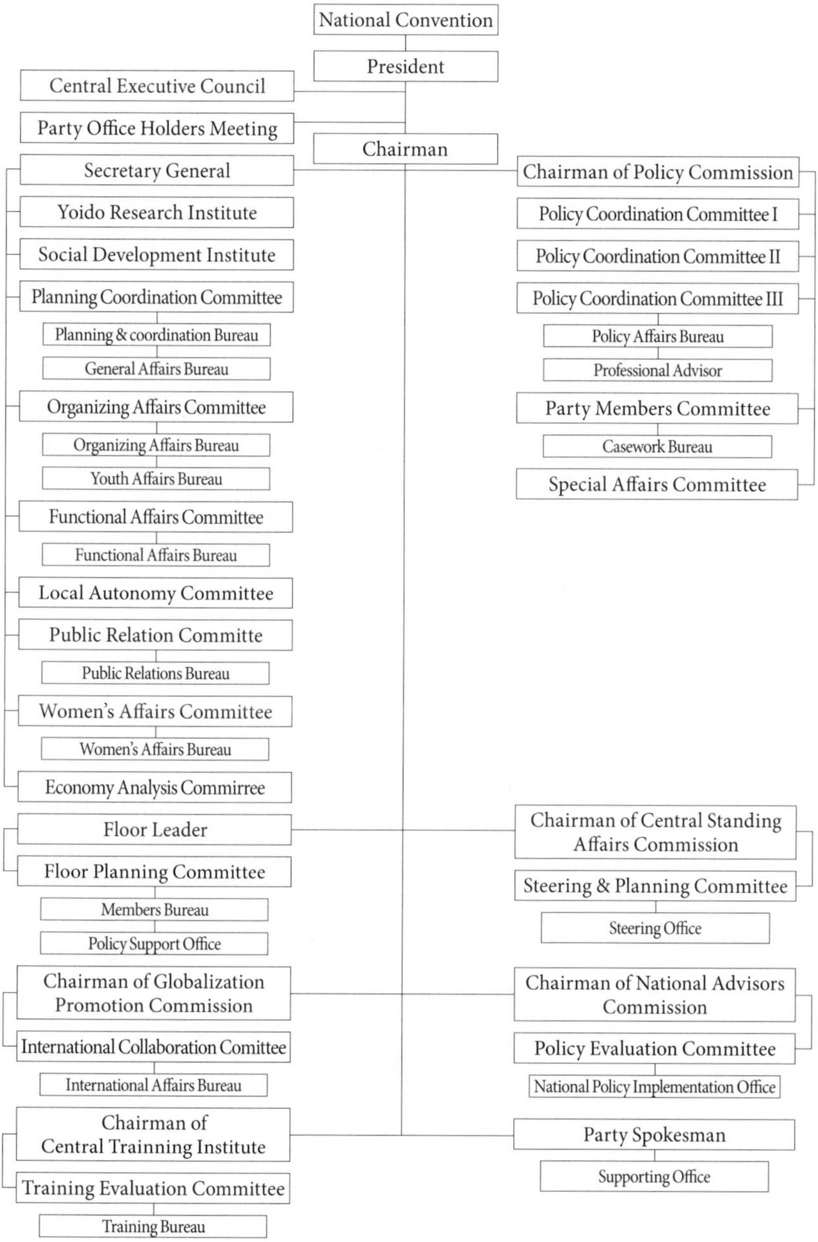

Source: Drawn on the base of Korea Democracy Foundation Archive Document No. 00208383(2012.08.20).

well, and very few of them are recruited on the merit system. Thus, the reliance on the party bureaucracy in the opposition parties is relatively lighter than that of the ruling party. In other words, the party bureaucracy of the opposition parties is more flexible than that of the ruling party and most of the party works are initially carried out by the members of the National Assembly, who are belonging to the political parties. Such phenomenon takes place since voter mobilization is the prime focus of interests for the political parties in Korea. And policy formation and interest articulation are secondary and even tertiary focus of interests to them.

In case of the NKP, city and provincial chapters and district chapters are organized as the regional apparatus of the party. The city (and provincial) chapter is consisted with convention, its organization and secretariat. The city (and provincial) convention is composed by the delegates elected from district chapters and those selected by the steering committee of the convention from functional groups under its jurisdiction. The organization is consisted with chairman, steering committee, and standing committees. The secretariat is composed by chief secretary, networking bureau, public relations bureau, local autonomy

<Chart 2> Organizational Chart of the NKP's City and Provincial Chapter

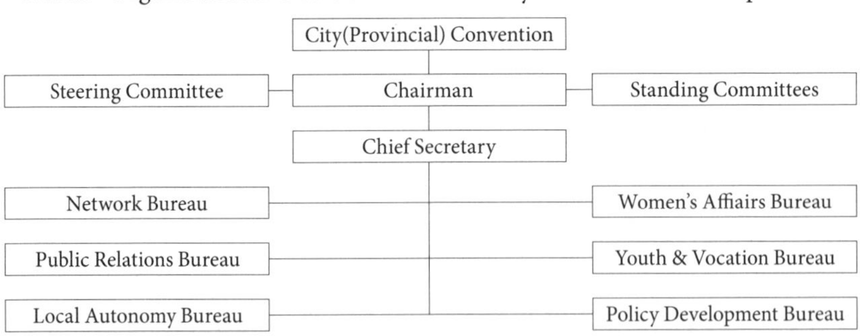

Source: Official Documents of the Secretariat of the NKP.

bureau, women's affairs bureau, youth and vocation bureau, and policy development bureau. The organizational chart of city and provincial chapter is shown at <Chart 2> above.

The district chapter consists of a district chapter convention, its organization, secretariat and relevant liaison offices. The district chapter convention is composed with delegates elected by the party affairs council and those selected by the steering committee of the district chapter convention from functional groups of the district. The district chapter organization is consisted with two tiers of key membership and senior membership. For the key membership, there are chairman, vice chairman, advisors and councilors, steering committee, standing committees, and secretariat. And the secretariat is composed by district secretary general (DSG), women's affairs bureau, and youth affairs bureau. For the senior membership, there are liaison affairs offices. For the

<Chart 3> Organizational Chart of the NKP's District Chapter

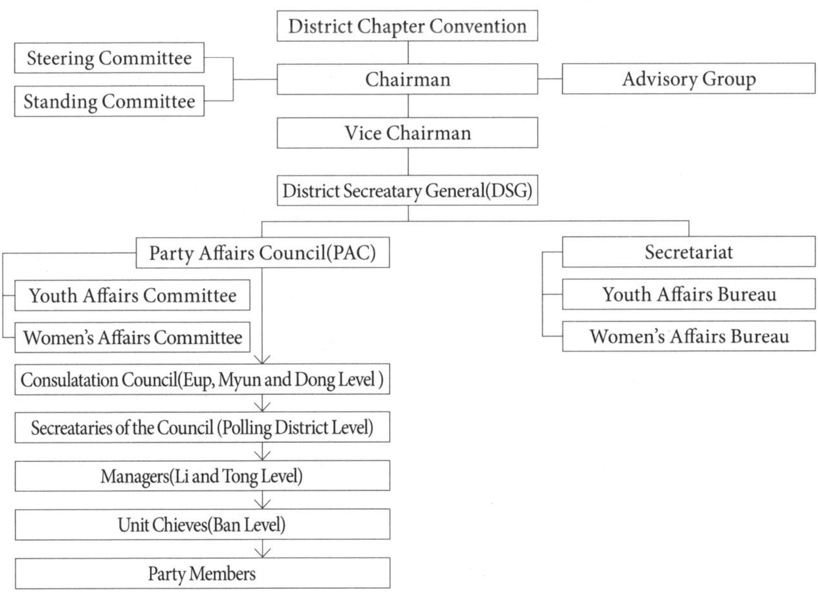

Source: Official Documents of the Secretariat of the NKP.

liaison affairs, there are party affairs council (PAC) organized at each level of government administration: Eup, Myun, and Dong under the jurisdiction of the district chapter. At each party affairs council, there are three different kinds of party officials. The ones are responsible for party affairs of each polling district (PD) under each Eup, Myun, and Dong. The others are managers at each Li (sub-village) and Tong (sub-village) level under each polling district. And unit chiefs responsible for the management of Ban level affairs. Such organizational structure of the NKP district chapter is shown at <Chart 3> above.

As such the local chapters of the NKP are very much sophisticated and well dispersed deep into the right neighborhoods of voters. They have a highly developed grass root apparatus to mobilize voters, and the level of bureaucratization of the party administration system is very high. In order to identify how many party officers are involved with the local party bodies and thus the level of bureaucratization, the number of party officials at district party chapters is traced since they are the forefront party officers directly facing and contacting with voters at the bottom of party structure. The result of the research is shown at <Table 3>.

According to <Table 3> below, it is very obvious that the NKP has a very highly developed district chapter system. At the upper echelon of the district party, they have 45,180 party officials organized all across the nation. Youngnam region has the largest upper structure of the district party officials in comparison with other areas. It is very natural since the officials are recruited according to the population size of each area. At the lower echelon of the district parties, they have 269,571 party officials scattered around the nation. And when we add up the whole district party officials joining to the NKP, it sums up to 314,751 persons. Since the total number of voters at the time of researching the number

<Table 3> Number of Party Officials at the NKP's District Chapter

Region Local Chapters			Seoul	Kyunggi (Incheon, Kyunggi	Kangwon	Youngnam(Pusan,Taegu,Kyungpuk ,Kyungnam)	Honam (Kwangju, Chunpuk, Chunnam)	Choongchung(Taejun,Choongpuk,Choongnam)	Cheju	Total
Key Mem-bership	Chairman		45	44	14	77	39	29	3	251
	Vice Chairman		842	757	115	1,168	580	546	52	44,060
	Advisors & Committees		1,140	1,426	431	2,043	1,552	1,717	99	8,408
	Steering Committee		4,264	2,138	201	2,441	1,070	912	111	11,137
	Youth		1,418	1,872	359	2,915	1,473	916	97	9,050
	Women		2,175	2,438	406	3,777	2,164	1,157	157	12,274
	Sub total		9,884	8,675	1,526	12,421	6,878	5,277	519	45,180
Senior Mem-bership	Chairman of PAC		499	676	126	1,196	793	502	55	3,846
	Vice Chairman	Youth	495	761	126	1,255	780	482	137	4,036
		Women	600	671	127	1,278	798	536	137	4,147
		PD	2,897	2,936	468	4,524	3,123	2,202	243	16,393
		Others	1,315	1,364	54	2,937	985	613	0	7,268
	Secretaries		505	682	125	1,174	798	474	55	3,813
	Managers		15,634	14,892	1,992	27,063	16,916	12,953	608	90.058
	VM		31,935	18,337	2,957	44,174	21,166	19,146	2,295	140,010
	Sub Total		53,880	40,318	5,975	83,601	45,359	36,808	3,530	269,571
Total			63,764	48,993	7,501	96,022	52,237	42,535	4,049	314,751

Source: Data compiled from International Affairs Bureau of the New Korea Party (1996: 436).

of the NKP district party officials is 31,488,294, the number of the district party officials indicates that the NKP has at least one district party official in ratio against 100 voters all across the nation. The NKP has mobilized a huge number of district party officials. However, the real number of party members is very small. And such situation is almost common to all of the other opposition parties. The only difference between the ruling party and the opposition parties is the size of party bureaucrats and officials engaged, and the natural result of such difference is the flexibility of party administration. Opposition parties are more flexible than the ruling party.

2. Membership of Parties

Since almost all of the Korean political parties are organized to decorate already established hegemonic power from top to down, the lack of real membership is inevitable. According to the official reports submitted to the Central Election Management Commission by the political parties at the end of 1996, party membership is not small in its size judging by its face value. But these figures shown on the reports are not representing real membership since only few members among them pay membership dues and actively participate to the party activities. Such situation is shown clearly at <Table 4> below.

According to <Table 4>, only 12.5% of the revenue is collected from membership due. It is a small portion of the revenue especially when we judge it in comparison with the large number of membership. In other words, only small portion of the membership reported to the Central Election Management Commission must have joined the parties with their voluntary

<Table 4> Membership Size and Membership Due

Party Membership	NKP	NCNP	ULD	DP & OTHERS	Total
Membership	3,760,948	541,531	1,874,448	414,830	6,591,757
Annual Revenue	211,196,381,657	34,373,537,613	28,793,649,290	21,794,599,169	296,260,167,729
Membership Due	14,068,226,700	12,875,600,954	6,841,045,358	3,279,747,082	37,064,620,194
Percentage Revenue/Due	6.7%	37.5%	23.8%	15.0%	12.5%

Source: Data compiled from official documents of the Central Election Management Commission.

initiation and most of the others only by name.

Such a lack of real membership in Korean political parties comes from many reasons. Since internal democracy of political parties is not established, there is seldom room for members to express their political needs and demands and particularly to be heard of their voices in the processes of party leadership selection and party nomination of candidates to publicly elected government positions. Most of the candidates to public positions are, in fact, nominated by the party leadership of central parties. Party leadership positions are not elected by the members but nominated by the chairman or president of the parties, and almost all of the other rank and file members are isolated from such process. Thus, the decision-making process of political parties is monopolized by a handful number of party leaders. Such a closed way of party management practices deprives interests of people of joining to political parties on a voluntary base. Internal management system of political parties is too much bureaucratized to join for a simple member of the party.

In addition to this, laws and regulations controlling political party activities forbid various important groups of citizens from participating to political parties. In Korea, central government officials, local government officials, journalists, and school teachers are not allowed of any participation to party politics. They are not eligible for party membership. But, in fact, they are opinion leaders in communities and capable of allocating resources for voluntary participation to party activities. They are those who may challenge to the party leadership and recommend candidates to the elected official positions and thus facilitate party politics. They are those who may penetrate into the community most effectively, communicate with people and convey information to and from the upper structure of society. Since such portion of citizen is excluded from party membership by intention, party membership is filled with either those who are mobilized by the heads of local chapters to decorate their hegemonic power or those who join to borrow political connections and exercise them as a leverage to lobby government. In such circumstances, the Gresham's law takes place here. Bad membership drives out good membership.

Moreover since social perception to party membership is negative and not easily receivable to the public, even those who might have an intention to join parties for developing social goods have inclination to stay away from political parties. Since party politics could be counted as a dirty job, those with noble ideas and self-esteem are prone to think that there is no need to taint themselves by joining political parties. Party politics implies bribery, plot, power game, irrationality, and selfishness in Korea. Even a social tendency of not willingly welcoming former party members has taken place nowadays. They shun them. It is very natural, in such a situation, almost all of the political parties are in the lack of real party membership.

3. Leadership Formation

In case of the ruling NKP, the party president is the single most important power source in selecting other leadership positions of the party including party chairman, secretary general, central executive council members, floor leader, chairmen of standing committees, and even Speaker of the National Assembly. Candidates for the National Assembly are decided by the party president upon recommendations of the party chairman according to the rules and regulations of the party. However, in fact, the party president nominates them at his pleasure. The same situation takes place even in case of the candidates for heads of autonomous wards, cities, counties and provinces. The president makes the final decision after deliberation by the central executive council in confirmation of the party chairman's recommendation. However, in case of the candidates for mayors of cities and governors of provinces, they are supposed to be elected by the electoral college of respective local party chapters. But those who are eligible to run for the election are reviewed by the party president and he decides who may run for the candidacy winning election. In other words, the competition to win a candidacy is supposed to be taken among those whom the party president favors. And even in the process of the election, it is not very unusual that the party president exerts a very subtle influence behind the scene to elect a candidate whom he favors most.

And in case of the leadership of the National Assembly, floor leader of the ruling party is supposed to be appointed by the party president in confirmation of the party chairman and with the consent of the members' caucus. But, in fact, the party president exercises arbitrary power. The chairman of the standing committee is elected by the members of the committee. But the party president's recommendation is the final in the sense that the ruling party members of the committee support the candidate recommended by the party president almost all automatically. And it is very natural that the majority of almost all of the committees with a very few exceptions belong to the ruling party. Such a confirmation to the recommendations suggested by the party president is an absolute imperative to the ruling party members of the committees, since party discipline is so strong and severe. Speaker of the National Assembly is elected in a similar process. Once you fail to observe orders extended by the leadership of political party then you should be prepared to face real hardship in being re-nominated for the publicly elected government positions and in some serious cases to be expelled out from the party. Since the ruling party has majority membership of the National Assembly, the election of Speaker is completely dependent upon the recommendation by the ruling party president, who in fact is concurrently the incumbent president of the nation.

In other words, the president of the government is placed at the apex of hegemonic power of the party and the National Assembly as well. He dominates and controls the ruling party, the National Assembly and thus the whole government. Thus, the National Assembly is subjugated to the executive and placed under indirect control by the bureaucrats. And the prime role of ruling the party is to carry out the orders of the president down to the people at the street level and not vise versa. The ruling party is a kind of unilateral political apparatus designed to serve to the personal interests of the president. Due to such a characteristics of the party, it is very seldom to observe any power shift among party leaders as long as the president of the state remains in his office as the top leader of the nation. However, when the president of the state steps down, whole party power structure moves to new leadership of the state and streamlines into a new power relations placing the new president at the power center. And such a power shift owes little to the political pressure from the people in most of the cases.

There has not been any smooth power shift between the presidents of the state in the Korean modern political history. Chun Doo-Hwan, the 11th and 12th presidents of the state, after grasping regime, consolidated his power base by purging completely almost all of the key political followers of the former president Park Chung-Hee even though he himself was a political pet to the president Park. He dispelled them out from the party and political arena as well by accusing of their bribery, corruption, and malfeasances but, in fact, their possible disloyalty to him. Roh Tae-Woo, the 13th president, also purged and dispelled close followers of Chun Doo-Hwan including Chun Doo-Hwan himself even though Chun Doo-Hwan handed his power down to him in an expectation that he would not betray the favors extended to him under his regime since he is the most reliable and credible follower and one of the close friends to him. Kim Young-Sam, the 14th president who succeeded presidential position from Roh Tae-Woo, also purged former presidents and their followers and put them in jail in a perusal to cut off any power base left behind their retirements from the party. Thus, there always is a severance of power, and political authority between the presidents who displace the former and a disconnection in the accumulation process of the party politics experiences. In other words, loyalty is the prime source of power shifts in the leadership structure of the ruling party and institutionalization of party system is not promoted in accordance with party history.

And according to the personality and in some cases due to the political environments requesting existence of sub-leaders in the party, factional leaders are given some share of power by the president. In that case, factional needs also are reflected when the president changes the power structure of the party. It is also true that he takes into account whether he or she may have a high possibility of winning the elections when he selects candidates for various publicly elected positions of the government.

Even the case of the opposition parties is almost similar to that of the ruling party. The party leadership structure is almost completely dependent upon the preferences of the party president. But the voices of the factional leaders are heard more clearly and frequently than the ruling party. It is because that it is rather frequent in the opposition parties that they are formed by coalitions among factional leaders. In other words, the factional leaders of the opposition parties have their share of power built upon the anti-government movement careers. And at the same time, since they have to cooperate each other in the face of the brutal oppression by the authoritarian governments, the opposition party president has to share party power with the sub-leaders. Thus, it is a kind of tradition for the opposition parties to elect floor leader at the members' caucus. And the party presidents are elected at the national conventions even though the results of such competitions, in most of the cases, are predetermined through bargains and compromises among factional leaders behind the scene.

IV. Roles of Political Parties

1. Linking Pin between Government and the People

Political parties in Korea are expected to function as a linking pin between government and the people, center and periphery within a nation, and the legislature and the executive branch of the government. Due to such a role expectation to political parties, it is very natural that the border lines demarcating political party system with its surrounding environments are not clear and, sometimes, even confusing. Therefore, the locus of political parties in Korea should be understood only in a relative sense and from the vantage point of dynamism. Even after counting such a dynamic nature of laying a political party on a certain locus of the Korean society, it is very much inevitable to mention that the locus of political parties in Korea is slanted towards certain directions.

In this sense, we can say that all of the political parties in Korea are highly centralized in their decision-making process and communication network. Thus, parties are working as a conduit to funnel down policy directions and strategic reactions to any politically salient issues determined by a handful of power holders within political parties. Party system is primarily a mechanism for cultivating and mobilizing political supports, but not for listening to the voices of the general people. And local chapters operate as a center for reaching and contacting voters of the community but not for policy development or interest identification and articulation. They simply reach the people primarily for a personal touch and to promote personal pride of those being touched. In other words, local parties are to establish personal network to be used as an electoral machine. They link people to the government not through policy articulation but personal and informal networks. Parties function as a linking pin but people are not linked to the government in the sheer sense of participation.

Due to this, parties in Korea have a very weak penetration power into the society and citizen participation to the political party is very weak either. In other sense, even though Korea now experiences flourishing development and upsurge of non-governmental and voluntary organizations, party politics in Korea in general shows how much they could be distorted when they are created from top to down. Party by nature has to be build from the bottom to up. But still there remains a problem of how to stimulate voluntary participation to party system even when we succeed in getting rid of other hindrances to the development of party politics laid by the vested interests groups with very weak ground and lack of voluntarism and public goodness in their perceptions. One of the possible solutions to this problem, although still in the process of examination, could be to boost up civil movement organizations and let them displace or provide with new blood into current party politics. Then, the next issue is how to promote civil movement organizations in developing countries like Korea. They normally lack voluntarism itself, concrete ideas to implement, funds to support their activities, open-minded leadership, and managerial techniques and technologies. At this point, we need a pumping strategy to water up by pouring basic resources needed through international cooperation and fraternity networks with sprouting NGOs.

2. Dramatizer of Interest Conflicts

According to Schumpeter, legislative democracy is based

upon parliamentarism and democracy. While democracy could be shortened into an integration mechanism between civil society and nation, parliamentarism is for compromise and coordination among such integrated opinions articulated by the political parties. In other words, if political parties play roles only as a political integrator among different and sometimes even contradictory opinions and interests, the outcome of such integration lacks legitimacy since the outcome is not refined and polished by any objective value system and is only for private interests. Only when the outcome produced by parties is brought into the legislature and accommodates other parties' opinions, party could play a role of authoritative distribution of national resources. Then Korean political parties have the intention of not being centrifugal to legislature and hold their respective standpoints without seriously trying to be baptized by legislative and compromising process. Such attitudes of parties by nature intensify tense relations among parties and their political followers. They simply count politics as a kind of zero-sum game not as win-win game. Korean parties in this sense are parties staying out of the legislature not in the simple sense of lacking serious dialog among them but real leadership of parties are placed outside of the legislature. Real power holders of major political parties are not matching with those of the legislature. Legislative leadership is controlled by party juntas not only in the case of ruling party but also opposition parties as well. Since real power holders of respective parties are not coinciding with leadership inside of the legislature, contents of dialog and compromises among parties sitting inside of legislature could not be effectively conducted. They have to get orders and directions from those remaining as real decision makers outside of the legislative deliberation process. Legislative coordination process is a kind of puppet play stringed to the hegemonic power holders of the political parties. Such a distance among the political leaders supposed to compromise inside of legislature makes it harder to arrive at meaningful coordination and compromise effectively. Such dissonant operation of the legislative process naturally leads to undermining of legitimacy for the legislature in particular and distrust with the political arena in general. Party plays a role of dramatizing interest conflicts, but not an effective tool to manage interest conflicts.

3. Legitimizer of the Presidential Leadership

The Korean constitution stipulates that the president is the head of state and the executive branch of the government as well. Meanwhile, the president wears the hat of headship of the ruling party also. Due to this double or tripple headship, the president supervises and controls not only the executive branch of the government but also the legislative branch via the ruling party members of the legislature. And since the president is, in fact, dependent upon information and professional advice provided by the bureaucrats of the executive, the legislature is controlled indirectly by the bureaucrats of the executive. The politicized bureaucrats exert their influence through presidential office over the ruling party and the ruling party controls their members in the legislature. Party discipline is very strong, and rank and file members of the legislature are strictly controlled by the party leadership. Block voting is a very usual practice in Korean legislature.

In this way, the power of the president is highly centralized. And there is almost none of controlling mechanism effective enough to counterbalance the presidential power. Even though the Korean government is constituted under the principle of presidential system, members of the legislature could be appointed to the ministerial position of the cabinet by the president crossing over the principle of tripartite power division of the government. Owing to this, those legislators who are appointed to the cabinet normally lobby their colleagues in the legislature with quite easy access and established personal network which have been cultivated while they serve as the members of the legislature. The principle of check and balance between legislators and the ministers of the government is not maintained.

Such concentration of power in the president could also be found by the fact that the constitution gives the power of bill initiation to both of the legislature and the executive. Almost 62% of bills introduced to the legislature are initiated by the bureaucrats of the executive. And slightly more than 90% of bills initiated by the executive have been passed bill examination process of the legislature with ease and without major revisions. Such a concentration of power to the president deprives of internal party democracy from the ruling party. Internal working mechanism of the ruling party is bureaucratized, and very few decision-making power is allowed to the party members.

In this context, political parties in general and ruling party in particular work as decoration and thus consolidation device of presidential leadership. The existence of political parties themselves upgrades political authority of the president in particular and the political system in general in which they are organized since any political system with political parties is taken as democratic. They provide the president with political shelter to protect him against any possible political accusations and criticisms raised by the people. They are reprimanded and blamed of political mistakes made by the president. They are soliciting public attentions to protect political safety of the president.

V. Financial Resources for Party Management and Campaigning

1. Party Expenditures

The actual expense of political parties could not be traced easily with accuracy since a lot of illegal money is given and taken through personal networks informally among party politicians and seldom information about it are recorded and released to the public. In other words, political parties spend a lot of extra money in addition to the official annual budgets reported to the Central Election Management Commission, which is requested to any political parties legalized by political party affairs act. And this extra expenditure is not known to the public. However, even we count only the official expenditures reported, the amount of party expenditures is not small particularly when we compare them with GNP of Korea. In other words, it requires a very expensive cost to run party politics in Korea.

When we look into the details of annual budget composition, however, it is known that most of the party expenditures are used for managing basic administrative needs of central party headquarters. In the case of the NKP, for instance, the personnel expense is the single item covering largest portion of the party's administration expenditure. The lion's share of the NKP's expenditure goes to monthly salaries for its paid party bureaucrats. Subsidies extended to the party district chapters are not a small amount neither. The current ruling party and the main opposition parties support party district chapters by about

<Table 5> Annual Expenditure Composition of Political Parties(Dec. 1996, unit: Korean Won).

Party Expense Item	NKP	NCNP	ULD	DP & OTHERS	Total
Basic Administration	110,954,865,556(57.4)	12,929,321,192(39.2)	9,387,698,113(34.8)	6,281,183,691(29.2)	139,553,068,552(50.8)
Policy Development	6,583,671,090(3.4)	629,919,961(1.9)	410,488,986(1.5)	74,673,558(0.3)	7,689,753,595(2.8)
Training & Education	6,339,686,005(3.3)	415,448,895(1.3)	305,912,690(1.1)	126,651,150(0.6)	7,187,398,740(2.6)
Program Running	17,809,435,000(9.2)	4,339,467,920(13.2)	2,199,674,731(8.2)	4,111,060,632(19.1)	28,459,638,283(10.4)
Advertisement	4,295,826,869(2.2)	3,619,641,512(11.0)	1,317,946,870(4.9)	1,927,501,302(9.0)	11,160,916,553(4.1)
Election Campaign	20,594,772,802(10.7)	8,807,889,924(26.7)	9,402,747,009(34.8)	8,354,106,116(38.8)	47,159,515,851(17.2)
Legislative Affairs	7,715,131,400(4.0)	860,548,456(2.6)	190,845,478(0.7)	150,124,670(0.7)	8,916,650,004(3.2)
Others	19,039,490,543(9.8)	1,389,096,078(4.2)	3,792,270,098(14.0)	480,359,596(2.2)	24,701,216,310(9.0)
Total	193,332,802,392(100.0)	32,982,333,938(100.1)	27,007,783,975(100.0)	21,505,560,710(99.9)	274,828,357,868(100.1)

Source: Data compiled from official documents of the Central Election Management Commission.

from 500,000 won (622$) to 1,000,000 won (1,244$) per month[4]. Operation costs are to cover expenses arising in holding seminars, paying rent fees, maintaining buildings and communicating with outside organizations and the general public, etc. Operation cost is the second largest source of expenditure next to the advertisement and campaigning expenses. And relatively very small amount of budget is allocated for policy development. Such an expense composition is clearly shown at <Table 5> above.

According to the above table, the political parties in Korea in general allocate only 2.8% of their annual budgets for policy development and 2.6% of them for training and education of the members. Meanwhile, they spend more than half (50.8%) of the whole budgets for basic management of political parties themselves and 17.2% for the election campaign. By such expenditure composition of the political parties in Korea, it is confirmed again that the political parties in Korea are basically for voter mobilization in the election cycles and not for policy development and interest representation of the voters.

Among the contemporary parties in Korea, the NKP spends more money for basic maintenance and administration of the party itself than the other parties. In other words, the NKP is the most bureaucratized party in Korea since a large portion of the basic administration expense goes to monthly salaries for party bureaucrats. For policy development, the NKP allocates slightly more money than the others (NKP, 3.4%; NCNP, 1.9%; ULD, 1.5%; DP & Others, 0.3%) when we compare the composition rate of the expense against the total expenditure of each political party.

---

4) In 1996 when the data was collected, there was a rapid devaluation of Korean currency through the year. Therefore, it is not easy to identify meaningful foreign currency exchange ratio but here I count 1 US dollar roughly equates to 804 Korean won.

Quite similar situation is seen for legislative affairs as well (NKP, 4.0%; NCNP, 2.6%; ULD, 0.7%; DP & Others, 0.7%). For training and education, the NKP spends a little more money than the other parties (NKP, 3.3%; NCNP, 1.3%; ULD, 1.1%; DP & Others, 0.6%) when we evaluate them from a comparative perspective. Relatively speaking, the NCNP (13.2%) and the DP and others (19.1%) are the political parties which allocate more money for running party programs than the other areas. And for advertisement and election campaigns, the NCNP and the ULD place more emphasis than the other political parties. The NCNP spends about 37.7% of its total expenditure while the ULD about 39.7%.

From such composition of the annual expenditures of the political parties, we can see that the ruling NKP relies highly upon party machinery meanwhile the opposition parties of the NCNP, the ULD and the DP and others on the creation of party image in mobilizing voters and soliciting political supports to them respectively.

2. Party Revenue

Turning to financial sources of party politics, there are five major legally recognized sources of raising funds. It is very obvious that the operational expenses for any political party should be raised from party members' dues. However, party membership fees can merely cover only about 12.5 percent of working expenses for any political parties in Korea. It is rare for ordinary members of a party to pay the party membership fee. The fee usually is paid by the chairman of the party, incumbent legislators, and party executives. In 1996, the ruling NKP, the NCNP, the ULD collected 14,068,226,700 won (17,497,794$), 12,875,600,954 won

(16,014,429$), and 6,841,045,358 won (8,508,763$) respectively.

Contribution by various supporters' association is another financial source of party politics. Central party, city/province branches, and district chapters, etc. of a political party, may designate a supporters' association respectively. Members of the National Assembly and those who have made the registration of candidacy for the National Assembly seat could also designate supporters' association. In the case of the central party supporters' association, the yearly amount of the contribution received by the supporters should not exceed 10,000,000,000 won (12,437,811$). The city/province branch, 1,000,000,000 won (1,243,781$). And the district chapter, 100,000,000 won (124,378$). However, in the year in which any of the following elections takes place, the upper limit of contribution amount goes up exceeding that of normal years by two times. Summing all those supporters' donations to the central party, city/province branches, district chapters, and legislators, the NKP received 36,878,458,493 won (45,868,729$) in 1996. In case of the NCNP, 10,941,699,841 won (13,609,079$). And the ULD, 3,052,632,130 won (3,796,806$).

Any person who wants to contribute political funds to the political party could deposit such funds under his or her name to the Election Management Commission. However, foreigners, state, state organizations, enterprises in which the state or a local government owns the majority of their stocks, journalists, labor organizations, educational foundations, religious organizations, and enterprises with a series of deficits are forbidden from donation. If he or she contributes by designating a certain party, his or her specification will be honored. However, when contribution is made without mentioning any specific party to receive, the Commission is expected to distribute according to seat ratio of the parties in the National Assembly. By the end of July in 1997, there are 58 cases of contributions which add up to 21,600,000,000 won (22,689,076$)[5]. And all of these contributions are designated only to the ruling party by donators. In other words, no opposition party has received any party contribution in recent years. Such phenomenon owes much to the social atmosphere of not having visible and close relations with opposing parties in the fear of plausible disinterests that might be triggered by ruling government.

The central government allocates each year subsidies to political parties. The total amount of subsidies is decided by multiplying the total number of electors in the general election for the National Assembly by 800 won. In the year when the presidential election, the general election for the National Assembly, or the election for the local council or heads of local governments are held, in which it is allowed to recommend candidates by the political parties, the subsidy goes up by 800 won for each election. And in case of the concurrent election for the local council members and the heads of the local governments, in which the political parties are expected to recommend candidates, 600 won should be added for each election. In 1997, the NKP is supposed to receive 18,900,000,000 won (19,852,941$) from the national treasury. The NCNP, 14,700,000,000 won (15,441,177$). And the ULD, 12,200,000,000 won (12,815,126$).

Each political party makes money by holding various fund-raising events and or running businesses including publishing

5) In 1997, there took foreign currency crisis in Korea and a very rapid devaluation of the Korean currency. Here I counted 1dollar equates to 952 Korean won

and selling party news-papers. The details of political parties' annual income composition are clearly shown at <table 6> below. According to official reports submitted by individual political parties to the Central Election Management Commission in 1996 respectively, the NKP has accumulated largest amount of party revenue while the ULD smallest among major three parties. The NKP has accumulated more than 6 times more money than that of the NCNP and 7 times than that of the ULD. The subsidy from the national treasury is the most significant financial resource for the political parties in Korea next to the unspecified source of funding. In the case of the NKP, the contribution donated by business circle is the principle source of funds next to the unspecified source. The donation by business circle, in fact, is the outcome of covert solicitations exercised by the ruling party leadership. In other words, the contribution could be an official version of black money donated at the exchange of policy favor or monopoly of vested interests for the donors by the ruling government officials. For the NCNP, however, party membership due is the prime source of revenue. For the ULD, subsidy is the most important source of funds. Such situation is clearly shown at <Table 6>.

3. Campaign Funds

In 1996, there was a general election to organize the 15th National Assembly. Political parties spent 17.2 % of their annual expenditure to support this election campaign. The NKP allocated 10.7 %, the NCNP 26.7 %, and the ULD 34.8 %. In other words, in an election year, total party expenditure is increased by 17.2 %.

<Table 6> Annual Revenue Composition of Political Parties (Dec. 1996, unit/won)

Party Revenue Source	NKP	NCNP	ULD	DP & Others	Total
Transfer from Last Year	21,148,831,687(10.0)	1,114,106,559(3.2)	1,321,273,161(4.6)	852,814,104(3.9)	24,437,065,511(8.2)
Membership Dues	14,068,226,700(6.7)	12,875,600,954(37.5)	6,841,045,358(23.8)	3,279,747,182(15.0)	37,064,620,194(12.5)
Contributions	34,079,305,441(16.1)	0(0.0)	0(0.0)	0(0.0)	34,079,305,441(11.5)
Subsidy	18,822,320,660(8.9)	10,034,202,920(29.2)	10,184,325,180(35.4)	8,702,204,370(39.7)	47,743,053,130(16.1)
Supporters' Donation	25,040,798,324(11.9)	5,954,102,310(17.3)	1,549,630,314(5.4)	1,062,466,031(4.9)	33,606,996,979(11.3)
Debt	4,293,898,675(2.0)	1,536,924,476(4.5)	3,664,250,756(12.7)	1,562,415,039(7.1)	11,057,488,946(3.7)
Others	93,742,980,170(44.4)	2,860,600,394(8.3)	5,233,124,521(18.2)	6,434,922,443(29.4)	108,271,627,528(36.6)
Total	211,196,381,657(100.0)	34,375,537,613(100.0)	28,793,649,290(100.1)	21,894,589,169(100.0)	296,260,157,720(99.9)

Source: Data compiled from official documents of the Central Election Management Commission.

However, such increase is measured only on the base of official records and informal and illegal expenditures are not counted.

When it goes to the campaign expenditures for individual candidates, it is believed that about 30,000,000,000,000,000 won (38,461,538,461,500$) is spent for the 1992 presidential election according to unofficial records[6] And from about 1,000,000,000 won (1,243,781$) to about 3,000,000,000 won (3,731,343$) is spent for a seat of the National Assembly in case of the 1996 general election. Even for a seat in local county council, it is heard that about 1,000,000,000 won (1,243,781$) is necessary when one wishes to win the campaign.

However, legal expenditure allowed for each election is relatively very small. According to election for public office and election malpractice prevention act, legally afforded expense for an election campaign varies in accordance with population size of each district. In the case of 1996 year general election, however, the average amount of legally restricted election expenditure for a seat of the National Assembly from electoral district is 81,000,000 won (100,746$). But average actual expenditure for a seat reported is 46,254,000 won (57,530$), which amounts only up to 57.1% of the upper limits of the legally allowed average expenditure. However, it is an open secret in Korean society that actual campaign expenditure far exceeds such reported amount of official expenditures and legally restricted upper limits of campaign expenditure. In other words, election for public office and election malpractice prevention act is not observed with high conformity and not enforced effectively.

In fact, the act requests any political party or candidate to appoint a person to be in charge of the receipts and disbursements

6) In 1992, 1 dollar equates roughly to 780 Korean won.

as to the election expenses for each election campaign. And the person in charge of election expenditure should report about receipts and disbursements of the election expenses to the Election Management Commission together with the details of dealings in the deposit account. And if it is demanded necessary to confirm the receipts and disbursements of the election expenses, the Election Management Commission is conferred with a power to inspect the account books, examine into political parties, and demand a submission of related documents and materials.

However, such legal framework to control campaign finance and expenditure is not enforced effectively. They simply do not report all the campaign expenses and submit fabricated materials and documents to support their reports. And since almost all of the political parties and candidates violate such legal requirements, and it is very hard to trace whether one violated campaign laws and regulations or not, the violators are seldom prosecuted in actuality. Such a practice, in turn, induces, promotes and instigates them not to observe the laws and regulations further.

Due to this almost unlimited campaign expenditure, any prospective candidate has to be dependent upon slush funds provided by the political party leaders. Even to organize supporters' association, it is inevitable for rank and file members of the National Assembly to depend upon party leaders' care and personal supports since there are few real volunteers joining supporters' association. They need party cadres who solicit businessman to extend his or her assistance to the supporters' association. Thus, excessive campaign fund drives politicians to be dependent upon party leaders and makes the internal structure of political parties highly bureaucratized and authoritative. And since party leaders are in the needs of providing such extra funds to their followers and the leaders, in turn, are obliged to secure political funds as much as possible in order to expand or at least to maintain their political influence. Naturally political party leaders could easily be seduced to corruption, bribery, and other unethical conducts to mobilize unlawful political funds. There have been frequent incidents in Korea of getting political funds out from foreign loans transaction, and national projects biddings, etc.

In order to get rid of such vicious circle, it is advised to cut down political expenses including campaign expenditures. The basic idea of fighting strategy against "high cost but low-efficiency politics" is to downsize demands for political funds. In order to meet to this suggestion, it is advisable to cut party bureaucrats down and reduce basic administration expenses which are the principle source of party expenditures. We need to cut down party district chapters which have required a large sum of expenditures in order to maintain huge staffs. When it goes to campaign, it is necessary to expand a publicly financed and managed system of election campaigns to make expenses of election campaigns more transparent and encourage politicians to spend less on campaign. And it is recently agreed upon among the political parties to forbid any outdoor mass rally, which has long been criticized in Korean public as the main source of a large sum of campaign expenditures. It is told about 30,000,000,000 won (37,313,433$) is requested in order to hold an outdoor mass rally since it necessitates to mobilize attendants all across the nation, provide transportation, and install mechanical equipments such as large speakers, and podium.

For the abolishment of environmental conditions soliciting for the slush funds providers to supply such funds to political party leaders, it is necessary to deregulate drastically and thus prevent power of government officials and politicians from being involved with specific interests protection. It is also advisable to make business management more transparent and make it harder to make slush funds by adopting outside trustee system and labor participation system to management.

And to make flow of political funds more transparent and easier for the general public to observe, it is necessary to make it compulsory for any politicians to keep records of and report all of the incomes to the Central Election Management Commission once a quarter of a year.

VI. Public Perceptions of Political Parties

Political parties in Korea are perceived by the general public as one of the most untrustworthy organizations. They take it as a symbol of irrationality, bribery, corruption, collusion with capitalists, and unpredictability. Such an attitude is well shown at a survey result conducted in August 1996 by one of the leading polling organizations in Korea. According to the poll, only 17.4 % of respondents count political party as an institution to trust. At the same poll, big enterprises received 39.1 %; NGOs, 74.4 %; educational organizations, 58.5 %; legal affairs institutions, 57.5 %; military institutions, 72.7 %;, religious organizations, 58.4 %; mass media, 54.9 %; medical institutions, 65.3 %; police, 43.4 %; and civil servants, 47.3 %. Political parties are evaluated as the most unreliable institution among other leading ones in Korea.

Such an attitude of the Korean people is also confirmed by a poll conducted on May 1997. The poll asked the respondents to present a political party which he or she evaluates better than the other ones from a comparative perspective. The NKP has received 19.7%; the NCNP, 19.5%; the ULD, 6.7%; others, 2.6%; no party to support, 43.8%; and no reply, 7.8%. Such a result of opinion survey clearly shows that how much the political parties in Korea are distrusted by the general public. There is no political party receiving more than 20% of political supports from the people in Korea. And almost half of the people do not support any political parties in Korea. In other words, among the Koreans, there is a strong distrust to the political parties which must have been accumulated through the modern history of Korean politics.

To make things worse, such an attitude of the general public is extended even to civil and voluntary organizations. They fear to cooperate with the parties openly even if they feel great needs of siding with a certain party to get through a certain policy position that they have insisted for the general public. They prefer an easy way of not tainting themselves by standing aloof from the close interactions with political parties. They assume their normative role is to watch, criticize, keep tension and not to cooperate with parties.

Such an attitude of NGOs and other civil movement organizations owes much to the fact that still the non-governmental organizations in Korea are not strong enough to pursue their goals on their own feet as well. They are highly concerned about what the others would like to think about what they do. They are very much sensitive to what the people might think about them and still not strong enough to maintain their values and positions unilaterally. In other words, non-governmental organizations in Korea are not playing a role of linking pin between the grassroots and the political parties and disconnected from the official interest representation system even though they become more dynamic and energetic and are in the process of expanding their role jurisdictions rapidly nowadays. And such an anti-political party stance is clearer and vivid when it goes with ruling party since any cooperative relation with ruling party has been perceived to support illegitimate government backed by coercive power during the past regimes. Even when they have very subtle and friendly relation with opposition parties, it is not between institutions but only between leaderships on their personal basis.

However, the NGOs and other civil movement organizations have played a role as a recruitment conduit to political parties. Key figures who have worked for the NGOs and other civil movement organizations have been recruited as candidates for the publically elected positions and party bureaucracy. Political parties buy and try to mobilize clean and purely voluntary image of those who have been involved with the NGOs and other civil movement organizations in order to make up their dirty and power seeking image. Therefore, there takes place an irony and a kind of contradiction between the NGOs' basic attitude of criticizing political parties and joining to the political parties by those who criticized them. In other words, the more the civil movements' leaders criticize political parties, the better chance of joining to political parties takes place. And such a social practice obviously undermines legitimacy of the NGOs and other civil movement organizations and political parties as well.

Generally speaking, the military and civil servants are known to favor bureaucratic rationality instead of political rationality since they conceive bureaucracy in terms of efficiency, economy, and modernity. On the other hand, they see politics in terms of corruption, bribery, parochialism, and inefficiency. This has been particularly the case in the Korean society since, as Henderson suggests, Korea has had a long Confucian tradition of "strong, centralized, uncontested bureaucratic rule even to the extent of retarding pluralistic, democratic development." (Park & Lee, 1976: 92). And it has been true that "the word of compromise in the Korean language carries a slightly immoral connotation and the Koreans in general think little of political compromise not understanding that democratic politics is the politics of compromise and dialogue" (Hong & Lee, 1976: 145). Such a social orientation to politics has led the military and civil servants to regard political parties and politicians as one of the most unqualified, immoral, and unreliable components of the society. Naturally, there takes place seldom interactions between the military and the political parties. And particularly between opposition parties and civil servants, they seldom exchange information and opinions. It is inconceivable that these two groups cooperate each other for the interests of the state. They simply do not trust institutional capability of the opposition parties in terms of managing and keeping records and personnel resources in addition to the natural inclination of bureaucracy of not sharing information with others. In fact, the military and civil servants as well are forbidden from joining to party politics in Korea yet.

VII. Future of Political Parties

Owing to the wide-spread of television and other information and communication technologies, political information is shared widely with speed and accuracy all across the nation. And as a result of this and partially because of the growing influence of regionalism in voting behavior, the traditional voting pattern of so-called "Yerchonyado", which means that voters in rural area have a tendency to support ruling party while those in urbanized cities to support opposition parties, is no longer working in recent elections. There is no difference found between voters in the rural area and those in the urban area in their voting patterns nowadays. The television and new information and communication technologies must have provided the voters in rural area with better information and thus better insights to evaluate political alternatives and cultivated a critical perspective to measure the world from a more objective point of view. They also must have protected voters in the rural area from bare and direct persuasion and mobilizations by the government officials, who have been eager to support ruling party candidates.

Replacing "Yerchonyado" phenomenon, however, there takes place a new voting pattern. In the past days, upper and middle class people had an inclination to support opposition parties which signify liberalism and strong agitation against authoritarian regimes in a relative sense, while poor and low class to support ruling party which stands for the vested interests. Such a twisted voting pattern was one of the characteristics of Korean voters. But nowadays, a reversed situation begins to take place. The rich and upper class people, including capitalists, medium sized businessmen, and shop owners, and etc., become to aspire for political stability and gradual change of the society rather than rapid and overall reform and alterations. Then it is very natural for such people to support ruling conservative party instead of relatively radical and progressive opposition parties. And because most of the well-to-dos live in urban cities rather than in rural areas, there is an inclination that those living in urban cities prefer ruling party more than opposition ones. In this sense, we can say that "Yerchonyado" phenomenon has now a tendency to be reversed.

And the wide-spread of television and other new media across the nation also have brought a negative impact to the functional weight of political parties in the Korean political process. The increasing reliance upon TV debates and campaign advertisements reduces the importance of party cadres and networks in mobilizing voters' support during various election campaigns. The proliferation of polling organizations replaces the conventional role of opinion identification and interest articulation, which have long been performed by the political parties in the past days. The advent of information society undermines the conventional roles played by the political parties and brings the people to a more direct contact with the political leaders. Thus, the role of political parties as a mediator and in some cases a buffer zone between the people and the government is now challenged. Or the political parties are placed under a competition with new technological devices of the information age.

Such a shrink of roles and political weight assumed by the political parties in turn and the general public's pressure criticizing political corruptions have brought a mounting request to downsize the central party bureaucracy and the local party networks. It has been counted inevitable to raise slush funds as long as they maintain the contemporary size of party organizations and staffs. And the needs to maintain the current size of party organizations and staffs as an election machine has also been decreased since the direct mobilization of voters by party cadres is not so effective as it were any longer. Such a change owes much to the very fact that vote-buying campaign strategy is not so effective as it were.

Korean political parties have long been organized and maintained as an electoral machine and money politics has been a very typical quintessence of the politics. Thus, parties have been used as the extended hands to buy votes and to distribute favors to those who promise to support their party candidates. However, nowadays, there takes a very clear symptom that money is not an effective vote buying resource any longer owing partially to the change of laws related to elections and continuous campaigns engaged by civic movement organizations heralding the importance of fair and clean elections.

The growth and rapid proliferation of civic movement organizations, on the one hand, enforce the political parties to compete with them in terms of articulating interests, raising and promoting social issues, and closely observing and criticizing the government operations. In other words, the growth of civic movement organizations is not confirmative to the consolidation of legitimacy of the political parties but vies, in some sense, against each other in soliciting people's supports. The rivalry relation between the two institutions is getting intensified as time goes on, and the civic movement organizations establish deeper grass roots. On the other hand, however, the strengthening of the civic movement organizations bring a positive impact of upgrading the quality of services and policy development function of political parties as the civic movement organizations suggest programs and policies to the political parties and ask them to join with their efforts to get them through the legislative process. The political parties are enforced to compete with the civic movement organizations in developing policies and programs and thus upgrade their service quality. Thus, new phenomenon has started to take place in Korean political arena.

< Appendix > List of Interviewees

Chung She-Kyun, Member, National Assembly, NCNP
Ham Suck-Jae, Member, National Assembly, ULD
Jun Yong-Won Jun, Member, National Assembly, NKP
Kim Eun-Ock, Individual Members' Staff to Namkung Jin, Member of National Assembly, NCNP
Kim Jai-Mock, Reporter accredited to NKP, Moonhwa Daily News

Paper

Kim Yong-Duck, Chief, Network Bureau, Central Party, ULD

Lee Jae-Chang, Reporter accredited to NKP, Saegye Daily News Paper

Lee Jae-Do, Vice Secretary General, National Assembly

Lee Shin-Bum, Member, National Assembly, NKP

Lee Soo-Hyung, Ph. D. in Political Science, Individual Members' Staff to Kim Jin-Jae,

Nam Boo-Won, Executive Secretary for Program, Asia and Pacific Alliance of YMCAs

Oh Hyun-Joo, Chairman, Public Relations Committee, Central Party, DP

Shim Wi-Pyo, Director, News Center, Korean Broadcasting System

Sin Seung-Keun, Reporter accredited to NCNP, Hangyerae Daily News Paper

Part Two

Building Civil Society in Globalizing Era

Chapter 06

Negative Impact of E-Governance on NGOs

I. Introduction

E-governance has become a part of our daily lives. It is no longer confined to the networks between government and citizens (B2C). It has developed into other spheres of our society. It is particularly so when we refer e-governance to any collaborations to enhance public interests by the use of information and communication technologies (ICTs), that have the ability to transform government's relations with citizens, business and other arms of government.

Among the collaborative partners of e-governance, NGOs have shown an exponential growth in their numbers and magnitude in policy-making process all across the world in these days. Korea is not an exception from such trend. After the advent of "87 system"[1], Korea has observed a rapid and flourishing development of NGOs in their number, diversity and voice to the governing process. NGOs in Korea have grown up even as one of the major political sources of hegemonic power steering directions of public policy and mobilizing citizens' supports.

There is, however, little research on NGOs' use of ICTs in general and impact of e-governance to NGOs in particular. We know from studies of firms that the introduction of new technologies can substantially impact on organization's internal and external relations (Orlikowski *et al.*, 1995). The internal structure of NGOs could reflect the collaborative and less hierarchical organizational forms observed in firms that have introduced ICTs to their interactions with government (Kahn, 2000; Stark, 2000). It also can be argued that NGOs would undergo organizational changes and allow themselves to more flexibly address the competing demands placed upon them and better exploit ambiguity.

This chapter aims at exploring what are the real impacts of ICTs to NGOs engaged in e-governance. There has been an assumption or normative expectation that the use of ICTs can stimulate innovative capacity within and among NGOs. This innovative capacity, however, could lead NGOs into new forms of hybrids that do not easily map onto conventional images of NGOs. This brings with it the risk that NGOs will encounter problems of accountability that undermine rather than enhance their responsiveness to social change.

---

1) July revolt by citizens in 1987 against then government's intention to change constitution in order to enable indirect election of the president is counted as a historical milestone in the process of democratization of Korean politics. And the successive governance from that time on is called as the 87 system in comparison with the previous ones.

Therefore, we need to understand the changes and possibilities that ICTs bring to the work of NGOs and how they affect the mission of NGOs. It becomes very important to find a way to work out how to adapt to the changes while maintaining the integrity of furthering the NGOs' objectives. We need to address and meet the changing expectations of the people with whom the NGOs work every day.

II. Role of NGOs in Information Society

The advent of information society has direct bearing upon the social and institutional environments in which NGOs operate. Being able to take advantages of ICTs in such a circumstance, NGOs expand their web of social interaction dramatically, increase its density, and promote new connections among diverse and dispersed social actors. They could solicit "wider participation" of citizens by locating people with far more ease than before who share same values and objectives with them, providing accessibility for those who are disabled, living in remote areas, and thus discouraged to join in advocacy process, and distributing information tailored for the interests of individual needs and aspirations.

Increased participation serves as a source of political legitimacy for NGOs to identify social issues, raise dissident voices, develop alternatives and thus advocate and represent the interests of people. Such a role is particularly demanding since political agents could not aggregate, transmit, and represent the interests of principles with such accuracy and speed that they were expected to be due to increased turbulence of information flow and bureaucratic structure of government. NGOs could thus be considered as an alternative conduit for citizens to deliver their messages to government. They become essential to the vibrant functioning of a democracy.

NGOs also become able to compete their professionalism and subject matter expertise with government officials since the monopoly or dominance of information by government could not be maintained any further in information society. Demarcation line between government and civil society becomes blurred and a tension to hold a sort of equilibrium between them takes place. NGOs become able to functionally complement or replace administrative agents, whose authority owes much to their professionalism and accumulation of information, relying much on "deeper participation" of citizens. Magnitude of NGOs as a gatekeeper or a third party judge has upgraded.

NGOs in the information society described in the literature cited above are not only to set priority of policy agendas but also to evaluate and interpret policy alternatives from objective and scientific standpoint. Along the line of understanding NGOs as such proponents or promoters of policy alternatives, there is an assumption to equate NGOs with citizens as if they were same identity. It is true that NGOs are associated on the base of voluntary participation of citizen, however, they are not citizen themselves. Between NGOs and citizens, there are almost same working mechanisms that we see in e-governance between government and NGOs and those between government and citizens as well. Associations imply an existence of internal working structure meanwhile individual citizens are isolated from each other and free from such working mechanism.

Discussions about issues regarding the impact of the advent of information society in general and e-governance in particular to NGOs most start from normative premises about technical properties of ICTs, even at the scholarly and policy level. They naturally arrive at emphasizing positive impact and or by ignoring negative one. Yet while assumptions about ICTs' social effects provide good rhetorical ammunition for debates, they tend, in most cases, to outstrip our knowledge of how ICTs are actually influence (ÖMahony and Barley, 1999) the relationship between NGOs and citizens. The social practices that evolve around the use of ICTs tell us more accurate information about their effect than assumptions based on their properties alone (Bijker 1997; Giddens, 1984). It becomes an imperative to correct such a bias by conducting closer research on the working mechanism between NGOs and citizens.

III. E-Governance between NGOs and Citizens

Three different categories of e-governance could be discerned from theoretical schemes dealing with e-governance and interactive collaborations among and between the major components of a society: e-governance between government and citizens (a), e-governance between government and NGOs (b) and e-governance between NGOs and citizens (c). Among these e-governance models, e-governance between NGOs and citizens (c) has seldom been discussed in the literature. Without e-governance between NGOs and citizens (c), however, e-governance between government and NGOs (b) could not function as an alternative conduit or a complementary funnel to e-governance between government and citizens (a). Communication and networking between NGOs and citizens are integral to NGOs' basic tasks of aggregating citizens' aspirations and needs, evaluating policy alternatives, transmitting them to government and coimplementing them together with government.

Such a relationship could be outlined as follow.

<Diagram 1> Three Different Models of E-governance

In other words, e-governance between government and citizens (a) depends upon what relations NGOs develop with citizens in their confrontations with newly introduced ICTs. ICTs are designed and adopted as a tool for processing information, increasing communication and facilitating networking. If ICTs are seen as such a tool, then NGOs seem organizationally ideal for adapting to them.

The problem of counting ICTs as a tool, however, is that once new technologies are introduced to solve problems, and then, the problems themselves change. E-mail may enable an NGO to increase its level of communication, but it may also create such a flood of requests for information that the NGO becomes paralyzed (DiMaggio *et al.*, 2001). The gap between institutional capacity of NGOs and exploding political participation by citizens makes their response so slow that the citizens who clicked on NGOs' internet may turn their way to government and communicate directly with government overpassing e-governance system between NGOs and citizens. There is no sufficient time to respond to rapidly erupting changes and flood of information incoming from citizens to NGOs. It becomes further serious when NGOs are not able to keep abreast with changes in a society in their technological edge and furnished with insufficient staff to work on such incoming requests.

One of the major reasons that have induced citizens to join in e-governance with NGOs has been their trust and reliance on professional knowledge and judgment extended by NGOs. It becomes, however, difficult for NGOs to maintain such a relative supremacy in their support of professionalism and expertise that could hold further reliance of citizens after the advent of information society since wider spread of ICTs enable citizens easily access to various sources of professional information and knowledge and enjoy higher quality of information by reaching directly to professionals and experts and circumventing NGOs via ICTs. For NGOs, there is no sufficient time to respond to the requests from citizens as long as they maintain conventional working mechanism. It is a routine way of providing professional expertise for NGOs to consult with subject matter experts at their initial stage of developing policy position, which inevitably requires some time to drag before responding to the citizens' requests.

It is obvious that ICTs accelerate communication, promote networking, and upgrade collaboration among NGOs. Widening gap between NGOs with advanced ICTs and those with outmoded computers and still depend largely on regular mail and faxes, however, makes collaboration far more difficult and uneasy to establish coalition front among NGOs. The main barriers causing such a different institutional adaptability to information society have been the relative lack of funding, relevant training, and accessibility to ICTs. The fast pace of change in ICTs has also contributed to such disparity among NGOs.

In other words, role of NGOs as an intermediary between government and citizens rapidly decreases and thus functional locus of NGOs is seriously challenged. Such change implies a working mechanism that may take place in the process of government's shrinking into civil society, which have been projected by some futurists in their discussion of changing relations between government and civil society. Even though it has been argued that technical properties of ICTs will eventually bring in auto-administration, there has been a paucity of information about how such change would be realized. Knowledge about how e-governance between NGOs and citizens (c) gradually degraded and e-governance between government and citizens (a) eventually replaces e-governance between government and NGOs (b) will furnish further understanding on this process of change.

IV. Impact of ICTs to National Council of YMCAs in Korea

Korea is well known for its vibrant NGOs activities among other Asian and Pacific countries. Such dynamic growth and operation of Korean NGOs owes much to their historical evolution led mainly by civil society organizations (CSOs)' leadership and standing staffers, most of whom once have engaged in student movements against dictatorial regimes in the past. Among such NGOs, there are four major ones, which exercise leadership in setting agendas, advocating against government, formulating public opinion, and thus directing CSOs movements in Korea: People's Solidarity for Participatory Democracy (PSPD), Korean Federation for Environmental Movement (KFEM), National Council of YMCAs in Korea (YMCA) and Citizens'

Coalition for Economic Justice (CCEJ).

Among these "big four"s, YMCA enjoys the longest institutional history, largest volume of standing staffers, membership, annual budget, and the greatest number of local movements. In other words, YMCA is the most established and institutionalized one among them. It does not necessarily mean, however, that it has kept technological edge in the adoption and use of ICTs. Yet, it is true that after the upgrade of internet equipment, YMCA has become more responsive to social issues than before. In the previous days, local movements have enjoyed almost complete autonomy in their initiation and responses to social issues, and thus there seldom has occurred unified confrontation against social problems and difficulties at national level. ICTs have opened up further networks and wider communications. Instead of a "one to one" relationship among the movements, individual local chapters began to formulate networks of common interest using an email, list serves, and chat rooms among themselves. This does not replace meeting face to face, nor does it dis-intermediate YMCA from its relationship between government and citizens. In fact, it has enhanced the work of YMCA. It has become more competent in putting people in contact with each other, facilitating, listening to discussions, summarizing, placing the personal issues in a political and historical context, monitoring and lobbying for change. This is done now online.

But it also threatens to dis-intermediate the existing lively and timely responses of YMCA to recurring requests of citizens. Conventional way of encountering and responding to social issues at its initial stage in YMCA has been to put an issue on an open and public debate inviting professionals and subject matter experts in a perusal to call attentions from the public and to take account of the professional knowledge and expertise into its work of analyzing impact of social difficulties, evaluating current policies and developing alternatives. It, thereby, could have been able to enjoy the role of leadership in the fields of developing issues, building public opinion and guiding Korean NGOs front. Citizens' Forum (simin nondan) marked its 400th meeting anniversary last October of 2004, which meets regularly at least once or twice a month for the last 20 years to enrich and promote such discussions and exchanges of opinions among professional experts and other related parties. This meeting, however, is rapidly declining nowadays in its magnitude in mobilizing public attention, drawing larger attendance of audiences, and soliciting standing staffers to rely more heavily in their daily works of advocacy building, which contrasts to the glory of heydays in 1970s and 1980s.

One of the major reasons of such decline owes much to the wide spread of ICTs in Korean society. Meanwhile those who are equipped with ICTs could access directly to professional expertise, research relevant knowledge with much more ease and speed, and develop their own forum to formulate opinions and alternative solutions to social issues, YMCA should go through such conventional procedures to attract expertise and bear on internal bureaucracy less flexible to respond to such rapidly popping issues. KTX café's are excellent examples.

With the historical opening of the express rail (KTX) in April 2004, Korea has joined the league of France, Japan, Germany and Spain and entered into the super high-speed train era, operating at speeds of 300 km per hour. Opening of the express rail, which has been referred to as the biggest national policy project since the national foundation, will not only bring enormous changes to the lives of Koreans by enabling them to reach anywhere in the country within three hours, but it will also have a huge influence on the economic, social, and cultural aspects of the country.

However, it turned out to be not very much fast, safe, convenient and environmentally friendly, which is almost completely different from what has been insisted by the government. Citizens disappointed with such a poor service began to criticize the government and look for solutions not by reaching to major NGOs this time which have exercised a strong leadership in mobilizing political pressure upon government but by forming anti-KTX café's in cyber-space by themselves. In fact, major NGOs in general and YMCA in particular had intentions to deal the issue with higher priority but the citizens were not able to wait until these bureaucratized organizations began to respond since they were evaluated to move rather slowly than they were expected to be.

Similar cases are observed more frequently nowadays. The long-term stabilization of the National Pension Fund became the overriding concern since the introduction of the National Pension Scheme in 1988 that was initially designed to provide high benefits against low contributions. Accordingly, the centerpiece of the full-scale reform which was made to extend its mandatory coverage to people in the urban area in April 1999 was a set of measures taken to stabilize the fund. In an effort to stabilize the fund, financial recalculation is advised to be made every 5 years from 2003 to adjust contribution and benefits level appropriately and maintain the long-term balance of Pension Fund. In the process of reforming the pension system, the transparency, specification and profitability of Pension Fund management have been questioned and become the focus of strong social concern and criticism. YMCA was concerned about the problems encountered by the recipients of the Pension and tried to launch a reform campaign. Its civil society movement committee was called upon to review the issue. Citizens, however, didn't wait until YMCA takes an initiation and develops a campaign program. There popped up many anti-Pension café's by themselves on the internet almost instantaneously and run reform campaigns without waiting the assistance from major NGOs. Such internet café's requested viewers and participants of chat rooms to join in e-protest against Pension authority and to drive sit-in demonstration in front of the building. If it were in the past, citizens must have tried to reach and rely on major NGOs leadership including YMCA.

Such a change implies that YMCA is now placed in tighter competition with other NGOs and citizens' self-help than before. In the case of YMCA, it has not been able to invest enough financial resources to develop ICTs and train standing staffers to adapt to such changes. When the whole Korean society has become mainstreamed into ICTs application and civic participation, YMCA, as like the other NGOs in Korea, has barely traced after such change and had not have enough resources to invest for the increase of its staffers' capacity in the effective use of ICTs. Let alone to build the capacity of their volunteers and those with whom they work. Such a reluctance to develop institutional capacity has drawn direct e-democracy. And it should be reminded that such a direct e-democracy where one by one, each individual reacts to an entire arm of government bypassing YMCA's mediation, threatens to ignore the experience, knowledge, institutional memory, grassroots connection, and expertise of YMCA in particular and Korean NGOs in general.

V. Conclusion

Therefore, it is an imperative for the major Korean NGOs in general and YMCA in particular to increase their capacity to work online more effectively in many ways such as by being able to select the most efficient method according to the needs and requests of participants, the communication processes, and the content. They need to upgrade internal and networked work as well as communication processes that can be used to respond to the online consultations. They need effective online report-back mechanisms for internal review of both process and content. They should keep abreast technological edge with other components of the society and reform internal working mechanism by reflecting requests for division of labor and rather flat organizational structure, thereby overcoming bureaucratic nature of conventional working system.

It has been argued that the ICTs build social capital by enhancing the effectiveness of community-level voluntary associations and by establishing powerful organizations watching on the works of government (DiMaggio *et al.*, 2001: 319). Such a prevailing optimism over the role of ICTs owes much, however, to the unilateral perspective reviewing the phenomenon from vantage point of NGOs rather than from that of citizens. When we approach to it from the side of citizens, it becomes very natural to arrive at a self-reflection that we need to widen our perspective and to correct our projection over the impact of ICTs to e-governance to more balanced view that there is an inclination not to allow room for NGOs to intermediate communications between government and citizens any further and citizens' direct communication capability to government increases far beyond our expectations. We should overcome research bias or disproportionate emphasis on NGOs implicitly treating the nature of ICTs as fixed.

And it should also be concerned that when citizens' direct communication with government circumventing NGOs becomes a rather recurrent and common phenomenon, there could take place a danger of populism dominating government policy formulation process. The normative role of NGOs in policy process is not simply to provide and transmit citizens' opinion without filtering it but to furnish professional expertise and judgment together with information about citizens' preferences and, thereby, to satisfy both premises of value and fact in decision making process. It should be reminded that for a rational decision-making it requires not only to prioritize citizens' preferences but also to make a professional evaluation on the base of scientific and objective rationality. We need not only "detectors" but also "effectors" as well in order to make an ideal decision.

The accumulation of knowledge about shrinking mechanism of NGOs' role as an intermediary between government and citizens could provide a base to enhance our understanding about final stage of government disappearance argued by Marx and emergence of real self-autonomous government projected by Kooiman (2003). Those arguments were in the lack of presenting intervening variables that connect cause and effect in the process of developing their theoretical schemes. The result of this research could be a grinding stone to correct such paucity in theoretical constructs of these assertions.

But such shrinking role of NGOs as an intermediary between government and citizens, however, does not necessarily mean that citizens will completely stop to interact with NGOs. On the contrary, they still continue to communicate and interact with NGOs and such relationship will continue to exist. NGOs will never lose their institutional trust and legitimacy as an intermediate between government and citizens since NGOs play a role as a gatekeeper evaluating and filtering citizens' opinion and initiating identification of social issues without waiting input from citizens.

Chapter 07

Alternative Tourism as Social Movement

I. Introduction

The advent of postmodern society has brought double-sided impacts to mass tourism; it offers opportunities and perils at the same time. As borders between nations have become blurred, and the movements of people have increased, resulting in the growth of travels to more various regions, mass tourism is in its groundbreaking heyday. As of 2009, it has been grown by 4.4% each year for the last 10 years and accounts for 9.2% of the total global GDP, and about 235 million people are employed in mass tourism. By 2020, it is expected that the number of people working in mass tourism will be increased to 300 million, which is 9.2% of world's working population, and that its share in the global GDP will grow to 9.6% (WTTC, 2010: 1).

This considerable proliferation of mass tourism, however, has caused several problems too. There is the high risk of assimilation and integration into the global culture biased toward western culture in that the travel of western people are far more active and that more frequent contact and exchange stimulate cultural assimilation among different regions, which has caused numerous cases of local cultural identity being damaged. The decrease in cultural diversity surely will reduce authentic local attractions and is very likely to lower the demand for mass tourism.

As the movements of people for hobbies and leisure have explosively expanded, carbon emissions, which is a likely cause of climate changes, have increased. Changed climate will cause damages or floods in cultural relics with heavy or acid rain. This, however, is just one of many ways of environmental destruction accompanied by mass tourism. Mass tourism depends on mass-transaction system that promotes the construction of large-scale recreational facilities or resorts and leads to disruption of local ecological environment. It causes the destruction of species and forests, making difficult to keep sustainable ecological environment.

The crisis of mass tourism is also caused by the fact that it seeks profit. The more competitive industrial environment that has been intensified by the globalization of economic activities pressures companies to strive for profit maximization. When they disregard residents' participation in their process of business management or keep decision-making process closed, by reason of excessive expense, it will be hard to establish tourism industry that is based on local community and community-friendliness (Suresh, 2005: 8-9). It won't be easy for the tourism industry without regional or local foundation to last long.

When the maximization of simple profit is focused, infringement of human rights is often done without hesitation; paying low wage to local workers, hiring unskilled workers, exploiting women and children, forcing the native or lower class to move out, and the like. And this causes a high rate of economic leakage unlike the initial expectation that it will contribute to the vitalization of the local economy (Suresh, 2005: 8). It increases the dependency of local economy on the tourism industry, brings uni-polarization or unbalanced growth and stimulates the transition to the economic system dependent on imports.

Mass tourism, on its way to expansion, can trample over the sustainability of culture, society, environment and economy of local community, and consequently be trapped in self-contradiction that confines its existence denying the sustainability of its own. We cannot expect sustainable mass tourism industry with this (Serrano & Carranza, 2005: 6). This recognition worked as a critical motive to search for alternative tourism at the opposite side of mass tourism. Alternative tourism, however, connotes various meanings depending on the aspect of mass tourism to which alternatives are looked for.

Alternative tourism is not an established term into a frame of refined theory yet, but rather a kind of collective term that involves very various concepts like "sustainable tourism (Beck, 1992)," "ego-tourism (Schveyens, 2002)," "new moral tourism (Butcher, 2002)," "eco-tourism (Nowaczek, 2010)," or even "new tourism (Poon, 1993)," "post tourism (Urry, 2002)," concepts that include all above terms.

Tourism or alternative tourism consists of tourists, hosting local community, and intermediary institutions that arrange or mediate tourism. Literature review reveals that most of the previous researches on alternative tourism have been focused on two former components and seldom on the last variable. Being reminded of the fact that tourism is a series of behavior patterns that is stimulated by motivational factors of tourists and that aims to achieve some goals through the touring process, there have been many discussions about motivational factors at individual level and the desired goals to achieve at hosting local community level, but not about the process of touring which connects these two.

Not a few perspectives have seen the relationship between tourism and social change as the latter is a passive consequence or a byproduct of the former, but there have been few attempts to recognize and to approach tourism as an active means of social change. However, with the construction of global civil society and increasing demand for social movements transcending borders of nation states, there have been growing needs to utilize tour or travel as an opportunity or a means to change social structure of hosting local community. Especially YMCA, as an INGO (international non-governmental organization), has shown the initiative in recognizing and coping with this matter.[1]

Being aware of this reality and problems, this chapter will approach the process of tourism that connects tourists and hosting local communities with a focus on arrangers or mediators. It is also examining whether YMCA, which wants to stimulate and support social movements transcending borders among nation states, has appropriate qualifications for an intermediary institution to mediate or organize alternative tourism as a social movement. For this, I will consider the process of reconstruction or de-differentiation that current global society is experiencing corresponding to social demand and characteristics of postmodern times.

1) Asia Pacific Alliance of YMCAs held the workshop for the construction of Global Alternative Tourism Network (GATN) to discuss the validity of adopting a role of mediating tourism at Chiang Mai, Thailand on July 27-30, 2009, and World Alliance of YMCAs passed the resolution about promoting global alternative tourism and researches on them at Hong Kong on July 19-24, 2010.

II. The Post Modern Era and Approaches to Alternative Tourism

The difference between post-modernity and modernity is that general principles of the past are not working anymore. We are in the need of new paradigm because changes in modern lifestyles have caused self-contradiction. With the dissolution of structuralism, dominant feature of modernity, grand theories, unitary projects, and mega-narratives have lost their persuasiveness and risk society has emerged, which has characteristics of poly-atomism, specialization, mobility, anonymity, insecurity, and the like. There also have been changes in tourism, which have altered existing orders and basic structures of tourism at least, with the advent of new ways of tourism. The rise of various types of motivational factors that stimulate tourism can be seen as one of these changes.

Alternative tourism, started as a way of passive resistance to mass tourism, has evolved to cover various meanings and contents and entered into the stage of constructing of its own identity, suggesting new viewpoint and perspective as itself and not as simple opposition to existing ways of tourism. And if we closely examine the pluralistic characteristic of alternative tourism, we can see that generally two approaches have coexisted depending on whether to focus on: tourists or host local communities and motivational factors about tour at the individual level or ultimate goals of tour at structural level.

First of all, according to postmodern consumption theories, alternative tourism is a way of conspicuous consumption (Veblen, 1994) or consumption of superfluities, which recognize alternative tourism as a means to show off one's social status or standing. Originally in traditional society, it was common to keep a lifestyle that was familiar or inherited corresponding to one's inborn social status or relationships. However, with the rise of industrial society, hereditary social class or the caste system collapsed and, as a result, lower social class could imitate lifestyles of higher class.

When lower class people realize that they can not afford the desired level of consumption, however, they become to identify consumption as a social privilege or a symbol of social status. As for higher social class, when they have no leisure time to enjoy spending for themselves, they also show off their standing or status by making their proxy, wife or children, putting on expensive clothes or jewelries. Consumption is transformed into a goal-oriented action that aims for consumption itself, not a means to satisfy physical needs (Mustonen, 2006: 35).

These kinds of phenomena have been intensified in post-modern times, and consumption now became a means that represents one's lifestyle (Miles, 1998: 16-18). Displaying one's identity or differentiating with others is attempted through ways of consuming (Scott, 2002: 23). Therefore, the demand for consumption is not about the utility of some product anymore but about difference (Baudrillard, 1998: 77-78) or signs (Featherstone, 1991: 85). Esthetic value (Lyon, 1999: 72), rather than functional aspects, of a product and ecstasies of hyper-reality, not of actual reality, become to be emphasized more.

From this perspective, leisure travel today is not merely for unknown natural phenomena or visual stimulations, rather it is motivated by symbols or meanings accompanied with them. It is not about existential reality of host local communities but about seeking the encounter with ontological existence, and in that sense, it can be considered as an effort to find authenticity (true one's self) escaping from the pressure of everyday life. In this way, travel can be described as experiencing truly new things through encountering one's true self and real experience (Wang, 1999: 364), not exotic attractions of something.

This perspective, however, has been criticized as egocentric and egotistic, calling for volunteer approach. Volunteer approach recognizes alternative tourism as voluntary action driven by altruistic motivation (Ackerberg & Prapasawudi, 2009), often focusing on conducting development and changes in a society or others, such as the development of host local community, improving sanitation conditions, enhancing the sustainability of ecological environment or cultural heritage, democratization, or reducing social-economic inequality. But this does not mean that voluntary participation in tourism is driven only by altruistic motivation.

Volunteering for tourism involves different kinds of egotistic motivations other than altruistic motivation. A person may volunteer for tourism to enjoy the development of humane solidarity while empathizing or sharing sentiments with others who participate in tourism with altruism or to develop solidarity among family members who are traveling with or to experience self-satisfaction from altruistic services. However, if alternative tourism wants to focus on the development or improvement of host local community, it would be reasonable to see it as a manifestation of altruism.

There surely are numerous factors for that, but we can find the main factor in the structural characteristic of postmodern era among others. Post-modernity has the characteristic of consilience of vertical and horizontal structure, and of the fusion or extinction between their boundaries through the process of regressive differentiation. Consequently, tourism and other domains of society influence each other and we can observe the effect of tourism or quasi-tourism in other domains of society. Tourism is no longer something distinct that is separated from other domains of society, and it becomes to materialize or to be interpreted while being dissolved with other values or standards of judgment and interacting with them.

For example, it is the reason for inpouring intellectual ability or professionalism that enables the invention of new concepts such as eco-tourism easily to the domain of tourism. As Beck (1992) asserts, the rise of risk society in post-modern era and the formation of introspective society in accordance with it are some of the reasons that motivate travelers who participate in tourism to reflect on various kinds of negative effects of modern mass tourism and to search for new alternatives. The de-differentiation of specialized social structure forces us to think about the contradictory reality and, as a result, it increases absorptive capacity for knowledge or information related to ecology leading to the enlightenment that we should contribute to the preservation of environment and ecological health of host local community.

Most volunteers share altruistic motivation even though they are not participating in tourism due to its fundamental characteristics (Pedicini, 2008). Therefore, volunteer approach perceives alternative tourism as a more ethical way of tourism in essence (Guttentag, 2009). Moreover, it can be said to be on the extension of a developmental perspective in that it intends to stimulate the development and changes of host local communities (Scheyens, 2007: 130). It aims to contribute to the diversification of lifestyles, social development, and the empowerment of people in host local community.

However, it's not easy to have a positive answer to the question of whether this kind of ethical and voluntary service of travelers always helps host society and whether this service is really what a local community needs. It means that without understanding of and communication with a host society, well-intended voluntary service can be a source of disaster. Such a problem could also be seen with the postmodern consumption theory. Consumption is not always working with someone's identity and rather it could be a kind of social behavior that is not made alone, but in relationship with others. Consumers are often influenced by common lifestyles or culture of the society they belong to without even recognizing it.

Post-modern consumption theory and volunteer approach focus on motivational factors of individual tourists and the structure of host local society respectively, but in reality, they are interconnected and in a relationship that can constitute more appropriate way of understanding or interpreting alternative tourism. It means that postmodern consumption theory and volunteer approach can improve the degree of their perfection when they are in a complimentary relationship. Discussions on alternative tourism, however, have only focused on motivational factors of individual tourists and/ or changes in the structure of host local society so far, and have rarely paid attention to the interaction between them or the process of tourism. They have simplified elements of tourism as tourists and host local communities only.

For a tour to be made, we usually need a tour organizer that connects tourists and destinations, and even bag packers and drifters, which are done individually and independently, need some kinds of mediators to be connected to destinations. An analysis of tourism should contain discussions on the process of tourism, and when we focus on that, it can give us the advantage that helps the construction of an integrated perspective that link tourists and host local communities since the process of tourism includes both. This is the reason we should give attention to social movement approaches that aim to promote the development of host local communities through organizing tourism.

III. Alternative Tourism from the Perspective of Social Movement Theory

Social movement theory generally tends 1) to deny established orders, 2) to criticize opponents with other perspectives 3) to have the group identity or solidarity and 4) to keep these attributes (Tarrow, 1994). Therefore, participants in social movements are mostly who have more aggressive motivation for works to change society by changing established orders and creating new ones. Researches on identifying the nature of social movements have shown two conflicting views, depending on what they perceive as the active motivation bringing participation in social movements.

First, according to classic theorists with social psychological approach, people who have psychological problems, such as cultural fringers, structurally neglected people, socially frustrated people, irrational or emotional people, and people with personality disorders, participate in social movements as a means to overcome what they have failed in having their way through existing orders. Participants in social movements are described as impulsive, irrational and volatile (Smelser, 1969). This approach, however, has limitations in that it is class-oriented and prejudiced. Concepts like exclusion, deviation, and irrationality are themselves the result of self-centered, subjective standards and judgments.

Most of all, it has a critical problem that it does not match the empirical reality. We can often see representative intellectuals in certain times have participated in and lead social movements. Various empirical works also have confirmed that participants in social movements are rational, reasonable, systematic, and are not only from fringe groups of a society. And the more fundamental problem is that it does not consider social structural factors.

It is this kind of reflection that brings resource mobilization approach. When we examine the social and economic background of participants in social movements, they are not irrational people or social fringers, but rather, they make rational choices that maximize utilities by rationally distributing limited social resources (Wiktorowicz, 2004). The reason for them participating in social movements is that they think it is the most rational and reasonable choice given social and economic conditions. Participants in social movements are not seen as extreme psychological deviations but as the most rational and reasonable agents.

It can mean contextual approach to social movements, which understands it from relativistic perspective. According to rational choice theory, however, the most rational choice is the free riding to social change without paying any opportunity costs. And if everyone chooses free riding, social movements cannot exist from the first. Rational choice theory assumes that there are some a priori models or standards for rational choice, agreed and accepted by all human beings. These are flaws resulted from counting on socio-structural factors too much (Jasper, 2004: 3).

Both social psychological approach and resource mobilization approach are not able to explain social movements completely. They are in a complementary relationship in that they can complement each other's weakness and problems. Moreover, they are not in a conflicting relationship in that social psychological approach focuses on individual level and resource mobilization approach focuses on social structure. They are in an interacting and interconnecting relationship in that social structure is formed through the process where individual perceptions or actions are transformed into the collective being and that individual psychological condition is formed with the influence of social structure.

Therefore, when we take an integrated approach that fuses both approaches, understanding and explanation that can embrace both become possible. As the former is the result from micro-approach and the latter is from macro-approach, it can be said as middle range approach, bridging and embracing both. From this integrated perspective, social movements can be understood as the formation of group identity in the process of interactions between socio-structural factors at macro-level and individual factors at micro-level.

This kind of group consciousness will stimulate the sharing of structural pain or problem awareness at the individual level, and furthermore will become the critical motivation for participation in social movements. When the relationship between individuals and social structure is examined around this group identity, we can see that group identity, which appears in a dynamic evolutionary process of continuous interaction between individuals and social structures where they belong, encourages individuals to develop self-efficacy and problem awareness and enables social structure to extend its network.

Group identity has characteristics that increase individual confidence that they can solve social problems with their own efforts, stimulates the concept of boundary that distinguishes between "I" and "Others" or we and them, and encourages self-confidence about the group or the class they belong to. As this kind of process recurs repeatedly, a kind of network is formed among individuals who share a group identity. We can define the analytic nature of social movements as interactions through this network among people who share group identity.

According to this integrated approach to social movements, alternative tourism transcending national borders is the process where tourists or travelers who belong to a society make the introspective development or change while interacting with the structure of different societies and make the structural change in these societies while building a group identity with members of host local communities. Conspicuous consumption in a certain society transforms into an ethical action or volunteering service in another society and produces the outcome of social movements. Certainly, mediator or mediating process that connects different societies is necessary for social movements transcending borders of different societies.

From the perspective of this mediator or intermediary, tourism can mean the administrative project and instrumental way or resource for social movements. It is the reason mediating alternative tourism is considered as a process or an effective means of social movements.

IV. Development Process of Alternative Tourism and Intermediary Institutions of Tourism

1. Demand for Mediator in the Development Process of Alternative Tourism

Before alternative tourism can be organized and managed as a means of social movements, the most urgent task, from the socio-psychological viewpoint, will be to detect, lure, recruit, and keep people who want to do volunteering service through tourism, developing the self-awareness about social problems and achieving self-development. It is the same reason customer segmentation is important in pioneering a new market. Human beings live up to expected value or preference they seek. To sort out people who prefer altruism or the value sought in alternative tourism as a social movement, there should be an understanding and identification of these people (Kotler & Andreason, 2000: 273).

Otherwise, there will be a gap between tourists' understanding of tourism and host local communities' understanding of tourism. Moreover, it will be hard to keep the balance between egoism and altruism, self-development and volunteering services, recreational and value elements, recreational effects and the contribution to host local communities, all of which are involved in tourism. Certainly, this will become a reason that causes difficulty maintaining or managing alternative tourism as a social movement. Therefore, it will require institutions, understanding both the society where tourists come from and the society where tourists visit, to connect or mediate the relationship between these societies. This means that it is calling for the mediating role of institutions, which have the foundation of movements in each society and the international networks.

In order that recruited tourists can do volunteering services through the contact with host local communities and, as a result, induce positive changes, there need to be a decision making process for tourism industry policies where consumers and producers, and employers and employees of tourism participate in together. And for this, it is required to release relevant information host local communities and local governments have, to guarantee the transparency in decision-making process, and to decentralize the structure of relevant policy making process (Thongma, 2009). It's because, for the realization of the value of social movements, it is absolutely necessary to communicate through local residents' participations and to take holistic approach denying the unilateralism that is inherent in centralized, top-down policy-making process.

If tourism industry is not developed from the viewpoint centered on host local communities, it cannot be the one for local communities; if it is not tourism for local communities, it will be hard to realize tourism that is value-oriented and, moreover, social movements-oriented. In that sense, participatory tourism can be another name for tourism centered on host local communities. Since there should be primary efforts creating and promoting the participatory space in order to stimulate local communities' participation, institutions, which are rooted in local communities and capable of mobilizing resources in those regions, should be active in mediating.

First of all, in respect to economy, tourism centered on local communities can target tourism industry utilizing regional specialties like local food, and consequently can diversify local communities by lowering economy leakage and increase self-containedness of local communities. This kind of the nature-friendly tourism will enable tourists to experience a trip adhered more to the reality of local communities, to become aware of the reality and social characteristics of these regions, and finally to reach self-development. This is called as edu-tourism by people who focus on these properties. Edu-tourism includes realizing the value of cultural pluralism or cultural relativism through the exposure to local, native culture and experiencing the importance of environmental conservation, as well as recognizing the reality of local communities.

It also includes indirect education through experiences and the case where education itself is the object of visiting. English education, skill education for economic development, history education, human rights education, and peace education are examples of the latter where education itself is an immediate purpose for tourism. In addition, when exploratory tourism, exploring historic sites or examining ecological environment is aimed, self-confirmation of intellectual ability and self-efficacy can be developed while applying social research methods, building networks, and acquiring information resources.

Even though this kind of process can stimulate changes and development of local communities and self-efficacy and problem awareness of individual tourists, still there needs to examine whether it can work as a fundamental factor that encourages and pressures the continuous participation in social movements. To induce the continuous participation of people who have never participated in social movements before, one or two times of tourism experience or the exposure to host local community would not be enough: consistent management and follow-up measures are required. From the perspective of social movement theory, continuous participation in social movements can mean the new way of life to participants in tourism, and thus needs resolute determination. This is why it needs intermediary institutions in charge of consistent management and follow-up measures.

2. Self-contradictory Task for Mediating Process of Alternative Tourism

Alternative tourism is certainly more eco-friendly than mass tourism. However, it has self-contradictory factors in that eco-tourism as alternative tourism, in whatever forms it is crystallized, cannot but contribute to environmental destruction eventually.

It means that there is no tourism like eco-friendly tourism in the first place. The movements of population naturally come with transportation which causes the increase in the amount of carbon emissions, and the fact that eco-tourism aims for the ecological environment in host societies as an object does make tourism eco-friendly as a matter of course. It can increase the risk of destruction or disturbance of an ecosystem with in-depth experience in or more frequent visits to ecological sites. It might be true that tracking is a lot less destructive than the construction of large resorts, but that does not mean it has no negative effect on the preservation of natural ecology. Instead, the tour close to ecological sites can have more regressive effect on the preservation of ecological sites.

The same thing can be said about the alternative tourism that intends to protect tradition or culture of local natives. The increase in outside visitors will cause different kinds of cultural shocks, in whatever forms it might take, to host local communities, and in that sense, it cannot be positive to the protection of traditional culture. It has clearly shown in the case of U.S. Indian policy that sets up Indian reservations and turns into them tourism assets for their livelihood, which has not contributed to the conservation of traditional culture of Indian societies or to the vitalization of social communities but rather has acted regressively on their cultural identity bringing the destruction of personality and the loss of self-esteem in people living in reservation areas. When these points are considered, the task is that organizing alternative tourism as a social movement should be done on a small scale and not so frequently.

This is self-contradictory task in that alternative tourism needs to be organized more frequently and to be encouraged for more participation from more people if it wants to devote to the realization of values that social movements aim. The sustainability of intermediary institutions is critical task to keep the sustainability of host local societies at ecological, cultural, and economic levels and to secure the sustainability of tourism itself. For this, intermediary institutions should be able to reinvest at least in alternative tourism, and in order for reinvestment to be possible, the work for mediating tourism should be able to guarantee the payability or economic profit that needs for reinvestment. From the perspective of resource mobilization theory, this leads us to the conclusion that the larger the scale of tourism, the better.

However, if they focus on producing economic profit, they will certainly lose the meaning of the existence of alternative tourism or the spirit as a value-oriented tourism mediator or a social movement intermediary. In addition, tourism as an industry has itself characteristics that commercialize culture, tradition and environment of host local communities (Wall & Mathieson, 2006). Values of host local communities can be undermined by the commercialism that tries to transform culture and tradition into easily salable goods for creation of income or increase of household income. This is the reason that the pursuit of values of social movements will be hard when alternative tourism mediator takes the form of pure business weighing only the profitability.

Therefore, we face the task that the process of mediating tourism as a social movement should be done on a small scale and keep its value-oriented character. In the field of tourism industry, however, alternative tourism is not the only one existing or marketing. It needs to compete with established mass tourism as well as other alternative tourism. Intermediary institutions for tourism here face another different task to keep appropriate service quality and reasonable price in the middle of a competition and to achieve the value-oriented goal as a means of social movements.

From the perspective of resource mobilization theory, there is a problem of whether participatory tourism can guarantee democratic participation when an opportunity space for residents' participation is made in the place which has not enough cultural and social resources for residents' participation. It will be like expecting democratic decision-making process and direct democracy to flourish in a place where social capital is not accumulated. The influx of foreign comprador capital might be able to be blocked with local residents' participation but there is a high possibility of false participation or mobilized participation by a small number of local businesses or wealthy local powers.

This implicates the risk of forming another kind of exploitation structure inside local communities. Cutting off the relocation of fruits from local economy to outside local communities and consequently reducing the rate of economic leakage does not promise fair share or equal distribution to all participants in tourism industry in host local communities. Rather, there is a high possibility that it will rationalize or perpetuate the exploitation of lower class by higher class in local communities. The problem that the trickle down effect of economic development implicates will also work inside local economic communities.

Same problems are suggested in protecting human rights of socially inferior groups through alternative tourism. In its management process, alternative tourism intends to exclude all kinds of activities that treat women as the subject of sexual amusement, exploit child labor, or neglect legitimate rights of minorities or natives. This is so natural that there would be no one giving different opinion about it. However, there still remains the problem of what would happen to their livelihood in that case. Being unable to put up with the pressure from civil society movement organizations blaming the exploitation of child labor, handmade carpet factories in Turkey had to lay off all the child labor. The fact that these children, all of a sudden, lost means of livelihood, entered into human trafficking market, and had to live even more miserable life has great implications.

This leads us to the conclusion that we should not recognize or deal with tourism as a separate domain isolated with the pluralistic structure of society. This means that an institution, which copes only with tourism itself or the work of mediating tourism separately, should not run for tourism mediation. Intermediary institutions for tourism should be able to take an organic approach to social movements through tourism at the holistic and pluralistic level and should have conditions for that. And this means that it should be institutions that can have empathy for host local communities and have resources and the will to approach social policies multidimensionally.

V. YMCA as an Intermediary Institution for Alternative Tourism

1. Civil Society Movement Organizations as Intermediary Institutions

The works organizing and mediating alternative tourism or alternative tourism as a social movement is facing multidimensional self-contradictory tasks. This means that there is a high demand for the role of intermediary institutions as a coordinator or balancer. Therefore, we can expect the higher possibility of problem solving and even the multiplier effect when civil society movement organizations go to mediating works for alternative tourism as an ancillary means for realizing the existing goals or expanding the power of movements, rather than existing intermediary institutions like travel agencies or hotels that has commercial characteristics.

First of all, they have an advantage at capturing target groups to solicit participation in alternative tourism as a social movement. Volunteer-type tourists, who focus on the reflection of self-identity or the development of host local communities, not limiting them to hedonistic motivation simply enjoying leisure time, are different with participants in commercial mass tourism in social and psychological conditions such as hobby, personality, values, and economic status. Civil society movement organizations can relatively easily capture this kind of value-oriented person. They can easily figure out the target for promotion because they are close to people who already support and participate in civil society movements of their own, and they can expand the target group based on these people.

Since people recruited through civil society movement networks are more homogeneous, it is easier to construct and keep the network among participants. Moreover, they have the advantage that they can consistently manage people after participations in tourism, develop follow-up works and connect to existing works of civil society movements.

From the perspective of resource mobilization theory, there is a relatively less demand for additional resources or costs in the case of civil society movement organizations, since they can organize or mediate alternative tourism as an extension of social movements they have already done and carried forward. The sunken cost related to social movements has already been accumulated, and they can utilize established manpower, resource, organization, and value system. As a result, civil society movement organizations are in an advantageous position for keeping small-scale tourism while maintaining sustainability of intermediary institutions. It is easier for them to tune the profitability per unit in the mediating process of alternative tourism due to the sunken cost.

When existing commercial organizations try to take the mediating works for tourism, there is high possibility that they will aim to expand continuously the scale of tourism due to the nature of the capital and the attributes of business. On the other hand, when civil society movement organizations organize and mediate tourism, they have the limit of their own because they try to work within the range that is sponsoring, encouraging and complementary to the achievement of established goals of movements, not the basic desired value of commercialism.

In the sense that the cooperation adhered to and supporting local regions is possible when institutions that are well-acquainted with the tasks and demand of host local communities mediate tourism, civil society movement organizations are definitely in an advantageous position. They know well what are needed and where these are needed through civil society movements in local regions. They also have the advantage that they can mobilize human and material resources with relevant networks. These strengths are the factor that makes hard for market, which excludes value orientation, to compete with them. And of civil society movement organizations, one that is based on global networks would be mostly appropriate because it should be well-acquainted with both the society where tourists are recruited and the host local society.

Mediating activities of civil society movement organizations, especially of comprehensive civil society movement organizations, are urgently needed when we consider the fact that there is need for residents' participation in host local communities and that the accumulation of social capital is the precondition for that. The accumulation of social capital cannot be done in a day, requiring hard efforts to be made intentionally, which is one of the works that civil society movement organizations have carried forward as ordinary tasks. Especially for the case of comprehensive civil society movement organizations that run very various kinds of relevant programs, it would be easier to make cooperative efforts through their solidarity with each domain of society. Local civil society movement organizations can be even more effective for monitoring deviation or distortion after participation.

After all, mediating alternative tourism, as a social movement would have greater efficiency when it is developed by comprehensive civil society movement organizations, which are value-oriented, adhered to fields, oriented to locality, and equipped with networks for solidarity activities in each domain of society and around the world.

2. YMCA as a Civil Society Movement Organization

The Young Men's Christian Associations seek to unite "those young men who, regarding Jesus Christ as their God and Saviour, according to the Holy Scriptures, desire to be his disciples in their faith and in their life, and to associate their efforts for the extension of his Kingdom amongst young men. In its way of operation, it has maintained the openness principle, the young men priority principle, and the Christ-centered principle." This is to open the door of YMCA to everyone regardless of their class or beliefs which cause the division in society. This also means that YMCA does not limit the qualification for membership only to Christians and that it embraces all levels of society and all occupational social classes (merchants, office workers, students and the like). For areas of works and programs, it does not limit itself to religious programs in a narrow sense and seeks comprehensive openness that deals with all kinds of tasks for social policies facing local communities, cities, rural areas, and/or the whole nation with a sense of mission.

Therefore, YMCA can be said as the movement organization that is highly value-oriented and also emphasizes the solidarity of movements in that it is organized and operated with ecumenism and the Christian sense of mission to build God's Kingdom on earth. It is also the comprehensive civil society movement organization in that it is trying to cope with various tasks for social policies comprehensively. This can be confirmed in various works for social policies YMCA has been carried out, which includes numerous tasks such as keeping the life and peace, reducing the poverty, protecting environment, enhancing human rights, promoting fair trade, improving public health and sanitation, eradicating illiteracy, and providing the emergency relief. YMCA is one of the most representative civil society movement organizations in the world.

For YMCA, mediating alternative tourism is just one of various social movement programs it organizes and runs. Mediating alternative tourism is not the sole work, but one of the many works that contribute to the nature and determines the existence of YMCA.

The diversity of its movement tasks is influenced by the fact that YMCA is an international civil society movement organization with global networks. YMCA is the oldest international non-governmental organization (INGO) established at the 1st World Council of YMCA in Paris. At the time of its foundation, it was active around Europe and North America, and now it has over 45 million members from 127 countries. This massive network will work as a very effective device for promoting the exchange of human resources and information that are needed to mediate supply and demand of alternative tourism.

Meanwhile, YMCA has maintained the field-first spirit. While it seeks common global values, about the way of the realization, it intends to respect contextually the spatiotemporal characteristic that each YMCA faces. This shows the flexibility and adaptability of YMCA movement that is trying to correspond to changes in environments of the times and the tendency of being socially relevant that respects and embraces the characteristics and traditional values of local societies. This is also shown in the Kampala Principles, one of the universal guides for YMCA movement. It has its origin in supporting and encouraging individuals who live in postmodern society to be developed into healthy human beings who are created equal in His image, without being pressured by the structural contradiction of society. It is to say that the priority goal of the movement is building a community in local society. This makes the way of developing movements focusing on encouraging residents' participation and being centered on local society. And this is the movement organization that is adhered to fields and regional sedentary.

Since its foundation for the realization of these values in 1855, YMCA has made efforts to achieve them mostly through education and experience. It has been equipped with various and extensive facilities and equipments and accumulated management experience in fields through running them for a long time. It has built hostels, cafeterias, campsites, swimming pools, and gyms and maintained cooperative relationship with local societies and local governments to operate them more effectively. This means that it has accumulated necessary facilities and management experience for alternative tourism and that it has the high sunken cost required for mediating and managing alternative tourism.

More importantly, mediating alternative tourism itself has the very significant strategic value for keeping the sustainability of YMCA and for realizing its objects for the social movement. YMCA has been able to keep its consistent viability as a civil society movement organization, continuously growing for a long time because it has operated on the base of an internal structure of revenue mobilization than other NGOs. YMCA has promoted social movement programs for the development of various local communities and at the same time, it also has run fitness facilities like gyms and swimming pools for the spirit, body and mind development of children, outdoor training facilities like campsites, and accommodation facilities like hostels. This kind of internal resource mobilization structure makes YMCA different from other civil society movement organizations that depend on raising funds and donations from outside for the most part of its revenue. In that sense, YMCA can be said as the first social enterprise.

In postmodern times, however, it became hard to keep its exclusive position, and competitiveness of the past as the market of social sports had been diversified and private companies and other NGOs had entered into this area. The structure of creating revenue inherent in the institution cannot work properly anymore, which have caused financial difficulties in many YMCAs all over the world. There has been an increasing pressure from inside YMCA that claims to build aggressively the new internal structure of mobilizing resources.

Moreover, there has been continuous questioning regarding the problem of whether it would be appropriate to keep pursuing social development in postmodern times from the closed perspective of the past that gives priority to local communities. In the postmodern times of globalization where boundaries between village and village, boundaries between region and region are being blurred, the strategic view that concerns the development of local community over other things can encourage conflict and confrontation between region and region or between nation and nation, emphasizing 'our' village first. Or, at least, it has a fundamental weakness that makes it hard to settle the conflict. This kind of reflection on philosophical principles of YMCA movements has spread the argument that they need to find the direction for more legitimate movement.

It was at the 16th World Council in 2006 when the resolution was passed, which adopted global citizenship as the direction for movement considering the whole globe over villages or local communities, based on the above recognition. Moreover, the 17th World Council in 2010 adopted thematic slogans for the coming quadrennial years as "Striving for Global Citizenship for All" (World Alliance of YMCAs, 2010: 14-19). Mediating alternative tourism as a means of social movements is the task that closely corresponds to this kind of global citizenship spirit and consequent global movements and interactions of people over the world. And it is one of the works that YMCA mostly needs to do in that it mobilizes financial resources. Mediating alternative tourism is a new alternative that makes YMCA movements in times of globalization sustainable.

VI. Conclusion

Multidimensional interpretation becomes possible when we approach alternative tourism from the social movement perspective. Alternative tourism is the outcome of social movements in that it appeared as one of the actions to report and correct harmful effects of mass tourism. It is an instrumental method for social movements in that it intends to alleviate or rectify the structural contradiction in host local societies through alternative tourism. It also can be a way of social movements in that it corrects the frame of participants' recognition of introspection or social tasks.

Therefore organizing or mediating alternative tourism from the social movement perspective naturally becomes multidimensional. Approaching to alternative tourism from the social movement perspective began as the opposition to the fact that alternative tourism still includes residues from mass tourism even though it started from the critical assessment of mass tourism, which makes this approach itself one of outcomes of social movements. On the other hand, it is strategic means of social movements in that it promotes and stimulates social movements through alternative tourism. It becomes a way of social movements when it corrects the frame of recognition of alternative tourism in the process.

Considering these multidimensional aspects as a social movement, if we deal with mediating alternative tourism as an extension of social movements, it is all too clear that it will be more effective with civil society movement organizations that have been active bearing social movements as their aims. They have relatively advantageous conditions in mediating alternative tourism; favorable position in capturing and recruiting the target groups for alternative tourism participation, abilities of understanding and adhering to host local communities, the power of global solidarity and international networks, the ability to connect to other various policy tasks, the high accumulation of the relevant sunken cost, the ability to act organically as comprehensive movement organizations, and the perspective that approaches as promoter and supporter. Especially YMCA has shown these advantages very clearly.

However, approaching alternative tourism from a social movement perspective is not always eurhythmics. Even though it is for overcoming alternative tourism, more specifically the problems of alternative tourism as an extension of social movements, it is difficult to completely get over hedonistic aspects of tourism, which is the core of criticism to mass tourism. Actually, one of the motivations in approaching alternative tourism from the social movement perspective is that alternative tourism can have the factors attracting participations because it still has hedonistic elements in spite of its value-oriented characteristics. In that sense, the key in an effort to mediate alternative tourism from the social movement perspective is how to keep a balance between hedonistic elements and value-oriented elements with what standard of distribution.

This is also a phenomenon that appears multidimensionally over egoism and altruism, leisure-oriented and volunteering-oriented, socio-psychological and socio-structural factors, and rationalism and emotionalism. Nevertheless, alternative tourism from the social movement perspective or the works of mediating it should be more strongly value-oriented than existing tourism because it is the way of being defined and it intends to make as the driving force of social movements. In this respect, mediating alternative tourism from the social movement perspective involves normative elements. And this is why promoting these kinds of ethical travels in the real world is not always successful.

It can cause a disturbance in local labor market or the decrease in the quality of labor by stimulating inflow of tourism participants or volunteers into host local society. There also is the possibility to harm the self-sufficient socio-economic structure of host local society increasing dependency on outside aids. Most of all, there is a serious problem that it is helpless in making tourists overcome the notional boundary of 'othering' host local society. In order that tourism can move desired value to the realization of values through volunteering, not the enjoyment of attractions, it is premised on conspicuous consumption, that is, differentiation with others, in post-modern times. Due to the attributes of tourism, the exposure to host local societies cannot but have short-term effects basically, and as a result, time perspective for volunteering or participation in the development of local society is also short-term, which implicates problems.

In this sense, there are criticisms that value-oriented alternative tourism and the works of arranging and mediating it are nothing but detouring or misleading individual guilt for the third world. It even faces wary suggestion that it is just a manifestation of imperialism in postmodern version, stimulating the nostalgia for the colonial period (Harkin, 1995: 652). These differences in recognition can be seen as the demand for efforts for more communicating with the surrounding environment and fully sharing information in the process of alternative tourism and mediating it. Alternative tourism and the works for mediating it themselves are self-contradictory tasks in that they are the kinds of ways and means of cultural, racial, human, and social communication and, at the same time, without communication it will be hard to achieve their goals.

However, we can find some comfort in that postmodern society does not coerce the general guiding code anymore. Diversity and pluralism are now like the nature of this age. Coexistence of many different things and warm desire for coexistence are the code of postmodern times. It is transforming from times where the relationship between people were about being together with others into times where it is about caring for them. The former relied on the power while the latter relies on love. In that very sense, it is well-timed and appealing suggestion that YMCA intends to act as an intermediary institution for alternative tourism.

Chapter 08

Climate Change and Alternative Tourism

I. Introduction

Over the past decades, tourism has expanded and diversified continuously, becoming one of the largest and fast-growing industries in the world. In 2012 only, over one billion international tourists traveled world, generating over US$1.2 trillion dollars in export earnings (UNWTO, 2013: 1). Technological advances in air transport are the key factors for such a rapid growth of tourism in addition to the rise of middle class, the growing wealth in emerging countries, government's supports to promote foreign travel and the forces of globalization instigated largely by the advent of information society and the fall of socialist bloc.

Such a rapid growth of tourism has produced no small problems. There took place a high risk of cultural assimilation and integration biased toward western society as the travel of western people is far more active, which led to the abrasion of local cultural identity. As the tourism industry looks for profit maximization under the severe competitiveness of the world market, infringement of human rights as like the exploitation of youth workers and aboriginals is often done without hesitation. High rate of economic leakage from host community leads to the increased dependency of the local economy to the outside capital.

More than anything else, it causes increased emission of carbon dioxide leading to climate change and global warming. Higher dependency on mass-transportation system requires high energy consumption. Expanded number of travelers promotes construction of large scale recreational facilities and resorts leading to disruption of local ecological environment. Frequent visits to the sites of natural beauty and environmental protection increase human footprints there. Expanded tourism has become a remarkable source of climate change and global warming.

Increased awareness of such trend in climate change and global warming and negative impacts contributed by expanded tourism as well calls for the role that alternative tourism could play as a tool to mitigate. Here arise the social needs to develop concrete ideas and strategies from which we can design programs and policies for such combat purpose. Korean cases will anchor our discussion further.

II. Impacts of Tourism to Climate Change

Global warming and climate change have become a usual phenomenon nowadays. We have witnessed a very steep rise of such a trend in recent decades. According to the international forecasting report (UNWTO, 2007), such a trend will be further aggravated. Average surface temperature will go up by 6.4c° at its maximum and sea level by 59cm in 2100. In each decade, average global temperature is projected to rise by 0.2c°. When such a pace of warming is kept, it is predicted that, in 2050, 1% of global GDP is required to adapt to such a changing situation, 4 billion people will experience shortage of water, and 500 million people will be stricken by hunger.

Such a changing pace of climate brings in wide-ranging impacts to our natural environments: retreating glaciers, longer growing seasons, higher speed wind as like cyclone, shifts of species ranges, increasing drought, more frequent torrential rain falls, and health impacts due to the unprecedented heat wave (Mishev & Mochurova, 2008: 1).

Climate change brings about a very serious impact not only on such natural environments but also on the world industries as a whole. Tourism industry is not an exception from such negative impacts. It alters attractive traveling destinations and brings in damages or floods to cultural relics and heritage sites with heavy or acid rain. Clean environment and favorable weather conditions are crucial to visitor satisfaction and fundamental factor for the development of tourism industry (Mishev & Mochurova, 2008: 1). When climate change destroys such attractive conditions of frequently visiting sites, decrease of tourists becomes an inevitable outcome. Nature-based tourism is more sensitive to climate-induced environmental changes. In addition to that, degree of such impacts to a hosting community varies according to the rate of economic dependency to a tourism industry. Thus, poor community becomes more vulnerable to poverty. Tourism is more a victim than a vector of climate change in this sense (Mishev & Mochurova, 2008: 1).

However, it is not deniable that tourism contributes a higher share to climate change. It contributed 4.95% of the whole CO2 emissions of the world in 2005. Among them, transportation of tourists makes 75%, accommodation 21%, and activities 4%. Out of 75% of transportation, air transportation contributes 40%, car transport 32% and other means of transport 3%. In other words, aviation traveling is a single most important contributor to the CO2 emissions (Scott *et al.*, 2010). Such a situation would aggravate further in the future. According to a research outcome jointly conducted by UNWTO-UNEP-WMO in 2008, air transport is projected to contribute 52% of CO2 emissions from the tourism sector in 2035. Accommodation will make 25%, car transport 16% and activities 7% (UNWTO-UNEP-WMO, 2008).

It is very natural in such a situation that people start to think about alternative way of "Traveling with Climate in Mind", which refers to a more fortified response than "Green Tourism" movement, implying a call for "Low Carbon Tourism" with the development of more strengthened mitigation policies against GHG(green-house gas).

III. Tourism to Combat against Climate Change

"Traveling with Climate in Mind" is a multidimensional task by its nature since tourism covers whole dimensions of human life. When we approach traveling from its outward dimension, it could be defined as a visitor's behavior taking place within certain environmental conditions of hosting community. And one of the major determinants of hosting community's social structure is government and its policy directions. In other words, traveling takes place within the network of tripartite concentric circles consisted with traveler's behaviors, government policies and community structures. In addition to these environmental determinants, when we approach traveling from its inward dimension, traveler's mindset plays a critical role in determining behavioral attitudes of travelers. Basic components of the human mind are intelligence, personality and moral character (Dweck, 2008). Intelligence is interrelated with information and knowledge. Personality interlinks with one's value system. And moral character is interlocked with spirituality as its ultimate and supreme form. Therefore, we can think of six determinants — three outward ones and three inward ones — affecting modes of "traveling with climate in mind."

From such a scheme discussed above, we can devise six different approaches to combat against climate change: for outward dimension, 1) social movement approach, 2) political process approach and 3) community-based approach and for inward dimension, 4) technological approach, 5) epistemological approach and 6) religious approach. Social movement approach aims to redesign behavioral patterns of traveling and thus perform alternative modes of travel in order to mitigate climate change, implying similar philosophy and performances as well of the new social movements in 1970s and 1980s in other fields of the world as like gender, peace, and anti-nuclear movements. Adaptation of the modes of tourism to mitigate climate change is the practical prime strategy of this approach. Political process approach focuses on and prioritizes government mitigation policies as a prime tool to combat against climate change believing that government policies have a direct and strong power to control social interactions and thus traveling modes. Therefore, it has an inclination to deal with relatively wider range of issues going beyond the boundary of mitigating CO2 through or by traveling. Lobbying and participation to the political process are the strategies to realize its objectives. And community-based approach emphasizes the importance of community structure and network in which tourism takes place. They try to alter outside conditions of tourism to make it more responsible to the needs and demands arising in the process of mitigation.

Technological approach assumes that without scientific information and knowledge, they cannot trace the cause and effect relationship between traveling and CO2 emission precisely and thus cannot develop adequate and relevant mitigation strategies. Researching and analyzing the technical side of traveling are the prime foci of interests. They want to produce and provide relevant scientific information to the development process of adaption strategies to change traveling modes to mitigate. Epistemological approach intends to change conceptual framework and value system of the stakeholders engaged in tourism by sharing experiences and deepening of understanding of the phenomenon relevant to the reduction of CO2 emissions. Doing and learning are the mottoes of this approach. Religious approach believes that without changing life-style to eco-friendly ones, we cannot change the basic nature of traveling and make it more fit to mitigate CO2 emissions. The ultimate way of changing life patterns from the contemporary mechanism of mass production and mass consumption to the alternative way of slow life could be possible when we go through with very serious self-reflection and such reflection needs spirituality which ultimately controls moral character of stake-holders engaged in tourism.

When we take social movement approach, it becomes very obvious from the above discussion that the longer we travel, the more we produce CO2 emissions. At the extension of such logic, it could be advisable to travel short. However, such a scenario of "staying at home" contradicts directly to the basic nature of traveling abroad looking for opportunities to be released from daily routine ways of life and thus seems to be unrealistic as well as unattractive. Even if they are fully aware of the dangers of global warming, they will not be able to give up their well-deserved holidays and unable to find any practical climate-friendly alternatives. However, it could be advisable to travel wisely. "Traveling wise" is to shorten total traveling distance by combining multiple travel needs into fewer traveling opportunities and ultimately reducing traveling frequency and so distance.

It also should be noted that most tourism trips are relatively eco-efficient as 80% of the whole trips — by rail, coach and car (except air) — cause just about 20% of the GHG emissions. And further prospects for increasing fuel efficiency of air transport are relatively low at present since the technology of jet aircraft is already mature and reflected. Alternative fuels will not be introduced on a large scale within the next three to five decades (Zussman, 2007). In such a situation, there is no other option, but to alternate transport mode from air to rail, coach, ship or other conventional means in order to mitigate emissions by choosing adequate tools of transportation.

As far as the length of stay is concerned, the shorter, the better to make the trips eco-efficient since accommodation is a higher source of emissions. However, such suggestion establishes an adversarial relationship with the frequency of travel. There is an inclination that the longer you may stay, the less frequently you may travel resulting shorter total distance of trips. Therefore, it is recommendable to stay longer once you make a trip. For the mode of stay, it is advisable to prefer nature-friendly and so eco-efficient accommodations. Instead of high energy consuming accommodation at luxurious tour resorts, it is advisable to choose home-stay or hostels consuming fewer energy.

Political process approach requests the stakeholders of tourism as like travelers, travel agencies, and advocacy NGOs to collaborate in campaigning and lobbying against government officials to develop stronger mitigation policies regulating higher standards for eco-efficient transportation, accommodation and activities. In order to design such policies, we need to know further in detail about the economic costs of climate change and that of adaptation at local level. They want to ask the government to make further in-depth researches and disseminate relevant information to the public and the stakeholders of tourism as well. In fact, national mitigation policy frameworks are emerging but slowly and uncoordinated yet (Gössling, 2010: 25). Facing with a rapidly globalizing world and tourism expansion crossing over the national boundaries, it becomes further important to urge global integration of tourism policies throughout the world and mitigation policies as well for more efficient supervision and promotion of combating programs against climate change.

When we take community-based approach, it becomes important to redesign a community and its nature as an object of travel attraction to make them more adaptable to climate change mitigation. Under this scheme, we can think of many programs as like reforesting barren land, promoting local food program, creating slow city, constructing pilgrimage route, campaigning no garbage movement, building bike-only road, and etc. They would like to create living conditions in which travelers could lead eco-friendly living at the hosting community and make such living condition as an object of tour or point of attraction for the visitors. It is very natural that, without supports and collaboration from the residents of hosting community, any intentions to mitigate CO2 in the walks of traveling are useless.

When we take a technological approach, it is important to

strengthen institutional capability of government and advocacy NGOs as well to review the causal relations assumed by conventional approaches to mitigate climate change in terms of scientific knowledge and data. Establishing collaborative network with scientific experts, therefore, is required to produce and amass information relevant to this checking. For instance, planting tree has been suggested and implemented by the conventional approaches as an appealing program to offset CO_2 emissions produced in the process of traveling and counted as a tool to teach tourism stakeholders through doing and learning about the importance of fighting against climate change. When it is checked from the technological point of view, however, it is known that planting tree does not help to the work of mitigating CO_2 emissions. Even if we agree it helps, it takes too long a time to grow up to offset by producing O_2 meanwhile climate change is a very imminent issue. For the grown up trees, whether they are cut down and burnt or go through natural decaying process, they are destined to produce CO_2 at their end. Reviewing from the technological point of view, trees are not efficient, immanent and scientific tool to combat against climate change contradicting to our conventional wisdom. It is very important to check, thus, scientific viability of any alternatives suggested as a tool to mitigate climate change caused by traveling.

When we approach from the vantage point of epistemological perspective, we can make use of travel as a template or an opportunity to share the idea of carbon reduction to mitigate climate change. Tour programs could be designed to teach and learn eco-friendly ways of life as like taking local foods, planting vegetables for their own consumption and thus spread and promote environmental awareness in hosting communities and among the travelers as well. The prime goal of this approach is laid upon spreading new value system to the stakeholders of tourism believing that without new value system we cannot easily promote the idea of mitigating against climate change and thus adapting to new modes of travel.

Taking a religious approach, in order to promote alternative ways of life and eco-friendly value system it becomes important to internalize the concept of ecological right and environmental sovereignty. It believes that strong power and energy of oneself come basically from self-reflection and self-centeredness and not from being compelled by the outside forces. Therefore, moral obligation could be counted as an efficient tool to drive people to eco-friendly life. One of the best ways to promote one's sensibility to moral obligation is to bring the issue into the realm of divinity. For instance, especially for the YMCA movement, it becomes important to emphasize a life leading a self toward Christlikeness. At the extension of such a thought, we could devise and carry out programs as like pilgrim tour and sacred tour programs to promote spirituality in the process of and by way of traveling. Such a rather fundamental strategy to promote mitigation idea is to make the travelers experience, self-reflect, and communicate with their inner minds and, thus, transcend into new ways of life. Providing opportunities to contemplate over one's own life and to grasp ultimate value of life, they believe, could instigate people's mind to prioritize slow life over greediness and thus to upgrade sensibility to eco-friendly modes of life in general and those of traveling in particular.

IV. Mitigation Programs in Korea

Several local governments and community based NGOs in Korea have strived to take the rising demands to mitigate global warming and to combat against climate change not as a crisis of tourism but as a momentum or opportunity to proactively renovate tourism itself and to promote tourism industry as well. At the extension of such a thought, they tried to promote green tourism as one of the major locomotives of the green new deal project coined and run by the central government. They approached the idea of "traveling with climate in mind" not as a simple instrument to mitigate global warming but as the power source of driving local economic growth, recognizing it as a high-value producing service industry. Below are the model programs designed and implemented by such local governments and NGOs in Korea

1. Chang Won City of Kyung Nam Province (Kim, 2009: 13)

They hosted the 10th Meeting of the Conference of the Contracting Parties to the Convention of Wetlands - Ramsar List of General Assembly - in 2008 and proclaimed the city as a "Capital of Environment" in order to build up the image of city as an attractive traveling destination with beauty of nature and environmental preservation. Obviously they wanted to draw attention of the general public to the importance of environmental protection and preservation of nature. At the extension of such a strategy, they built eco-town and restored ecological function of streams running through the city. They drove a very strong campaign for riding bike instead of a car, CO2 offset program throughout the city and developed tour program visiting Woopo wetland near to the city. The tour program to wetland is designed to emphasize the importance of preserving ecological settings.

2. NGO Olle kil of Jeju Island (Jeju Olle, 2014)

A former journalist, Ms. Suh Myung-Sook, developed trail courses called "Olle kil(narrow path)" in Jeju island for the first time in 2008 as a part of people's voluntary movement for eco-friendly travel after visiting and getting idea from Santiago Pilgrimage route(Camino de San Tiago) in Spain. Now there are 22 courses developed carefully avoiding artificial touches, preserving ecological settings and being friendly to nature. Each course covers a trail running 10 to 20 kms requiring about 3 to 6 hours of walking. The trails run either alongside the seashore or through the deep forests of the island canvassing history, mythology, culture, and gender issues of the island. One of the beauties of the Olle kil project is that it has diversified travel destinations from mass tourism centers developed by major conglomerates of Korea into small villages of the island and thus has started to divert inflow of economic earnings from mass tourism centers to the residents of local communities in addition to providing eco-friendly travel modes to mitigate CO2 emissions.

The NGO supervising and promoting "Olle kil" runs a couple of sister programs aimed to mitigate climate change. They run a program called "Gran Mum's Guest Room." The program is to support and develop private rooms left behind after kids grown up and leaving home town as guest rooms for Olle kil travelers. This program contributes to the reduction of CO2 emissions by curtailing needs to build additional accommodations for expanded travelers and utilizing already existing rooms left vacant. Another program is to engage in a campaign of not using disposable products as like paper cups, disposable tooth-brushes, and paper towels while traveling, which is called BYO(bring your own) drive. They also run a joint campaign together with National Trust Fund for Nature Preservation, one of the most active NGOs to protect environment in Korea, which calls for donations from the Olle kil travelers to offset their own footprints left behind due to their trail walking and to buy private forests in the island to preserve from any profit-seeking development. "Clean Olle kil" program is to advise the trail walkers to pick garbage bag at the starting point of the trail, to collect trashes left behind by other visitors and their own along the trail walking, to take proving shots by cellular phone and to go for competition to win prizes donated by business circle. They also run a green tourism academy in order to share eco-friendly philosophy and way of life among the stakeholders of tourism and the general public as well.

3. Jeju Special Self-Governance Province (Kim, 2009: 15)

Jeju province hosted World Conservation Congress in 2012 organized by the International Union for Conservation of Nature, which is the only NGO bestowed with observer status by UN, where they agreed to work for making Jeju as world environmental hub in 2020. From that time on Jeju province started to accelerate its green tourism policies in order to get qualified for such status in 2020. They would like to increase target share of green tourism up to 30% of total tourism inflow of the island. Understanding that simple number of green travelers could not make such target qualification, they began to emphasize quality side of green tourism. Green tourism policies they consider to introduce are: to provide incentives to the eco-friendly tourism sites and destinations designated officially by the government as such, to adopt prior-review system for the eco-friendly tourism resources development projects, to collect carbon tax according to the estimated carbon emissions produced by individual tour programs at their initial stage of development, and to provide tax reduction benefit to the eco-friendly tourism facilities and programs.

4. NGO Good Travel (Good Travel, 2014; Na, 2010)

Good travel is a social enterprise registered with the Korean government, which looks for promoting and realizing the idea of sustainable, responsible, ecological, fair and ethical tourism. They believe world alternative tourism development paradigm has been changed from nature preservation and environmental protection tourism in 1990s to sustainable tourism in 2000s especially after the Davos Declaration in 2007 jointly adopted by UNWTO, World Meteorological Organization, and UN Environment Programme, which emphasizes low carbon emission instead of no carbon, optimal utilization of ecological resources instead of simple preservation of ecology, and balance between economic benefits and energy consumption. Following such a shift of paradigm, they develop and carry out eco-friendly tour programs as like home stay at Vanho village of Vietnam and Hmong tribe's village of Cambodia, cyclo tour in Cambodia, joining to talk shows run by professors in Vietnam and Laos about ecological travel and anti-sex tour issue. They also run "Tree-House" program jointly organized by Good Travel and local NGOs from 2012 which provide opportunities for the good travelers to stay, learn and participate to the hosting community works as like planting trees and developing local mitigation programs. They cover mainly travels to Mekong river basin as like Yunnan of China, Vietnam, Cambodia, Laos, Thailand, and Burma.

5. Temple Stay by Chogye Order of Korean Buddhism (Temple Stay Center, 2010)

Temple stay is a cultural and religious tour program which is designed to let the visitors experience the life of Buddhist practitioners at traditional temples scattered in mountains across the nation. It was developed in 2002 and run by the national order of Korean Buddhism in response to increased foreign visitors to Korea to learn about Korean culture and recognized as one of 5 most successful tour programs by OECD for 8 successive years in 2010(Our Buddhism, 2010.10.11.). A typical program entails an overnight stay at a Buddhist temple, and participation in religious rituals as like ceremonial service, Zen meditation, monastic meal, tea ceremony and strolling along the forest path. Zen meditation is a way to discover the Buddha mind and a true nature of oneself. It is considered as one of the ways to reach supreme enlightenment of oneself. Monastic meal is designed to eat ecologically, in complete silence and with no wasting of food at all. The meal is served with complete vegetarian dishes and allows one to live in harmony with nature. Through the practice of tea ceremony, one can find true stillness and tranquility in a cup of tea. While walking along a peaceful forest path in the vicinity of temple, one can listen to one's own inner voice and through the practice of 108 prostrations one can learn the technique of putting down one's inner desires and attachments.

V. Conclusion

When we review whole spectrum of tourism, we can easily note that only a small part of all tourism as like aviation trip, in fact, is responsible for the main share of GHG emissions. This means that it would be better to prioritize our mitigation efforts to this relatively smaller part of tourism (Zussman, 2007). Even if we agree to focus on this part of tourism, it is important to notice that mobilizing government mitigation policies is more demanding since they cover wider ranges and more efficient in responding to such needs. However, it also should be learned that few governments, in fact, develop adaptation policies specifically targeted to tourism. To the government officials who are trained to look into the world from the perspectives of efficiency and economy, it is costly and uncertain to combat against negative impacts of tourism only since the returning impact loops of such policies are too long, interconnected and complex to trace. Not many government officials are well and fully exposed to the importance of developing adaptation policies. And sometimes government policies are not applicable throughout the world and thus curtailed for global collaborations. For instance, high rate of the carbon tax for aviation is more significantly effective in reducing fuel use in OECD countries than in the others (Sterner, 2007).

In addition to this, it becomes clear that any adaptation policies require additional costs and financial resources. Such increased travel costs caused by the adoption of adaptation policies as like incentivizing the reduction of GHG emissions could curtail tourist mobility (Assimacopoulis, 2013). Knowing such limits of political process approach, we may prefer social movement approach requiring changes of travel modes and behavioral patterns. However, alternative modes of travel, which are designed to combat against CO2 emissions, have inclinations to curtail hedonistic pleasure of tourism by their nature. Without changing value system of the stakeholders of tourism, it would not be easy to keep tourist inflow level as usual. Therefore, it becomes important to teach and learn about alternative way of life and to change one's value system into prioritizing eco-friendly mode of life ultimately. Even if we take community based approach, we have to rely on inward dimension oriented approaches also as like altering way of thinking and value system as well since community people's way of thinking and preferences and their subsequent collaborations determine whether to succeed in obtaining supports from them or not. The close collaborations from the community residents cannot be guaranteed without changing their value system into eco-friendly ones.

Therefore, it becomes evident that information relevant to green tourism and eco-friendly life as well should be shared widely since education, learning, and contemplation start from sharing information. Korean experiences confirm to such practices. They hold either international gatherings as like Ramsar meeting and WCC, seminars as like Green Academy and Tree House, or meditation in retreats in order to promote and share the idea of eco-friendly way of life widely. From such interrelatedness of outward dimension oriented approaches and inward dimension oriented approaches tackling over traveling and its mitigation strategies, it becomes clear that six approaches suggested above do not establish displacement relations but complementary and supplementary ones as well. Thus, there is no single approach accomplishing the job of mitigation but collaborations among the multiple approaches could lead to the success of mitigation programs.

And it also should be noticed that we cannot work on alternative tourism only isolating it from the rest of the world since whole social network is interconnected. In other words, it is important to draw attention of the whole community and the world as well. Therefore, it is also advisable to collaborate further throughout the world since any country cannot be detached from the rest of the world as long as climate change and its mitigation strategies are concerned. They are interrelated further in this rapidly globalizing world.

Chapter 09

Disaster Relief and Social Capital in Asia

I. Introduction

Occurrences of disasters are unequally distributed around the world. Natural disasters are threatening our lives more frequently in Asia. For the last couple of years alone, serious floods swept eastern part of Sri Lanka, Bangladesh, Myanmar, Thailand, Pakistan, the central part of Vietnam, and North Korea. When it goes to earthquake, situation is more serious. For the year of 2011 alone, for the last six months only, Java Island and Sumatra of Indonesia, Hunchun and Yunnan provinces of China, Myanmar and Tofuku of Japan were hit by strong earthquakes and history record tsunami.

In addition, man-made disasters also take place more frequently in Asia. For China alone for the last couple of years, bridges have collapsed in Fenghua city of Hunan province, Xijiang river of Foshen city, Nanjing city of Jiangsu province, Hastings river of Sichuan province, Kunming city of Xian province, Foshan city of Guangdong province, etc. Buildings and apartments have collapsed in New Delhi of India, Hong Kong, Guiyang city of China. And the Fukushima nuclear power plant accident stands as a culminating symbol of a combination of such man-made disasters and natural disasters in Asia. Disasters of this region are expected to keep rise owing much to global warming and relative lack of social safety checking system.

In the midst of such a vortex of various disasters in Asia, it has been reported that 9 out of 10 adults in Korea feel anxiety that such large-scale disasters may happen in Korea. One of the online portal sites in Korea asked 1,198 adults whether they feel anxiety that large-scale natural disasters might take place in Korea and 89% of the respondents replied positively. Among them, 59.4% felt a little bit while 29.4% very much so. And in addition, 82.5% of them replied their anxiety and uneasiness had been escalated after the recent earthquake in Japan. They indicated that factors contributing to such feeling of uneasiness come primarily from the very fact that they cannot predict when and with what scale such disaster might take place. Second one was that their life safety would not be guaranteed in such disasters. They also were concerned about the insufficient preparedness and incomplete disaster alarm and response systems in Korea (Moon, 2011.03.23.).

It seems to be very natural, in such circumstances where Asian countries in general and Korea in particular are relatively more vulnerable to large-scale disasters and not sufficiently prepared yet to respond to them, that the people of these countries are concerned about protection of people and properties more than any other part of the world. But the contemporary situation shows us that such concerns and aspirations of the people are not well taken. The damage occurred by disasters is very serious in Asia. Asia accounts for 38.95% of the whole natural disasters occurred in the world for the last 30 years, but casualties mount up to 89.85%(Kim, 2010). Recognizing such a situation in Asia, many ideas and assistances have been extended from the outside especially from the West to meet the challenge. It is not clear, however, to what extent such ideas and services regarding disaster relief transfer to either cross-cultural or international settings. This lack of attention to such cross-cultural settings may have resulted from a view of disasters as random, isolated acts of God, so that the disproportionately high risk of Asian countries and their societal differences have been ignored. It is very natural in such a situation to be interested in learning about major reasons of bringing in such incapability of responding to large-scale disasters in Asia.

II. Quintessence of Disaster Scene and Epistemological Dilemma

Large scale disasters are so unpredictable by their own nature that any relevant preparation to respond could not easily be made in advance, and it is difficult to develop any a priori responding models or strategies. There is a very low level of the predictability ratio available to any serious observers of disaster occurrence. There is no other way, but to respond to each occurrence in the consideration of individual case and requests arising from the scene and be very much flexible in responding and developing strategies to cope with disasters. Success of such contextual and contingent approach is highly dependent on how much live and concrete information from the scene could be debriefed and gained. The closer goes to the disaster scene, in this context, the better for the success of disaster relief response.

Disasters take various forms, sizes and characteristics, arise in different environmental settings and bring in different level of impacts to the social, economic, and political templates. Individual disaster relief target people, therefore, encounters with different need from one and another. Such heterogeneous needs for disaster relief service make any disaster responding systems or organizations difficult to meet and encompass all the expectations and aspirations arising from the scene with one fits for all services or policies. Such a need for individual customer-oriented responding service asks the service delivery systems and voluntary organizations be decentralized and be spread across the nation as much as possible. Role of local government is requested more than that of central government in this context.

Occurrence of disaster disrupts almost all of normal ways of living system all of a sudden. Disaster stricken area becomes isolated from the outer world and helpless. One disaster tends to bring in another one since whole social system is interconnected and intertwined. Damage will be serious and aggravated further when there is no prompt response to the disaster in such circumstances. Prompt response cannot be exerted, however, by being distanced geographically and politically from the disaster scene. That is why we need community-based response to the disaster for more effective relief works. Once located physically near to the disaster scene, community could mobilize resources required for recovery and political pressure to government decision makers for certain policy directions required by disaster victims with much ease.

On the other hand, multidimensional nature of a disaster leads to complexity of disaster response works. It is inevitable to interconnect and coordinate disaster relief organizations of different levels and sorts as well in order to meet this multidimensionality of a disaster scene. It becomes important to promote coordination of the network among these organizations during a disaster, as well as the mitigation process of destructive competition among systems and organizations committed for relief. More effective coordination is a focal point for improvements in disaster response. Coordination promises to make services accessible for vulnerable populations, as well as link services together to provide for improved continuity of care for victims of disaster (Zakour & Harrell, 2003).

Though the disaster response required from the scene may be extraordinary and lead to radically changed behaviors to meet the crisis, disasters may usefully be viewed as an extension of everyday events (Streeter, 1991). When we take a close observation, it is not difficult to learn that the natural and built in environments interact with societal variables and it may lead to disasters. Environment and society mutually affect one other all through the process of instigating disasters and perceiving subsequent crisis of the scene. That is why any disaster response needs or permits a long-term developmental orientation to be more efficient.

As such, there is a built-in dilemma in responding to disasters with more effectiveness. On the one hand, disaster relief response should be approached from a narrower perspective as we see from the requests to be closer to the individual disaster scene, decentralized, and community-based as much as possible. On the other hand, a wider perspective to coordinate diverse relief organizations and to take long-term developmental orientation. Taking the analogy of a camera, they request to zoom more in the disaster scene and to take more a panoramic view at the same time. Any disaster relief works encounter with such dilemma. Theoretically speaking, we can overcome this dilemma of responding to bi-focal requests when we alternate them very swiftly. Such a dynamism or mobility, however, can only be assured when the related shareholders trust each other, respect reciprocal norms and interact around nods of established network. In other words, social capital as of trust, norm and network is a critical prerequisite for overcoming the dilemma.

III. Social Capital and Response to Disaster

According to Bellah *et al.* (2007), there are two dimensions in the concept of social capital: cognitive and structural. Cognitive dimension of social capital refers to connections at the psychological level. It is a "habit of heart," which cuts across the different notions possessed by men, the various opinions current among them, and the sum of ideas that shape mental habits. It is about the way people think about themselves and their society and how their plans and thoughts are related to the actions. Structural dimension of social capital is a connection at the substantial level. It indicates networks, rules, organizational structures, and social systems. And when it goes to the structural dimension of social capital, there are three different types of networking. Putnam (2000) presented two different types of social networking: bonding and bridging. Bonding inclines to inward-looking with a tendency to reinforce exclusive identities and homogeneous groups while bridging is more outward-looking and encompass people across different social divides.

The former operates within and between community members - where they can bypass social niceties and operate as if they were members of the same family (Erikson, 1976: 187-188). It has been described as pre-modern in that they assume a high degree of familiarity and involve a willingness to give up some degree of privacy as like relations between family members, close friends, and neighbors. The latter links members of the group or network to extra-local ones, crossing ethnic, racial, religious cleavages. It links to external assets and generates broader identities by bringing individuals from different locations, identities, and language groups (Field *et al*, 2000).

Woolcock (1998), however, added a third type, linking social capital from the perspective of developmental assistance. It is made up of "networks of trusting relationships between people who are interacting across explicit, formal or institutional power or authority gradients in society" (Szreter & Woolcock, 2004: 655). Whereas bonding and bridging social capital primarily link individuals of the same status - whether neighbors and kin

<Figure 1> Bonding, Bridging, and Linking Social Capital

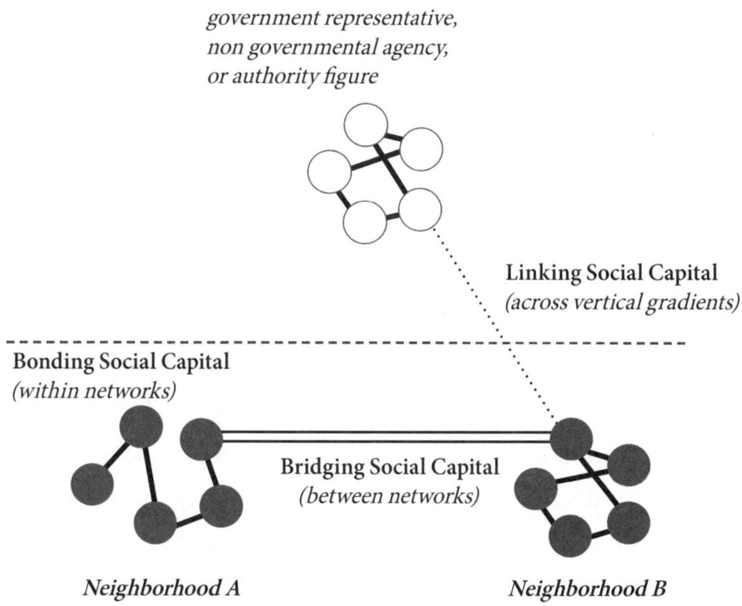

Source: Figure adopted from Aldrich (2011: 148)

with bonding social capital, or out-of-town acquaintances from another ethnic group with bridging social capital - this form takes into account vertical distance as well (Aldrcish, 2011: 148). DaCosta and Turner (2007: 195) point out that for developing or underdeveloped communities, linking networks are particularly important for economic development as they provide resources and information to otherwise off-the-grid cities and towns. Figure 1 above illustrates these 3 types of social capital models.

This social capital, however, does not always lead to a positive relation with disaster response and compose single dimensional relation neither. We can categorize four dimensional groups of the relations as we see at the below <Table 1> by crossing over two poles: one is whether to account social capital as an independent variable or a dependent variable in its relationship to disaster response and the other is whether to see the outcome as positive or negative.

<Table 1> Relationship between Social Capital and Disaster Response

Relationship \ Impact	Positive	Negative
Independent Variable	I	II
Dependent Variable	III	IV

Among the four dimensions categorized above at <Table 1>, dimension I denotes social capital as an independent variable to disaster response bringing in positive effects. Its analogy is that the more we accumulate social capital, the more we become capable of responding to disasters. This is a very much general understanding about the role of social capital in regard to disaster relief. However, it is not a panacea and encompasses negative effects too, which is shown at dimension II. Portes (1998) points out the downside of social capital as exclusion of outsiders while excessively claiming on group members, restrictions on individual freedom and privacy, and downward leveling of norms. Moreover, social capital is not equally distributed universally due to its cumulative characteristics. It is very evident in such situation that any disaster relief response would not be successfully accomplished and its societal integration impact neither.

In dimension III, the process of overcoming a crisis requiring disaster relief and recovery produces new social capital within and outside of the community. Norms of reciprocity become rooted in the affected area. And also a sense of solidarity could be fostered among citizens in the community. Networks of local government and disaster relief voluntary organizations could be consolidated. The disaster relief process consolidates social capital. And dimension IV implies that the way people experience disaster response affects social capital and influences disaster victims negatively. When many people fail to have their needs met through disaster response process, it will make a highly stressful situation to the society (Barton, 1969). When government fails to coordinate the inflow of goods and services from outside of the affected area, competition at crisis scene will be escalated and people will begin to feel as like they are isolated from neighbors, kin and the normal organizations and become distrustful and traumatic. Such situation leads to increased suspicion, disconnection and downward of societal norms among people. The disaster responding process results in undermining of established social capital. These four dimensions are neither separate from each other nor predetermined. They are interrelated and interact each other. Any actual scene is composed by these dimensional features. How much percentage of these dimensions, however, will compose the relationship between social capital and disaster response depends upon societal context in which such relation takes place. In other words, only when time and place are given, the actual composition would be determined. Actual relationship between social capital and disaster relief is dependent upon the structure of the social environment in which such relationship takes place.

IV. Vulnerability of Asian Countries in Responding to Disasters

When we review contemporary communities in Asian countries in general, many of them are experiencing difficulties in their efforts to respond to large-scale disasters. In most of the cases, it owes much to the relative lack of social capital accumulation. For the cognitive dimension of social capital, for instance, most of the Asian countries are relatively lacking emotional connections among themselves expressed by volunteerism and philanthropic value, which seem to be essential components of any individuals or communities in their responding efforts to large-scale disasters. It has been reported very difficult for community members to access relief service organizations during and after disaster when there are only few voluntary organizations and their programs available. Disaster response and mitigation programs are prone to be lacking in such communities where volunteerism and philanthropic value are lacking or poor. There is, thus, a high possibility that the populations most vulnerable to disaster due to relative lack of volunteerism are protected by fewer mitigation projects and served by fewer disaster relief organizations with relatively low service capacities (Zakour & Harrell, 2003). The relative lack of volunteerism and volunteer resources account for the reduced access to disaster response especially for the marginalized. Municipalities with more marginalized residents were reported to have the lowest level of volunteer resources during and after disasters.

Maslow (1970) introduced 5 different levels of individual needs: physiological needs, security needs, social needs, self-esteem, and self-actualization. He asserted that aspirations of individual human beings move from the lowest level of needs like physiological and security needs up to higher ones like social needs and self-esteem when the lower ones are satisfied. Likewise, we can assume communities or countries follow the same path of moving from aspirations for the lower ones to those for higher ones since they are composed by such individuals. Volunteerism and philanthropic values are related rather with higher aspirations of social needs, self-esteem and self-actualization by their nature. Meanwhile, they can be looked for only when they are satisfied with physiological and security needs, most of the Asian countries are located still at the level of striving for satisfying physiological and security needs. That is why many countries in Asia could not produce much volunteerism and philanthropic value yet.

When we look into the bonding network of structural dimension of social capital in many Asian communities, it can easily be detected that they have not accumulated enough social capital yet and poverty is one of the most telling variables leading to such low level of accumulation. Poverty is negatively associated with inward interrelatedness and thus to community survival and recovery during and after major and long term disasters (Sherraden & Fox, 1997). Furthermore, economically helpless individuals and households tend to reside in communities whose other residents and families have similar social and demographic characteristics. Partly because of such low-income communities tend to have a poor tax base; the degree of vulnerability of communities usually coincides with the vulnerability of populations (Zakour & Harrell, 2003) in their capacity to integrate each other and to upgrade their capacity to challenge and overcome disasters. Poverty does not mean simply unable to eat and be provided with proper nutrition. Poor people are easily exposed to the disease and suffer from not receiving adequate medical care. Educational opportunities are limited. Poverty brings in a vicious circle and puts people in traps of losing hope, falling in deeper despair, and being prone to nurture hatred and distrust among themselves. Due to these reasons when the poor people are hit by disaster, damage becomes fatal and penetrates to the whole process of their lives.

It should be reminded, in this context, that we cannot speak about the world poverty without mentioning Asia. In Asia where more than 55% of world's population live, there are many poor people. And most of the peoples living in these poor countries belong to the poorest level. According to the World Bank report, the world's poorest people living at the cost of lower than one dollar a day comprises 1,174 billion. Among them, 790 million people live in Asia (Dorling & Ballas, 2008). It reminds us that there are more poor people in Asia than in Africa where we have thought of as the poorest region of the world. Globalization brings in further aggrandizement of such regional economic disparity. Poverty is one of the many reasons for Asian countries to put themselves in the situation for striving for bonding.

When it goes with bridging, it is known that the more homogeneous a society is, the easier it is for bridging and outward looking action and the more profoundly people trust each other (Alesina & La Ferrara, 2002). Ethnic and economic fragmentations are reported to have detrimental effects on damage arising from disasters, leading to increases in fatalities (Kahn, 2005). The same logic is applicable to Asia as a region. Asian countries, unfortunately, have long been identified as being indifferent each other and maintained even an attitude of looking down to each other owing much to the lack of communication and thus information and understanding among themselves. It is not an unusual phenomenon that English is taught as a primary or secondary language in most of the Asian countries but not the modern language of neighborhood, which is quite different from that of the Western part of the world. Relative self-alienation among the Asians themselves hasn't been alleviated even after the advent of the information society.

Intensification of global economic system has brought a polarizing gap not only between the Asian and the Western countries but also among the Asian countries. Almost all of the Asian countries are encountered with serious polarizing gap in their income distribution. Economic dependency and manipulation inside of and among the Asian countries are getting worse and becoming a major source of political instability, social unrest, and even religious confrontation. In fact, Asia has long been identified as the most religious continent of the world. Almost all of the major religions of the world have their origins in Asia. Judaism, Christianity, and Islam came out from Western Asia. Hinduism, Buddhism, and Confucianism were born in Eastern Asia. Such a historical fact may not be a major factor but strong explanatory variable at least for the formation of contemporary multi-religious society inside of and among the Asian countries. These multiple religions have fortified religious fundamentalism, fanaticism, and even terrorism of this region. In such a fragmented and split region of the world, it is not realistic to expect close, efficient, and long term based collaborations among the Asian countries being encountered with disaster.

When it goes with linking network, according to the previous studies, it is found also that linking the governmental and nongovernmental sectors and establishing inter-organizational network is very much advantageous (Zakour & Gillespie, 1999) for efficiently responding to disasters. One of these advantages is the combination of the significant resources of governmental agencies with the greater information of community needs of local voluntary organizations. Other advantages include increasing the capacity of voluntary organizations active in providing services to geographically isolated neighborhoods and making the service delivery governmental organizations more accessible to community organizations and their constituents during and after disaster. It is also found that the total number of different types of organizations that a given disaster organization is linked to is significantly and positively associated with an organization's preparedness for disaster. They suggest that each type of organization, including smaller, informal organizations, have basically different resources in a disaster, so that linkage to a larger range of various organizations translates into an organization's access to different types of disaster resources.

In most of the Asian countries, however, government is not relatively ready to open their policy making and service delivery system to people and people also is not prepared yet enough to collaborate with government actively. For the formation of collaborative governance between government and people, the government should accept that they are not capable enough anymore, could not manage the public sphere alone and in the needs of assistance from outside of the government. They have to take a lower profile than before. For the voluntary organizations, internal democracy should be established and maintained. Otherwise, standing staffers and relatively small number of leaders of the organizations are apt to domineer decision-making process and choke out communication funnel. Inputs from the boundary of voluntary organizations would not go through the collaborative governance process and reach the decision makers of the government. Without real participation of the people to the voluntary organizations, collaborative governance could not reflect needs and demands of the people on the disaster scene and such real participation could not be affirmed when there is no complete political freedom of the people. Political freedom is an indispensable even though not sufficient condition for successful collaboration between government and the people. Without political right, no one can associate with others freely and equally without discrimination and thus could develop trust, norms and networks among themselves and thus social capital.

Unfortunately, Asia as a region could not be evaluated as a place of fully bloomed political freedom.According to the Freedom House report (2011), among 38 Asian countries 41% were rated free, 38% partly free and 21% not free. Roughly speaking only half of them are rated politically free. In the case of Europe which was rated as the freest region of the world, 96% were rated free, 4% partly free and no one as not free. Meanwhile in Africa, which was rated as the least free place, 6% free, 19% partly free and 78% not free. Global status shows 45% free, 31% partly free and 24% not free. In other words, Asia as a region is rated almost tantamount to the average of the global status. Such data shows us that most of the Asian countries are still in the process of striving for political democracy and accumulating social capital further. They are weak in their bonding, bridging and linking as well. And such low level of social capital has been perceived as one of the major sources of weakness in their response to disasters.

V. Conclusion

When we approach the relationship between social capital and disaster response from a dynamic perspective, dimension I is linked to dimension III and constitutes a virtuous circle. Meanwhile, dimension II leads to dimension IV and form a vicious circle too. Asia is placed in a vicious circle, in which poor social capital leads to poor response to the disaster and poor response to the disaster undermine social capital. Relative lack of volunteerism and philanthropic value, widespread poverty, heterogeneity of the social components, and comparatively lower level of political freedom were identified as major cognitive and structural sources of detrimental performance contributing to the formation of the vicious circle.

Such findings imply us that in order to break a vicious circle, we need not only physical infrastructure but also more importantly social infrastructure like " habit of hearts", increased communication, and political freedom, which require a long-term perspective for the development. And such social infrastructure can not be nurtured overnight and neither on the scene of disasters. And it cannot be nurtured by approaching from a narrower perspective of responding to disasters only but from a wider perspective of societal reform and reconstruction.

Lifelong and school educations as well are important strategies for the promotion of such societal reform since without self-reflection power of individual people we cannot open a new perspective and value system in approaching societal structure. And such reflexive citizen can only be nurtured when we provide them opportunities to review a society from a critical perspective. Such critically reviewing power does not grow naturally or automatically from one's selves but needs to be brought up by intended educational programs. One of the best ways of nurturing such power is to practice on the very scene of social needs. Participatory education is a prime source of learning such power. For real participation, however, we need political freedom and social capital as well. In other words, there is no royal road to overcome such dilemma that exists between accumulation of social capital and social reconstruction but to follow trial and error strategy in a zig zag manner until we reach to the point where we can collaborate with government with more ease and efficiency.

Any inter-regional collaboration in their response to disasters, therefore, should focus not only on physical needs of a disaster scene but more also on social infrastructure of the whole communities being stricken by large-scale disasters. The former requires a relatively shorter term perspective, but the latter needs longer term perspective. It also should be reminded that there is a contextual difference between Asian communities and those of the outer world in their ways of responding to disasters and even collaboration with other countries of the world. Contextual approach is required not only at the scene of disasters but also in their efforts to collaborate with other countries of the world in general and at the regional level in particular.

Chapter 10

Area Studies in Globalizing World

I. Introduction

Area studies in Korea have long been an academic colony monopolized by the Hankuk University of Foreign Studies (HUFS). No one can deny that HUFS has been a single most important provider of area specific intelligence and information required to protect national security especially during the Cold War era and to support foreign trade promotion alongside economic development process of the nation as well among the universities in Korea. Such motives of creating and promoting area studies in HUFS in particular and those of Korean universities in general at their early stages really remind us those of the United States, where area studies began to be established in the universities after the World War II by the alumni of OSS (Office of Strategic Services) organized under the leadership of Franklin D. Roosevelt during the World War II to coordinate collecting, sorting, and analyzing area specific materials relevant to the war (Dirks, 2012: 2). We are resembled with such intellectual trajectories of area studies in the United States in the sense that the area studies were established in the universities not as an outcome of self-reflection by academicians to overcome limits of segregated and thus parochial nature of individual disciplines and thus to launch interdisciplinary collaborations to cross over the boundaries but because of the market demands outside of universities to produce area specific information.

Demands for such area specific information made HUFS enjoy its heydays of area studies until 1990s when the civilian government run by President Kim Young-Sam began to drive economic globalization policies. As a very natural outcome of such strengthened outward-oriented policies of the government, they began to encourage universities to expand area studies and provide full supports for the creation of graduate schools focusing on area studies. Such a booming tide of area studies brought adversarial impacts to the area studies in HUFS. From the positive side of it, it has provided a momentum to upgrade social recognition about the importance of area studies in general and that of HUFS in particular. From the negative point of view, it has lifted the protective wall of monopoly enjoyed by HUFS and made the market of area studies more competitive. By being baptized with such increased competition among the area studies of universities, HUFS has been able to increase the institutional capability to cope with such changing environments on the one hand and enforced to strive harder to survive on the other hand. Encroaching of our area studies market, once monopolized by us, is not deniable nowadays. It is high time that we have to restore our pride and prestige in this field and to revitalize our heydays especially because the area studies are the intrinsic core of HUFS by their own nature.

More fundamental and serious issues we are facing today, however, are the challenges brought in by the advent of information society and subsequent globalization. Radical changes of the context in which we research the areas provoke multidimensional issues all around the world.

II. Advent of Information Society and Subsequent Globalization

All through the era of industrial society, a binary way of thinking has prevailed. We have been accustomed to or indoctrinated to accept such a way of thinking as a modernity and counted it "logical and rational" to crush and square certain social phenomenon into separate boxes. We have seen the world by grouping into the right and the left, this and that, here and there, and you and me. Such separations are, however, the beginning of comparison, competition, tense, distrust, and ego-centrism. This is the reason the industrial society has failed in salvaging human beings. This is why we have to develop new perspective other than the conventional way of thinking to meet the challenges of the next generation coming.

In fact, such juxtaposing or locating things border to border are available only when the world is relatively stable. We can draw a line of separation only when the objects are not moving around. However, nothing is static any further in this information society. Dynamism, fluidity, and flexibility are the quintessence of this contemporary society. We cannot analyze and understand the world from the perspective of dichotomy any further. We need to see them in a wholeness and as seamless or boundary-less objective. We are now no longer living in the world of mechanistic components, but that of trembling energies crossing over the borders since everything is constantly moving, interacting, interlocking, becoming, and changing.

At the extension of such an understanding of the world and its changing nature, at first, it is very natural that we have to approach area studies not as a collaborative work of individual disciplines but as a new and independent field of academia covering whole conventional academic divisions of languages, humanities, and social sciences. It is not first time that similar issues are raised inside of area studies as like the calls for interdisciplinary works. Instead of their professed way of interdisciplinary studies, however, they used to focus on micro and technical side of it and never challenged real convergence among them. Now we are calling for a holistic approach to area studies going over such compartmentalization pertinent to the conventional wisdom of disciplines.

Likewise, we have to approach an area as a single unit of research and not as a collection or collaboration of researches on multiple individual nations. It has been requested for area studies to focus on the interconnectivity among the nations. However, now, we have to go over even such interconnectedness of all nations belonging to the same area or region. The boundary separating the nation states is deteriorating. Supra-territorial interactions and the networks have interwoven the global society already, and the depth and the intensity of such activities will further be consolidated. Alongside such understanding, it should be reminded that simple collection of data and information gathered on the base of individual nations cannot makeup for the wholeness of the area to which the nations belong.

In addition, there has been a tendency in area studies not to discuss the theorization and/or methodological questions pertinent to themselves. We cannot avoid any further but to face with such challenges more proactively since we are already in the midst of paradigm shifting process of the world. From the methodological point of view, we should not approach areas from the stand-point of a third party any longer. We have objectified areas as "the other" and tried to learn and build theories from which to interpret areas we were aiming at. However, in this highly interconnected and thus complex world of information society, it is not easy to trace cause and effect relations of any social phenomenon by simply observing from outside of the very phenomenon. High density of social relations brings in "intervention effects" when we try to get into a phenomenon from outside. They do not afford any a priori models or theories built outside of the area since area phenomenon changes constantly and drastically in this information society. We need insider's view and knowledge engaged in the very scene.

As anthropologist Clifford Geertz argued once, village fieldwork is not a simple study of village or about village but a study in village. The view from the village is different not just from the view from the metropolis but the view from other villages or towns or cities as well (Dirks, 2012: 4). Today's increasingly interconnected world transcends the particularity of individual areas. But we should be cautious about assuming that abstract social theories are never affected by where they are read (Dirks, 2012: 4). We must study not just the connectedness of things, but the things that connect, what happens when they connect, and what connection looks like from specific places and to specific people(Dirks, 2012: 4). We have to be prepared to encounter with the information society and subsequent globalization seen from the perspective of individual places. Many of the global controversies spiraling around us today must be read through the perspectives of fundamental human values and enduring cultural realities of the very individual areas as well.

Moreover, we have to add new agenda to area studies responding to the emerging phenomenon of globality. We have to strengthen further our transdisciplinary and transregional responses to the newly arising thrusts of global issues as like fast spread of Ebola virus disease, aspirations for democratic polities, gender equity, environmental protection, anti-terrorism, and etc. Area studies should intensify their researches on the global issues, expand knowledge about global culture, and widen research unit in area studies up to the globe. Global world has become another area of studies adding to the existing conventional ones. When we approach wider area of a global world, it is obvious that we should approach it as a single unit of research crossing over the boundaries by which we used to separate areas.

Finally, since we have to empathy with the people of areas in order to make successful researches of areas in this rapidly changing world, it is inevitable to make ourselves to be "the others" and the others provide certain wisdom to us. Such a bilateral way of collaborations and understandings drive us not only to import models and theories developed by researching areas and enforcing us to adjust to such preset frames as we were in the past but also to think about exporting theories and methodologies developed by us to the areas outside of us. Therefore, researching and learning of globalization should go together with localization and indigenization of a certain area, and this requires context sensitivity about the historical totality of the area. We have to develop research languages that understand areas from the holistic perspective of globality and combine parochial and specific place oriented knowledge with horizontal and vertical interconnectivity of the whole world as well

III. Our Challenges against the Contextual Change of Area Studies

Understanding all those needs and demands arising in the process of studying areas in this rapidly changing context of information society and subsequent globalization, what are the prime thrusts that HUFS has to respond? One of the challenges that HUFS has to contemplate seriously for the future would be to establish area specific colleges at local places as extended hands or hubs of studying areas abroad as like the African College in South Africa, and Latin American College in Costa Rica for examples. Employing such glocalization strategy in studying areas and establishing institutions for such objective are more proactive ways of responding to the changing context of area studies. This is the way that we can assure and sustain our context sensibility of area studies with more confidence. This is the way that we can overcome obstacles brought to us by the advent of information society and subsequent globalization and can restore our glorious days of area studies in Korea and the world as well. This is the way that we make ourselves get prepared for the coming centennial anniversary.

The other way of glocalizing area studies would be to mobilize further participation of local experts to the study of areas. And one of the efficient ways of mobilizing such participants would be establishing expanded governance network between HUFS and local institutions and experts as well all around the world at the virtual world. It is an ideal way of keeping the local participants more vibrant to their local context sensitivity by not pulling them out of their home towns. HUFS is well known with its large number of foreign scholars in Korea, who have moved to Korea and by this way detached a little from their original localities in fact. Many of them are aligned with individual departments primarily focusing on individual nations and rather than areas. We need to establish further expanded human networks working on the base of areas providing us with more vivid insiders' views and judgments.

Another way of promoting area context sensibility would be to organize "travelling seminars" holding workshops regularly and more frequently beyond Korea in order to provide different contexts and frameworks for engaging theoretical issues with colleagues from the other part of the world (Kennedy, 2001: 3). This is to explore the sensibilities behind apparently similar phenomena and to use those unexpressive schemes to expose different kinds of questions and comparisons laden in study of areas. This is to seek and to make more explicit the limits to and value of studying in existing historiographic and cultural contexts. We ought to pursue also some study abroad, should it involve language study, personal network development, and full cultural immersion, short-term visits and interacting through fellowships and other kinds of exchange programs of this perusal.

For the inside of HUFS, we may have to establish research institution, as like Research Institute for Global Citizenship, to cover studies at global level, in this global context, and about global thrusts and to develop methodologies and theoretical foundations of global area studies. It could operate as an umbrella organization coordinating with the existing area study institutions of HUFS and anchoring external collaborations with outside research arms scattered around the world. It could contribute to the development of a new intellectualism required for the promotion of a paradigm shift as a tool to look into the world from a different and challenging viewpoint. It is also strongly requested to promote more frequent interactions and collaborations among the area study organizations existing already inside of HUFS as like what we are doing today. Increased interactions and collaborations crossing over the boundaries of individual departments are also requested.

IV. Conclusion

Area studies in HUFS are now placed at a very critical juncture in their responses to the changing context. Not simply because of the increased competition among the universities in Korea but because of the changing needs and demands signaled by the donors, students, and collaborators of the world. As Korea began to move into the center of globalizing world, it has become more important and demanding to abandon old practices of area studies in favor of new forms of global study. It is time for us to challenge directly to what we face today introducing students and collaborators of area studies to the complexities and haughty importance of global affairs. As the early bearers of area studies in America assumed that modernization was an unavoidable process that would lead to political and economic development alongside mutual understanding, shared interests and increased commercial exchange (Dirks, 2012: 3), it is high time for us to assume that globalization is an inevitable trend that would lead to expansion of mutual understanding, peaceful coexistence, and maximization of economic benefits for the Koreans and the rest of the world as well.

We have to put more efforts to turn those assumptions into the development of theories and methodologies not only to promote the Koreanization of globalizing phenomenon, but also to spread Korean standards more widely across the world.

In order to accomplish such an objective, it is important to build infrastructures to provide training for the students in regional languages, cultures, histories, and politics to breed a new group of future intellectuals and indigenous academics prepared to guide Korean attitudes and value systems toward a new world order. Area studies could help us clarify the conditions that make further international collaborations and a transnational expertise possible. It could identify why some places resonate with global visions while others remain invisible. Area studies could help us to remember the limits of Korean common sense also.

Area studies of HUFS will find revitalization not through laments about the loss of market and further flattering to the financial supporters but by moving to consider how to articulate our own expertise in this historical period of global change and at this particular place of Korea. We can accomplish this objective by exploring ways to build that grounding as a point of departure for elaborating the expertise that might move HUFS beyond the expectations of the world. Area studies should be able to clarify the conditions that make international collaborations more fruitful and transnational expertise more relevant and tangible.

However, one could assert that HUFS may not be ready yet for such a role since it may not have enough budget to promote glocalization strategies as like establishing localized colleges for area studies, organizing traveling seminars, networking insiders of areas, and etc. It should be reminded, however, that glocalization strategies are not simple source of expenditure, but a real base of earning further incomes rewarding us far more to offset such an investment. More than anything else, it is a very important agenda for HUFS since we may need it most among the stakeholders of area studies in Korea. Area studies would help us to remember the limits of globalization and to bring more of the world's diversity into our heart and to this university.

I strongly believe we are the ones, that are best prepared to lead area studies in the future, responding to this globalizing world with clearer vision and never-ending energies and determination as we have done so far.

Part Three

Reviewing Political Development in Korea

Chapter 11

Politics between Tradition and Information Society

I. Historical Political Legacy

Le Banquet: Let's start with the review of political development in Korea. Some scholars and political analysts assess that democracy in Korea is a miracle meanwhile others it should be further deepened. What is your view of the main successes in that regard and of some remaining shortcomings?

Park Jai-Chang: The Freedom House, an America based research NGO, has rated Korea as a free country for several years now, freer than India and Singapore and tantamount to Japan of this region. In terms of legal structure and procedural democracy, Korea is evaluated highly. However, it is not unusual to meet people lamenting over inability of party politics, clogged National Assembly, and skewed election process. Downsizing democracy is a pending issue in Korea. Before we discuss in detail, I think, we would be better to go through with the political development process in order to grasp deeper understanding of contemporary situation in Korea.

After World War II, we started to build nation state from scratch. There was no natural resources, no accumulation of capital, no trained bureaucrats, no previous exposure to democratic value and practice... For about 20 years after the independence from colonial rule, we struggled to build nation itself. By that time due to economic difficulties, we didn't have enough financial resources to run the nation independently. It was an usual phenomenon to make a deficit budget. Most of the national income had been supplemented by the economic aids from U.S.A., not only for the annual budget to run the government but also for the maintenance of standing army. So, when we define modern nation state in terms of being composed of political sovereignty, economic self-reliance and military power, Korea was not an independent modern nation until that time

Amidst of toiling for building nation state itself and political unrest owing much to chronic poverty, we met, in 1961, a military intervention into politics led by General Park Chung-Hee, who later turned himself into President of the 3rd Republic. He launched an economic development plan. Owing much to the success of the plans, for the first time in the history of Korea, it became industrialized and capitalist economy began to take roots. Even though the idea of capitalism was introduced earlier, the system of capitalism was not sustainable by that time. It was an authoritarian regime but the economy began to move and finally boom up. It is the only country that has succeeded in economic development after World War II. During his regime, however, President Park was challenged chronically by those who asked for expanded freedom of individual and fought for democratization of the nation. In the whirl of internal turmoil, he was assassinated by his own right-hand man, the head of Korean CIA. The regime was handed over to military leaders for two consecutive terms after a short interim government. They were an extension of authoritarian government. It was very natural that the regimes were under continual pressure to expand freedom and democracy. In 1987, there was a civilian revolt against the dictatorial regime organized mainly by the middle class white color workers. They succeeded in revising constitution to elect president by direct vote. We count it as a water-shedding symbolic incident of accomplishing procedural democracy and call the later on governing structure as "87 system." We succeeded in political development owing much to the economic development. It would be very ironical to those who had prioritized economic affluence over political freedom and democracy. The appearance of "87 system" has been counted as a symbol of success in political development, which is the only case achieved after World War II in global community.

Le Banquet: There was a sort of revolution cycle in Korea.

P. J.-C.: A Korean sociologist presented a theory of ten year cycle in the history of modern Korean politics. As I mentioned earlier, modern government was founded in 1948. In April 1960, roughly about ten years later, there was a students' uprising, triggered by rigged election, leading to the overthrow of the regime. New regime led by then opposition leader Yun Po-Sun took in. But the leaders of new regime were not able to manage the country effectively. There was a split inside of the ruling party and a lot of turmoil. One year later, in 1961, the military as an institution intervenes into politics replacing the government. It was led by General Park Chung-Hee. Even during Park's tenure, there were chronic political unrests and in 1969 President Park changed constitution to enable himself to run for 3rd term.

Amidst of increased voices and continuous street demonstrations organized by the opposition bloc, he promulgated an emergency action of the October Revitalization Reform in 1972, which came together with dissolution of the National Assembly and banning political activities. Again it was almost ten years later from the General Park's intervention into politics. In 1979, President Park was assassinated and then prime minister Choi Kyu-Ha became an interim president. But the actual power was exercised by General Chun Doo-Hwan and he showed a clear interest to succeed the presidential position. In 1980, there took place a strong revolt in Gwangju City, a very tragic event, uprising against political injustice and above the constitutional measures taken by General Chun. Hundreds of people were killed by the military. After repressing by armed forces, Chun became the president by indirect election. Roughly it was ten years after from the October Revitalization Reform. He reigned the country for about 8 years. In 1987, there took place again a strong citizens' uprising asking for the right to elect next president by direct vote. He surrendered and agreed to change the constitution to adopt direct presidential election system. And President Roh Tae-Woo was elected according to the new constitution. It was again roughly about ten years later from the death of President Park in 1979.

Such a pattern of occurring major political incidents at a certain span of interval reminds us that the Koreans are very reluctant in raising issues directly on the spot and fixing complaints through dialogue bit by bit. Even if they are dissatisfied with the political leadership, they put it down in their mind until they cannot tolerate any more and once it reaches to the critical point it erupts like an explosion. Lacking face to face culture could be one of the major quintessence of Korean politics. Someone told such a cultural legacy resembles that of France. Another one could be the highly centralized nature of the government.

II. Decentralization: New Commitment for Achieving Democracy

Le Banquet: Shall we move towards more decentralization?

P. J.-C.: Korean government is highly centralized probably due to the strong influence of Chinese culture. China was the origin of oriental despotism. And Confucianism was developed to legitimize such a power structure of the ancient Chinese society. Meritocracy has been regarded as an indispensible pillar to support and maintain such a highly centralized government by Confucianism. It has been taught that government should be run by the learned people and the political power be amassed into the hands of them. In addition to that, the modern governing system was introduced through colonial administration run by Japan, which was designed to centralize governing power for the effective exploitation of the Korean peninsula. When it comes to the modern Korea, the break out of Korean War also further legitimized the centralized power of the government. And the subsequent advent of development ideology in the process of modernization of the country also contributed to it since the development ideology goes with economy and efficiency and it has been believed such values could be realized by centralization of power more effectively.

However, as time goes on, recognizing needs to respond to the further arising requests for democratization, local autonomous government system was introduced in 1982. However, it was not a full-fledged autonomous local governing system. They cannot be counted as a local autonomy even at this point after more than 30 years since only 20 percent of the laws and 30 percent of the budget of the country are allocated to the local governments. Therefore, devolution of central government's power to local governments is a pending issue in Korea. It is so especially because today's citizens in Korea are no longer those of yesterday. They became more self-centered, self-respectful and self-confident owing much to the economic development and advent of information society. They are smarter than before. It is very natural such people begin to aspire for more autonomous governing system and increased opportunity to participate in decision making process.

From a structural point of view, Korean society has changed drastically. It cannot be managed effectively by a single apex or one fits for all system any longer. It has become a very much complex society. It has entered into industrial society from agrarian society before the completion of social transformation and from industrial society to information society in the same manner. In remote areas peoples still maintain agricultural way of life meanwhile the metropolitan cities are highly industrialized. Korea is also one of the leading countries in information society. There exist three different time zones at the same time. Discontinuity, disconnectedness, social alienation, and rupture of communication are not alien in such a multi-dimensionally fractured society. They are a sort of inevitable outcome of compact development that we have gone through within a relatively short span of time.

When you turn your head to European societies, for instance, situation is completely different. They have evolved gradually from agricultural society to information society via industrial society in a relatively smooth and linier manner taking enough time to melt down differences and complications arising in the process of social transformation. In such a society, it is relatively easier to build consensus since there are many commonalities that they can share among the members of the society. But in Korea they are experiencing very serious social structural cleavages, which cannot be easily managed by single measurement or one apex or centralized decision making power. There are pertinent needs to diffuse decision making power. And also the advent of information society fortifies such needs further since fluidity, speediness, and complexity of the social structure in information society require more prompt responses by decision making nods. It is better to place the decision making nods closer to the sites where social problems arise not only for the speedy response but also for the understanding and penetrating into the issues with more easiness, clarity and preciseness.

Such structural cleavages existing in contemporary Korean society is one of the major reasons leading to malfunctioning of democracy also. It has been told that for the efficient operation of democracy, the members of a society have to agree upon a fundamental principle of democracy at least once. However, it has not been easy for the Korean society to reach on fundamental agreement yet due to such multidimensional cleavages of the society.

Another fundamental cause owes much to the legacy of cold war era. Korea is a very exceptional case in the contemporary global community in the sense that two different political models of the world are under fierce experimental competition border to border. North Korea is built under the ideology of communism meanwhile South Korea capitalism in terms of economic system. And North Korea is in pursuit of totalitarianism meanwhile South Korea liberalism in terms of political system. These two pairs are representative models of governing system developed through the modernization process of human history. Both of them were originated from Christianity and democracy. In that sense, they vary and compete each other only in their methods to accomplish the same objectives judging at their nominal value. However, their competition for the excellence of governing methods is very keen and intense. The fierce rivalry relation between the countries squared by the super powers after World War II is so tense that they bring in really critical impact each other to their daily lives. Technically speaking, they have been on war foot even after signing on armistice ever since the Korean War in 1953. Due to such security threat and rivalry competition for supremacy of governing model, they cannot maintain ordinary pattern of daily lives. The existence of each other brings in negative impacts exaggerating usual ways of lives and especially political mechanism. South Korea places prime value on individual freedom but it is easy to legitimize any measurements violating such value by justifying as an efficient response to such pending threats from the North. Intervention by the government to the free market system giving exclusive favor to conglomerates could also easily be rationalized in the name of upgrading global competitiveness of our country at final to win over the North.

There was no way but to grow democracy in a relatively skewed manner. After the collapse of socialist bloc and the achievement of rapid economic development and democratization of South Korea, it has been proved South Korea has won over North Korea. But still, the security threat is pending and the inertia of Cold War era keeps on hovering over South Korea. People are prone to overreact to socialism and even to progressive party owing much to the legacy of North Korea. It is very natural when you are reminded of the very fact that about 3 million were killed during the Korean War and their family members are still surviving. Newtonian democracy developed in the West is based on rationality and mechanistic view of the world. When people respond emotionally to such a system, how could they succeed in running democracy successfully? There are about 30 percent of voters who favor conservative party no matter what they did as a simple response mostly motivated by hatred or fear to North Korea.

III. Family Values: Key Factor in Political Life

Le Banquet: What is your assessment of the political party landscape in South Korea? One often hears that, like in Japan, the political parties do not fit with the yearnings and expectations of most of the citizens.

P. J.-C.: As you know, Newtonian democracy, a concrete model of liberal democracy in contemporary world, was developed in the West and imported to Korea after World War II. Such an implantation of exogenous model to Korean society was carried on with many assumptions untested in practice. According to Putnam, social capital - trust, network, reciprocity - is an essential social base of Newtonian democracy, which is not nurtured yet in Korea. In fact, theory of Newtonian democracy itself does not count on environmental condition of democracy especially because of its mechanical perception of the world. But in fact, the environmental condition in which a democracy operates determines actual shape of democracy and whether to succeed or fail in realizing democratic principle in our daily lives. It is because actual outcomes of any legal and political designs are concretized through interactions between institutional designs and environmental energies in which they operate.

In that regard, Newtonian democracy is based on individualism. However, fundamental base of Korean social network is not individual but family. Family bandage in traditional Korean society had been very strong probably owing much to the legacies of agrarian culture and Confucianism. Some observers assert that such a strong bandage has been loosened passing through the modernization process but it is still surviving. Strong zeal of parents for their offspring's education is frequently hailed by many commentators across the world recognizing that high rate of recipients of higher education works as one of the major determinants of the success in economic and political development as well in Korea. Barack Obama, President of U.S.A, and Arne Duncan, US Secretary of Education, are the model cases lamenting that the US isn't anywhere near as serious about educating its young people as the Koreans. Such a serious commitment of Korean parents to their children's education verifies that strong loyalty to family and family based world view of the Korean society are still dominant. Once an American sociologist took a comparative research to measure the length of time perspective born by the peoples across the world and was astonished by learning that the longest one is one generation and it was Korean. Koreans go to work in the morning not for one's own hedonistic pleasure in coming Friday night but for the wellbeing of their children. Their world view is based on familism which runs through one generation.

Moreover familism does not fit well with democracy. It requires a strong commitment and loyalty to family and plays as a cause of exclusive favoritism to the family members and least and even hostile treatments to the non-members. Familism has a tendency to promote a society with "thick binding and thin bonding." Such discriminatory treatment could not go well with democracy which is in pursuit of equality, justice and fairness in front of the general rule of law. When you look into the world from the telescope of familism, it also becomes really difficult to distinguish the border lines separating formal and informal dimensions and public and private relations since family is a cradle of emotional comforts and intimacy, whose demarcation line is blur by its own nature. Familism has an inclination to approach public arena from the extension of private one. It prefers ascriptive relations rather than contractual ones and thereby, paternalism rather than rationalism. It tries to interpret official relations from the perspective of primary relations such as kinship. school ties, and regionalism. Such a high reliance on nepotism has turned familism into a tool to maximize one's own private interest as they go through dynamic industrialization and modernization process. As a political scientist asserts "*neo familism*" was given a birth as a strategic response to survive and to overcome extreme confusion of personal identity arising in the turbulent modernization process. Neo familism is an outcome of the framework of familism extended to outer social network.

Such Neo familism contributes a lot to the deepening of segregation of the society on the bases of regional ties, generation gap, ideological stance, and labor-management relations. In the process of modernization, there was a regionally biased accumulation of capital due to geographical conditions. Korea was exposed to Western society through Japan who tried to establish an inroad into the Korean peninsula to exploit effectively. The south eastern part of the peninsula was enforced to open to Japan prior to the other part since it is located nearer to Japan. As a natural outcome of exploitation process, the south eastern part has accumulated capital faster than the others. Meanwhile the south western part has become neglected from industrialization process which was the base of agricultural products. Such an imbalanced economic development between two regions has triggered a regional rivalry sentiment and they become to tribute almost blind loyalty to the politicians from the political parties symbolizing regional sentiment respectively. They become to identify the political parties from the perspective of family ties.

Quite similar situation is taking place in ideological confrontation between conservative bloc and progressive one. The brutality experienced during the Korean War left the people with incurable scars. Since it was a civil war triggered by North Korea who tried to establish socialist regime in the South, it is not surprising to see the general public in the South respond to any non conservative ideology in a rather unusual manner. In addition to that, in the process of modernization and industrialization of the country, they produced two rivalry groups of people. Those who led the industrialization process and economic prosperity have become a strong hold of conservative ideology meanwhile those fought for democratization, that of progressive ideology claiming moral superiority over the conservatives. Such confrontational relation between the two blocs has been hardened by the sense of Neo familism which claims for family like ties respectively. Neo familism aggrandizes confrontation by adding emotional touch among the bloc members.

The relationship between labor and management is also very hostile each other and enjoys a very strong ties among the members of the blocs respectively since they approach to the relationship from the perspective of Neo familism. As you might well know, Korean government adopted an imbalanced development strategy to rapidly boost Korean economy by providing exclusive favor to handful of business leaders, which have become major conglomerates of Korea today. Labor union leaders believe the accumulation of wealth has been available since the government intervened into the relationship between labor and management by force and gave landslide favor to management. In other words, they do not believe in the legitimacy of wealth accumulated by the capitalists and count it as an outcome of sacrifices by the labor immorally mobilized. And such a perspective is fortified by the framework of Neo familism.

There is a deep generation gap between the younger generations in their 20s, 30s and 40s and the older generations of 50s, 60s, and more. The younger generations are exposed to information society more widely and deeply. They have grown up while the Korean economy booms up. They have been nurtured in a relatively affluent environment. However, now they are experiencing real difficulties in finding jobs together with the shrinking economy and widening gap between the haves and the have-nots. Meanwhile, the older generations are relatively less exposed to information society yet. They have experienced real turbulences of modern history of Korea as like chronic poverty, the Korean War, political unrests, and even brutal oppression by the government. They have remained in labor market until recently while the market expands along side with the booming economy. It is not surprising when they have nurtured different world views and value systems. The former declines to progressive ideology meanwhile the latter conservative one.

As like the above mentioned, Neo familism in Korean society has played a really critical role in exaggerating the cleavages and segregating into the rivalry blocs in multi-dimensions. In such complex segregations, it becomes really hard to build consensus and reach out for compromise. It is not unusual that democratic institutions would not work well and produce infertile outcomes in such a context.

IV. Criticisms and Dissatisfaction

Le Banquet: What is your assessment of political phenomena like the movement that was launched by Ahn Chol-Soo or the successes of Seoul's Mayor, Park Won-Soon?

P. J.-C.: When you view the inner mind of general public in Korea, you will easily find that they are strongly looking for alternative to the established politics. According to a poll's result released a year ago, only 5.4 percent of Koreans trust National Assembly and 18.6 percent favor the executive. Another poll shows us that 64 percent of the people do not commit to any political parties. Such extreme dissatisfaction to the established politics is the major source of supports to Ahn Chol-Soo. It is a kind of explosive expression that they cannot tolerate contemporary Korean politics any longer. In that sense, you could be reminded of Parotism appeared in 1992 presidential election in U.S.A. Political popularity of Ahn Chol-Soo does not owe much to his personal cult or charisma but people simply took him as an icon to symbolize their strong aspiration for "new politics". Such recognition of problems pending in the contemporary Korean politics does not stem from simple displeasure to moral hazard or corruption or inability of the individual politicians but is drawn from far deeper frustration to the contemporary political system. They believe there is no way but to change paradigm of contemporary politics of Korea from palace intrigue typed power struggle among the political leaders to normal state of democracy seeking for the consensus to maximize the interests of general public.

They are looking for normalization of Korean politics. But what do they mean by normal sate of politics? It is very clear and obvious that the cultural and structural legacies of Korea do not fit well with Newtonian democracy. It has been told that we have to change or develop cultural and structural conditions to run the democracy more smoothly. It is still a very persuasive observation. After the advent of information society, however, they began to think about legitimacy of Newtonian democracy itself. In such drastically changed Korean society, we may need different version of governing system for more effective operation and more appealing responses to their needs and demands. Actually the Newtonian democracy model was designed or evolved in the process of industrialization as a natural response to the social needs arising by that time. Now, Korea has entered into information society and plays a leading role there in the global community. Without coining new designs of politics matching well to information society, we cannot salvage inability of Korean politics and frustrations of the general public. That is what they come to think about. With indirect democratic system, we cannot respond to the needs of the contemporary society which is highly complicated, changes rapidly, goes over the national boundaries, and very fluid. Instinctive recognition of such a need for new governing design, I believe, has drawn peoples' attention to Ahn Chol-Soo, who is taken as Steven Jobs in Korea by general public due to his professional achievement in IT industry and free sharing of vaccine programs developed by him.

Le Banquet: One says also that they are actually less engaged, vibrant and ready to be involved in, let us say, something like a revolution. Of course, it could be the result of the democracy since they don't need to fight dictatorship. However, it could be the consequence of another phenomenon, usually depicted as de-politicization. How do you analyze it?

P. J.-C.: We are in the middle of drastic change of human cultural history. They are highly disappointed with contemporary political system but at the loss of wisdom to alternate it with new one. They do believe we are in the process of paradigmatic change but do not know yet with what paradigm of governing system to alternate. New paradigm of governing system is yet to come. In such a situation, it is natural for the people to be very reluctant in aggressively agitating establishments. It is especially so when they become aware government is no longer a single most important alternative in solving social problems but opportunities for increased participation of people to the decision making process.

People has become smarter owing much to the advent of information society and they do not want to rely on frameworks developed outside of them knowing that in such rapidly changing world, any frameworks developed outside could not respond to the instantaneously out breaking needs of the society precisely and speedily. That is one of the reasons why we call contemporary society as that of the end of ideology. As such mass party systems could not function as they did in the past neither. Further fragmented interests of people could not easily be articulated into simple division of capital and labor. The role of political parties to transmit information from local to central is also challenged by many self initiated communication tools as like internet, SNS, and U-tube. The monopoly of communication role of political information by political parties is now strongly challenged. Majoritarianism, which has long been treated as a golden rule in decision making, is also challenged since de-massifying society becomes common and very hard to amass real majority.

As they become aware that the politics by themselves rather than by the delegates is the ultimate solution to the immobile contemporary politics, it becomes depoliticized in terms of not pressuring government directly but facilitating their own living politics in their own initiations. It is also very natural such a tendency is more vibrant among the younger generations as they are more exposed to information society. They have been nurtured when the country becomes affluent. Inglehart impact might also have worked for their de-politicization.

Le Banquet: If you had to make some forecasts about the future of Korea, what would they be for the fifteen or twenty years to come?

P. J.-C.: The political magnitude of Korea in the global community could be upgraded. There is plausibility that the Korean standard could be treated as a global one. Not simply because of the upgraded capability of Korea in both terms of economy and politics but because of the contextual change of the global community itself. Being situated at the leading edge of information society, there is no way but to lead frontier spirit in devising new way of responding to newly arising social needs. Deepening information society will, also, drastically change established global power structure which would not allow single apex but diffused power centers. As the magnitude of cyber community of the globe becomes upgraded where the territorial boundary of nation states becomes less meaningful, Korea could play better roles crossing over the conventional and territorial boundaries limiting its potentials and voices. It might have a possibility to be released further even from the impending threats from North Korea and pressures squared by the super powers surrounding Korean peninsula.

Interview in Seoul by Nicolas Tenzer

References

<Korean Books and Articles>

Ahn, Young-Sub. (1998). Behaviors and Reports by the Journalism about the Annual Auditing of the National Assembly. A paper delivered at a conference organized by the Korean Journalism Development Foundation. Press Center, Seoul.

Bill Drafting and Budget Office, Secretariate of the National Assembly. (1998). *Data Compilation on the Annual Auditing 1, 2.*

Central Election Management Commission. (1996). *A Comprehensive Report of the General Election for the National Assembly.* Seoul: Seyon Industry. 140.

Cho, Hee-Yeon. (2010). *Financial Crisis and the Nation as a Buffer.* In Park, Jai-Chang. ed., *Democracy in Korea and Civic Society.* Seoul: Arche.

Choi, Chang-Yerl. (2014.07.21.). Principle of Personnel Management, Emprise of Politics. *Hankookilbo*, <http://www.hankookilbo.

com/v/ 39d77c25c9014233951ae5b4c 166f57e>

Chung, Ho-Young. (2000). *Interpretation of the National Assembly Law.* Seoul: Bub-Mun Publishing. 614.

Chung, Chung-Kil. (1985). Policy Auditing : Concepts and Problems in the Process of Adaptation. *Quarterly Audit* 1:45-52.

Chung, Yong-Duck. (1985). Policy Auditing. *Quarterly Audit.* 1:40-44.

Citizen's Coalition for Economic Justice. (2013.06.25). Call for Effective Abolishing of Legislators' Privileges. <http://ccej.or.kr/index.php?document_srl=369021>

Digital News Team. (2014.08.01.). In Spite of Winning at the By-Election, Popularity Rate of Park Geun-Hae Is Still Low. *Pressian.* <http://news.khan.co.kr/kh_news/khan_art_view.html?artid=201408011625311& code=910100>

Good Travel. (2014). Good Travel. <http://www.goodtravel.kr/main.html>

Ha, Sun-Young. (2014.06.26.). Closed Session for Personal Lives and Open Session for Policies, Reform for Two Tracks. 2014.6.26. *Joongang Daily News.* <http://mnews.joins.com/news/article/Article.aspx?ctg=mobile_A1&total_id=15073750>

Her, Bum & Kim, Myung-Soo. (1998). *Application of Theories and Methods of Policy Evaluation to Auditing Process.* Seoul: Public Affairs Research Institute, Sungkyunkwan University.

Jeju Olle. (2014). Olle Travel. <http://www.goodtravel.kr/main.html>

Kang, Young-So. (1989). Measures to Reform the Settlement Bill Evaluation System of the National Assembly. In Kim, Kwang-Ung & Park, Dong-Su. eds. *The Legislature and the Executive. Seoul: Bub-Mun Publishing.* 654.

Kang, Joo-Hoon. (1996). A Study on Activation Strategies of Performance Auditing. *Audit Journal.* 1(1): 3-22.

Kho, Sung-Kuk. (1993), On the Road Towards Reform, Reorganization and Change in Situation, *Road of the Nation in the 21th Century.* 14 & 12.

Kim, Ewi-Keun. (2009). Climate Change and Tourism Policy of Jeju. Jeju Development Forum 30. Jeju Development Institute. Summer.

Kim, In., Lee, Eun-Ho., & Lee, Kyoung-Eun. (1985). The Specialization of the Standing Committee, In Park, Dong-Su. ed., *The Parliamentary and the Legislative Process.* Seoul: Bub-Mun Publishing. 399.

Kim, Jae-Il. (1992.04.02.). 14 Management Rules to Correct. *Sisa Journal.* 11.

Kim, Jin-Hyun.(2010). The Paradox of Democracy in Korea, In Park, Jai-Chang. ed., *Democracy in Korea and Civic Society.* Seoul: Arche.

Kim, Hang-Kyu. (1995). Ensuring Political Rationality in the Policy Making Process. *Korean Journal of Public Administration.* 29(3): 681-698.

Kim, Hyo-Jung. (1997). The Annual Auditing by the National Assembly as a Counter Balancing Mechanism to the Executive by the Legislature. *Legislative Politics Materials.* 24.

Kim, Hyun-Koo. (1989). Effective Linkage between the Annual Auditing of the National Assembly and the Auditing by the National Board of Audit. Public Affairs Research Institute, Sungkyunkwan University.

______________. (1996). Basic Directions and Tasks of the 1996 Year Annaul Auditing by the National Assembly. A paper delivered at the Seminar for the 1996 Year Regular Session of the National Assembly. September 1996. Members' Office

Building, Seoul.

________________. & Park, Joon. (1995). *Public Auditing.* Seoul: Daeyoungmoonhwasa.

Kim, Young-Kyun. (2010). To Reduce Natural Disaster in Asia and Pacific. < =ko&source=hp&q=%EC%A0%84+%EC%84%B8%EA%B3%84%EC%A7%80%EC%97%AD%EB%B3%84+%EC%9E%AC%ED%95%B4%ED%98%84%ED%99%A9&btnG=Google+%EA%B2%80%EC%83%89&gbv=2&rlz=1R2ADBF_koKR408&oq=%EC%A0%84+%EC%84%B8%EA%B3%84%EC%A7%80%EC%97%AD%EB%B3%84+%EC%9E%AC%ED%95%B4%ED%98%84%ED%99%A9&aq=f&aqi=&aql=&gs_sm=s&gs_upl=3743l9962l0l13411l28l27l0l21l21l0l294l1155l0.4.2l6l0>

Korea Democracy Foundation. (2012). Archive Document No. 00208383. 2012.8.20.

Korean National Assembly. (1998). Corrections and Treatments Items Requested as of the 1998 Year Annual Auditing by the National Assembly.

________________. (1998 a). Reports of 1998 Year Annual Auditing by the Committees.

Kwon, Oh-Don. (1997). Auditing System Reform to Upgrade Efficiency of the Audit : With Special Reference to Promoting National Competitiveness. *Audit Journal.* 2: 3-24.

________________. (1996). Performance Auditing and Auditing. *Job Education Material for Performance Auditing Course.* Seoul: Audit Education Board. 1-36.

Kwon, Young-Cherl. (2014.07.07.). Concurrent Job of Deputy Prime Minister for Economic Affairs with Legislators, Why Is It Controversial?. *No Cut News.* <http://m.nocutnews.co.kr/news/4054195>

Lee, Kye-Hyang. (1989). The Parliamentary Right of Inspection and Examination of the Administration: Issues and Suggestions. In Kim, Kwang-Ung & Park, Dong-Su. eds., *The Legislature and the Executive.* Seoul: Bub-Mun Publishing. 301-324.

Lee, Ki-Kon & Ahn, Byoung-Uk. (1989). The Parliamentary Right of Requiring the Submission of Information and Material. In Kim, Kwang-Ung & Park, Dong-Su. eds., *The Legislature and the Executive.* Seoul: Bub-Mun Publishing. 425.

Lee, Kwang-Jong. (1989). *Administrative Responsibility.* Seoul: Daeyoungmoonhwasa.

Lee, Kyung-Sub. (1994). Operation of performance Auditing. *Audit Journal*, 1: 45-53.

______________. & Kwon, Oh-Don. (1997). Approaches to Performance Auditing. *Job Education Material for Performance Auditing Course.* Seoul: Audit Education Board. 1-36.

Lee, Myung-Sun. (2014.08.01.). Lee Chul Hee Told Park Geun-Hae Era Is Over as a Matter of Reality. *Pressian.* <http://www.. pressian.com/news/article.html?no=118841>

Na, Ki-San. (1985). Role of the Executive in the Proecess of Examination and Correction of the Administrative Misconducts *Korean Journal of Public Administration,* 24(1): 277-316.

Na, Hyo-Woo. (2010). Travel Development Focused on Ethical Consumption. A Power Point Presentation at the 1st Policy Forum on Sustainable Tourism: Present and Future of Sustainable Tourism in and out of Korea. 10 September. Seoul, Korea.

National Assembly Steering Committee. (1992). *The Broadcasting System of the Parliament.* Seoul: Sung-Eun Publishing.

No, Hwa-Joon. (1985). Policy Evaluation and Policy Auditing. *Quarterly Audit.* 2: 29-35.

Oh, Moo-Keun. (1990). Role of the National Assembly in the

Process of Examination and Correction of the Administrative Misconducts. *Korean Journal of Public Administration.* 24(1): 317-400.

Our Buddhism. (2010.10.11.). Seminar on Temple Stay Development Held at National Assembly. <http://www.wooribulgyo.com/news_view.jsp?ncd=2999>

Park, Jai-Chang. (2014). *Political Reform 4.0.* Lee Books.

______________. (2010). ed., *Democracy in Korea and Civic Society.* Seoul: Arche.

Park, Dong-Suh., and Kim, Kwang-Woong. (1989). *The Legislature and the Executive.* Seoul: Bub-Mun Publishing.

Park, Jae-Wan. (1997). Productivity in the Public Sector and Rationalization of Public Auditing. In Choi, Kwang & Im, Joo-Young. eds., *Research on Improvement of Productivity in the Public Sector III.* Seoul: Korean Institute of Tax Policy. p. 125-283.

______________. (1997a). Social Efficacy and Costs of Public Auditing. *Korean Journal of Public Administration.* 6(2): 221-245.

Secretariate of the Korean National Assembly. (1999). *1998 Year Annual Audit Related Data Compilation.* 4-15.

Proceedings Bureau, Secretariate of the National Assembly. (1996). *Handbook on the Annual Auditing.*

Shin, Ji-Hong. (2014.06.30.). President Park Said to Make Extended Pool of Candidates to Government Offices. *Yonhapnews.* <http://www.yonhapnews.co.kr/ politics/2014/06/30/0501000000AKR20140630128200001.HTML>

Sin, Hyun-Jik. (1989). The Annual Auditing Power and the National Invenstigation Power. In Kim, Kwang-Ung & Park, Dong-Su. eds., *The Legislature and the Executive.* Seoul: Bub-Mun Publishing. 265-300.

<English Books and Articles>

Ackerberg, Igor & Prapasawudi, Parkpoon. (2009). An Analysis of Volunteer Tourism Using the Repertory Grid Technique (Master Degree Project No. 2009:65). University of Gothenberg, Sweden.

Addison, Maryse. (1979). Parliament on Camera. *The Listener,* 101(2602): 367.

Aldrich P, Daniel. (2011). Local Civil Society and Disaster Relief: The Role of Social Capital in Recovery. Proceedings of the 3rd International Forumon Disaster Relief, Civil Society and Global Solidarity, Seoul, Korea.

Alesina, Alberto., & Eliane La Ferrara. (2002). Who Trust Others?. *Journal of Public Economics*, 85: 207-234.

Almond, Gabriel., & Verba, Sydney. (1980). *The Civic Culture Revisited: An Analytic Study.* Boston: Little, Brown.

Antle, R. (1996). An Agency Model of Auditing. *Journal of Accounting Research*, 20.

Assimacopoulis, D. (2013). Climate Change Impacts on Tourism in the Mediterranian Region.<http://environ.chemeng.ntua.gr/en/UserFiles/files/04%20-%20Tourism%20v_3.pdf>

Bach, Stanley. (1981). Thoughts on Some Possible Effects of Permitting Television Coverage of Senate Floor Proceedings. *CRS Report*, 148.

Barton, Allen H. (1969). *Communities in Disaster: a Sociological Analysis of Collective Stress Situations.* Garden City, NY: Doubleday.

Barzelay, M. (1996). Performance Auditing and the New Public Management: Changing Roles and Strategies of Central Audit Institutions. *OECD. Performance Auditing and the Modernisation of Government.*

Baudrillard, J. (1998). *The Consumer Society: Myths and Structures.* London: Sage Publications.

Beck, U. (1992). *Risk Society: Toward a New Modernity.* London: Sage Publications.

Bellah, R.N., R. Madsen, W.M. Sullivan., A. Swidler., & S.M. Tipton. (2007). *Habits of the Heart.* 3rd ed. Berkeley: University of California Press.

Bijker, W. (1997). *Of Bicycles, Bakelites and Bulbs: Toward a Theory of Sociotechnical Change.* Cambridge, MA: MIT Press.

Bosley, Charles. (1977). Senate Communications with the Public. Commission on the Operation of the Senate, Washington D.C.: U.S. Government Printing Office.

Brown, Richard., & Ray Pethtel. (1974). A Matter of Facts: State Legislative Performance Auditing. *Public Administration Review,* 318-327.

Butcher, J. (2002). *The Moralization of Tourism: Sun, Sand -- and Saving the World?.* London: Routledge.

Caiden, Gerald E. (1982). *Public Administration.* 2nd ed. Calif.: Palisades Publishers. 92-93.

Collier, David., ed. (1979). *The New Authoritarianism in Latin America.* Princeton, N.J.: Princeton University Press. 41.

Cook, Timothy E. (1986). House Members as Newsmakers : The Effects of Televising Congress. *Legislative Studies Quarterly,* 11.

CNN Report. (2008.05.25). Candlelight Protest in South Korea and the Government's Violent Crackdown. <http://ireport.cnn.com/docs/DOC-26426>.

DaCosta, Elsa., & Sarah Turner. (2007). Negotiating Changing Livelihoods: The Sampan Dwellers of Tam Giang Lagoon. *Vietnam: Geoforum,* 38(1): 190-206.

Daivs, Dwight F. (1990). Do You Want a Performance Audit or a Program Evaluation? *Public Administration Review,* 50(1): 35-41.

Davidson, Roger H., & Walter J. Oleszek. (1976). "Adaptation and Consolidation: Structural Innovation in the U.S. House of Representatives," *Legislative Studies Quarterly*, 1: 38.

Dee, Thomas S. (2003). Are There Civic Returns to Education?. MA: National Bureau of Economic Research.

Diamond, Larry. (2005). Democracy, Development and Good Governance: The Inseparable Links. A paper delivered at Miaden Annual Democracy and Governance Lecture of the Ghana. Center for Democratic Development. British Council Hall, Accra, Ghana. March 2005.

Dirks, Nicholas B. (2012). Scholars, Spies and Global Studies. The Councile of Higher Education. <http://chronicla.com/article/Scholars-SpiesGlobal/133459/>.

DiMaggio., Paul., Eszter Hargitta., W. Russell Neuman., & John P. Robinson. (2001). Social Implication of the Internet. *Annual Review of Sociology*, 27: 307-36.

Dorling, D., & D. Ballas. (2008). Chapter 6: Spacial Division of Poverty and Wealth. In T. Ridges and S.R. Wright. eds., *Understanding Poverty, Wealth and Inequality : Policies and Prospects.* Bristol: Policy Process.

Dweck, Carol S. (2008). *Mindset : The New Psychology of Success.* Random House

Erikson, Karl T. (1976). *Everything in Its Path.* NY: Simon and Schuster.

Etzioni, A. (1967). Mixed-Scanning: A Third Approach to Decision-Making. *Public Administration Review*, 27: 385-386.

Featherstone, M. (1991). *Consumer Culture and Postmodernism.* London: Sage Publications.

Field, John, Tom Schuller, & Stephen Barron. (2000). *Social Capital: Critical Perspectives.* UK: Oxford University Press.

Frame, Mariko., & Khan, Haider A. (2007). Deep Democracy:

A Political and Social Economy Approach (CIRJE-F-469). University of Denver.

Freedom House. (2011). Freedom in the World Comparative and Historical Data/ Country Status by Region. <http://www.freedomhouse.org/template.cfm?page=439>

Geertz, Clifford. (2000). *The Interpretation of Cultures.* Basic Books (Paper Book).

Giddens, Anthony. (1984). *The Constitution of Society: Outline of the Theory of Structure.* Berkeley: University of California Press.

Gössling, Stefan. (2010). Tourism and Climate Change: Policies for Mitigation and Adaptation. A Paper Presented at Workshop on Sustainable Development Strategies and Tourism, 18 June. OECD, Paris.

Grumm, John G. (1979). A Theory of Legislative Reform. A Paper prepared for a delivery at the Moscow IPSA Congress of August 12-18, 3.

Guttentag, D. A. (2009). The Possible Negative Impacts of Volunteer Tourism. *Journal of Sustainable Tourism,* 15(5): 463-482.

Ha, Sun-Young and Kang, Jin-Kyu. (2014.06.27.). Speaker Seeks to Reform Hearings. *Korea Joong Ang Daily.* <http://koreajoongangdaily.joins.com/news/article/article.aspx?aid=2991234&cloc= joongangdaily%7Chome%7Cnewslist1>.

Harkin, M. (1995). Modernist Anthropology and Tourism of the Authentic. *Annals of Tourism Research,* 22(3): 650-670.

Hong, Sung-Chick and Lee, Young-Ho. (1976). Popular Perceptions of Political Leadership. In Suh, Dae-Sook and Lee, Chae-Jin eds., *Political Leadership in Korea.* University of Washington Press. 134-157.

Huntington, Samuel P. (1991). *The Third Wave: Democratization in the Late Twentieth Century.* Oklahoma: University of Oklahoma Press.

International Affairs Bureau of the New Korea Party. (1996). *A Handbook of the New Korea Party.* Seoul: Hyundai Co.

Jasper, James M. (2004). A Strategic Approach to Conflict Action: Looking for Agency in Social Movement Choices. *Mobilization: An International Journal,* 9(1): 1-16.

Jewell, Malcolm E., & Smuel C. Patterson. (1977). *The Legislative Process in the United States.* 3rd ed. N.Y.: Random House. 6-11.

Ji, Myung-Kil. (2014.06.29.). President Racing against Time to Win Back Support Ahead of July 30 By-Election. *Ariang News.* <http://www.youtube.com/watch?v=jWrM7kwtuWE>

Kahn, Matthew. (2005). The Death Toll from Natural Disasters: The Role of Income, Geography, and Institutions. *Review of Economics and Statistics,* 87(2): 271-84.

Kahn, Russel L. (2000). The Effect of Technological Innovation on Organizational Structure: Two Case Studies of the Effects of the Introduction of a New Technology on Informal Organizational Structures. *Journal of Business and Technical Communication,* 14: 328.

Kahne, Joseph. (2004). What Kind of Citizen? The Politics of Educating Democracy. *American Educational Research Journal.* Summer. 41(2).

Kennedy, Michael D. (2001). Globalizing Knowledge Through Area Studies. <http://quod.lib.umich.edu/j/jii/4750978.0009.107?rgn=main;view=fulltext>

Kooiman, Jan. (2003). *Governing as Governance.* L.A: Sage Publications.

Kotler, P and Andreason, A. R. (2000). Strategic Marketing for Non-Profit Organizations. In Baker, M.J. *Marketing Theory: A Student Text.* Cenagage Learning EMEA. 264-283.

Lyon, D. (1999). *Postmodernism.* Buckingham: Open University Press.

Maffesoli, M. (1997). The Return of Dionysos. In Sulkunen, P., Holmwood, J., Radner, H. and Schultze, G. eds., *Constructing the New Consumer Society.* N.Y.: St. Martins Press.

Manning, Preston. (1994). Obstacles and Opportunities for Parliamentary Reform, *Canadian Parliamentary Review,* 17(2): 2-5.

Marvin and Hedrick. (1974). GAO Helps Congress Evaluate Oversight. *Public Administration Review,* 36.

Maslow, Abraham H. (1970). *Motivation and Personality.* 2nd. ed. New York: Harper.

Miles, S. (1998). *Consumerism -- as a Way of Life.* London: Sage Publications..

Mishler, William and Rose, Richard. (2001). What are the Origins of Political Trust? Testing Institutional and Cultural Theories in Post-Communist Countries. *Comparative Political Science,* 34(1): 30-62.

Mishev, Plamen and Mochurova, Mikana. (2008). Climate Change Impacts on Tourism. A paper presented at International Conference on Global Environmental Change: Challenges to Science and Society in Southeastern Europe. 19 to 21 May. Sofia, Bulgaria

Moon, Ye-Bin. (2011.03.23.). 89 Percent of South Korean Adults Worry About Natural Disasters. *The Korea Herald.* <http://www.koreaherald.com/view.php?ud=20110322000954>

Mosher, Frederick C.(1967). *Governmental Reorganization: Cases and Commentary.* Indiana: Bobbs-Merrill.

Mustonen, Pekka. (2006). Postmodern Tourism -- Alternative Approaches (Sarja/Series A-2:2006). Turku School of Economics, Finland.

Newcomer. Kathryn E. (1994). Opportunities and Incentives for Improving Program Quality: Auditing and Evaluation. *Public Administration Review,* 54(2): 147-154.

Norris, Pippa. (2004). Deepening Democracy via E-Governance. The UN World Public Sector Report. Harvard University.

Nowaczek, A. (2010). Ecotourism: Principles and Practices. *Annals of Tourism Research,* 37(1): 270-271.

OECD. (1996). Performance Auditing and the Modernization of Government. Official Documents of the Secretariat of the NKP.

ÖMahony, Siobhan., & Stephen R. Barley. (1999). Do Digital Telecommunications Affect Work and Organizations? The State of Our Knowledge. *Research in Organizational Behavior,* 21: 125-61.

Ottawa Citizen. (1977.10.20.). TV in House: a Useful Tool. 6.

Orlikowski, Wanda., & Iacono. (1995). Shaping Electronic Communication: the Metastructuring of Technology in the Context of Use. *Organizational Science,* 6: 423-44.

Park, Dong-Suh and Lee, Chae-Jin. (1976). Bureaucratic Elites and Development Orientations. In Suh, Dae-Sook and Lee, Chae-Jin eds. *Political Leadership in Korea.* University of Washington Press. 91-133.

Park, Jai-Chang. (2012). Globalization and Challenges for New Social Order. *Responses to the Globalizing World.* Seoul: Lee Book.

______________. (1996). Confirmation Hearings for Appointees. *Korea Focus On Current Topics,* 4(6): 47-53.

Pattie, Charles, Seyd, Patrick and Whiteley, Paul. (2004). *Citizenship in Britain: Values, Participation and Democracy.* UK: Cambridge University Press.

Pedicini, Cary. (2008). Volunteering Australia: Submission to the Productivity Commission on the Contribution of the Not for Profit Sector. Melbourne: Volunteering Australia.

Poon, A. (1993). *Tourism, Technology and Competitive Strategies.*

Wallingford: CAB.

Portes, Alejandro. (1998). Social Capital: Its Origins and Applications in Modern Sociology. *Annual Review of Sociology,* 24: 1-24.

Putnam, R. (2000). *Bowling Alone: the Collapse and Revival of American Community.* New York: A Touchstone Book.

Rieselbach, Leroy N. (1978). *Legislative Reform.* Lexington, Mass.: Lexington Books.

Rutus, Steve. (1978). How Televised Floor Proceedings Might Afffect the House. *CRS Report.* 48.

Scheyvens, R. (2002). Backpacker Tourism and 3rd World Development. *Annals of Tourism Research,* 29(10): 144-164.

_______________. (2007). Exploring the Tourism --Poverty Nexus. In Hall, Michael. ed. *Pro-Poor Tourism: Who Benefits?.* Cleavdon: Channel View Publications.

Schick, Allen. (1976). Congress and the Details of Administration. *Public Administration Review,* 25: 526-551.

Scott, Daniel, Peeters, P. and Gössling, Stephan. (2010). Can Tourism Deliver Its "Aspirational" Greenhouse Gas Emission Reduction Targets?, *Journal of Sustainable Tourism.* 18(3). 394-408.

Scott, J. (2002). Social Class and Stratification in Lat Modernity. *Acta Sociologia,* 45: 23-25.

Seo, Ji-Eun. (2014.05.02.). Shipping Association Accused of Irregularities. *Korea Joong Ang Daily.* <http://koreajoongangdaily.joins.com/news/article/Article.aspx?aid=2988691>

Serrano, Helga., & Carranza, Pedro Humberto Armendariz. (2005). Community Based Tourism: An Ecuador Experience. In Rajan Solomon. ed. *Perspectives in Tourism 3.* Hong Kong: Ecumenical Colition on Tourism.

Shaw, L. Earl. (1977). A Prolegomenon to Responsible Legislative

Reform. *Policy Studies Journal,* 5(4): 396.

Sherraden, Margaret S., & Ellen Fox. (1997). The Great Flood of 1993: Response and Recovery in Five Communities. *Journal of Community Practice,* 4(3): 23-45.

Shin, Yong-Ho and Seo, Ji-Eun. (2014.04.24.). Disaster Sparks Calls for Major Changes in Korea. *Korea Joong Ang Daily.* <http://koreajoongangdaily.joins.com/news/article/ Article. aspx?aid=2988370>

Silk, Paul., & Rhodri Walters. (1987). *How Parliament Works.* London: Longman.

Smelser, Neil. (1969). *Theory of Collective Behaviour.* N.Y.: Free Press.

Stark, David. (2000). For a Sociology of Worth. A Paper presented at Santa Fe Institute Workshop on Heterarchies : Distributed Intelligence and the Organization of Diversity.

Sterner, Thomas. (2007). Fuel Taxes: an Important Instrument for Climate Policy. Energy Policy, 35(6). 3194-3202.

Streeter, Calvin L. (1991). Disasters and Development: Disaster Preparedness and Mitigation as an Essential Component of Development Planning. *Social Development Issues,* 13(3): 100-110.

Suresh, K. T. (2005). Democratizing Tourism: a Civil Society Call to Make Tourism Development Just. In Rajan Solomon. ed. *Perspectives in Tourism 1.* Hong Kong: Ecumenical Coalition on Tourism.

Szreter, Simon., & Michael Woolcok. (2004). Health by Association? Social Capital, Social Theory and the Political Economy of Public Health. *International Journal of Epidemiology,* 33: 650-667.

Tarrow, Sidney. (1994). *Power in Movement, Social Movements, Collective Action, and Mass Politics in the Modern State.*

Cambridge: Cambridge University Press.

Temple Stay Center. (2010). What is Temple Stay? <http://eng.templestay.com /contents/contents.asp?cid=7>

Tirole, J. (1986). Hierachies and Bureaucracies: On the Role of Collusion in Organizations. *Journal of Law, Economics, and Organizations*, 22: 181-213.

Thongma, Weerapon. (2009). Approaches for Developing Community Based Sustainable Tourism Products: Research for Development Approach. A paper delivered at the Workshop on YMCA Global Alternative Tourism Network. Asia and Pacific Alliance of YMCAs. Chiangmai, Thailand.

UNWTO. (2013). Making Travel and Tourism a More Effective Tool for Sustainable Development. A paper presented at the Sixth Meeting of Worldwide Air Transport Conference. 18 to 22 March. Montreal, Canada.

__________. (2007). World Tourism Organization, Tourism & Climate Change Confronting the Common Challenges UNWTO Preliminary Considerations. October.

__________ -UNEP-WMO. (2008). Climate Change and Tourism: Responding to Global Challenges.<http://www.unep.fr/shared/publications/pdf/WEBx0142xPA-ClimateChangeandTourismGlobalChallenges.pdf>

Urry, J. (2002). *The Tourist Gaze.* 2nd ed. London: Sage Publications.

Veblen, Thorstein. (2002). *The Theory of the Leisure Class.* McLean, Va: IndyPublish Com.

Wall, G., & Mathieson, A. (2006). *Tourism Change, Impacts and Opportunities.* Essex: Pearson Education Limited.

Walsh, Annmarie H. (1996). Performance Auditing and Legislative Oversight in the Context of Public Management Reform: the U.S. Experience. *OECD. Performance Auditing and the Modernisation of Government.*

Wang, N. (1999). Rethinking Authenticity in Tourism Experience. *Annals of Tourism Research*, 26(2): 349-370.

Wiktorowicz, Q. ed. (2004). *Islamic Activism: A Social Movement Theory Approach*. Bloomington, IN: Indiana University Press.

Woolcock, M. (1998). Social Capital and Economic Development: Toward a Theoretical Synthesis and Policy Framework. *Theory and Society*, 27(2): 151–208.

World Alliance of YMCAs. (2010). Work Book for 17th World Council of YMCAs. Hong Kong: YMCAs publishing.

World Travel and Tourism Council(WTTC). (2010). WTTC Forcasts Subdued Growth for 2010. <http://www.wttc.org/eng/Tourism_News/Press_Releases/Press_ Releases_2010/WTTC_Forecasts_Subdued_Growth_For_2010/>

Zakour, Michael J., & David F. Gillespie. (1999). Collaboration and Competition among Nonprofit and Governmental Organizations during Disasters. Zakour, Michael J., & David F. Gillespie. *Crossing the Borders: Collaboration and Competition among Nonprofits, Business and Government.* Alexandria, VA: Independent Sector. 495-506.

____________. & Evelyn B. Harrell. (2003). Access to Disaster Services: Social Work Interventions for Vulnerable Populations. *Journal of Social Service Research*, 30(2): 27-54.

Zussman, Tracy. (2007). ed., The Impact of Tourism on Climate Change: Does Tourism Add to Climate Change? <http://www.eldis.org/go/display&type= Document&id=43261#.VDcL1WAcTIU>

*** The chapters of this book are reprinted or revised from the following sources written by the author.**

Chapter 1: "Deepening of Democracy in Korea and Civic Education," A paper delivered at the Symposium on Beyond Society of Conflict: Civic Education for Sustainable Development, Asia-Pacific Forum on Civic Education, Emerald Hotel, Changwon, 2010.10.20. "Introduction: Deepening of Korean Democracy and Civil Society," In Park, Jai-Chang ed., (2010). *Democracy in Korea and Civil Society.* Seoul: Arche. (in Korean). "Theories of Democratization and Civic Education Strategies," In Park, Jai-Chang and Seliger, Bernhard J. eds., (2007). *Strategies and Issues of Democratic Civic Education.* Seoul: Oreum. (in Korean).

Chapter 2: "Korean Legislative Reform Directions and Issues: A Managerial Perspective," A paper delivered at the Symposium on Sustainable Development, Environmental Conditions and Public Management, National Institute for Research Advancement (NIRA) and National Academy of Public Administration, Keio University, Tokyo, 2002.07.26. Park, Jai-Chang. (2004). *Korean Legislative Reform.* Seoul: Oreum. (in Korean).

Chapter 3: "The Functional Locus of the Annual Auditing of the Executive by the Korean National Assembly," *International Review of Public Administration,* 4(2): 79-95. 1999. "Chapter 8: Operational Reality and Functional Locus of State Administration Inspection," In Park, Jai-Chang. (2003). *Korean Legislative Politics.* Seoul: Oreum. (in Korean).

Chapter 4: "Confirmation Hearings for Political Appointees," *Korea Focus On Current Topics,* 4(6): 47-53, 1996 11/12. "Il est ne'cessaire au re'former le syste'me des auditions parlementaires de Confirmation en Core'e," *Korea Analysis,* 4:

15-20. Paris: Asia Center. 2014.11.

Chapter 5: "Baseline Assessment of Korean Political Parties," A report delivered at the Project Meeting of Political Parties in Asia's New Democracies, National Democratic Institute(NDI) for International Affairs and Institute for National Policy Research, Taipei, Taiwan, 1997.03.04.

Chapter 6: "Negative Impact of E-Governance to NGOs: the Case of Korea National Council of YMCAs," A paper delivered at the 26th International Congress of Administrative Sciences, International Institute of Administrative Sciences, COEX, Seoul, 2004.07.17.

Chapter 7: "Mediating Alternative Tourism from the Perspective of Social Movement," A keynote address delivered at the Workshop on Pilgrimages in Search of Truth, Asia-Pacific Alliance of YMCAs, Lalitpur, Nepal, 2011.02.11. "Alternative Tourism for Social Movement," In Park, Jai-Chang ed., (2011). *Global Citizenship and Social Movement: A YMCA Perspective.* Hong Kong: World Alliance of YMCAs and Asia and Pacific Alliance of YMCAs.

Chapter 8: "Alternative Tourism as a Combat Instrument against Climate Change," A paper delivered at Conference on Climate Change, Asia and Pacific Alliance of YMCAs, Kuala Lumpur, Malaysia, 2014.10.24.

Chapter 9: "Disaster Relief and Social Capital: An Asian Perspective," A keynote address delivered at the 3rd International Forum on Disaster Relief, Civil Society and Global Solidarity, Korea Disaster Relief Association, Press Center, Seoul, 2010.07.13. "Disaster Relief and Social Capital: An Asian Perspective," *Korean Review of Crisis and Emergency Management.* 8(3): 235-248. 2012. "Disaster Relief and Accumulation of Social Capital," In Park, Jai-Chang. (2012). *Responses to the Globalizing World.*

Seoul: Lee Books.

Chapter 10: "Area Studies in HUFS: Retrospect 60 Years of Struggle and Prospect for the Centennial Anniversary," A keynote speech delivered at 60 Years of Foreign Studies, *Pro Centesimus Annus*, 60th Anniversary International Conference of Hankuk University of Foreign Studies, Seoul, 2014.11.07.

Chapter 11: "Political Life in Korea: Between Tradition and Information Society," Interview by Nicolas Tenzer, Editor of *Le Banquet,* Seoul, 2013.09.26.

About the Author

Park Jai-Chang is an Endowed Chair Professor at Hankuk University of Foreign Studies and was a dean of politics and law college at Sookmyung Women's University in Seoul.

Park, who earned his doctorate in Public Administration from the State University of New York at Albany, has served as president of major professional associations: Korean Association for Public Administration, Korean Association of NGO Studies, Association of International Area Studies of Korea. He was a Humboldt Foundation scholar at Free University of Berlin, Fulbright scholar at UC Berkeley, visiting professor at Doshisha University, visiting scholar at Chiang Mai Rajabjat University and a Congressional Fellow of the American Political Science Association.

He has led many civil society organizations as: president of the Ombudsman Forum, president of the Civil Society Forum, National Executive Board chairman of the Voters Association for Clean Election, co-president of the National Citizen's Alliance for Fair Election, and president of the Asian and Pacific Alliance of YMCAs. He has hosted several news commentary programs at four major radio broadcasting systems and contributed many columns to major daily newspapers in South Korea.

He co-chaired the Presidential Commission on Devolution Promotion for Local Authorities with the Prime Minister and chaired policy advisory committees at: the Ministry of Government Administration and Home Affairs, the Ministry of Environmental Affairs, the Korea Independent Commission against Corruption, the Ombudsman of Korea, and the Special Committee on Political Reform of the Ruling Saenuri Party.

He has authored and edited numerous scholarly books including Political Reform 4.0, National Remodeling in Governance Era, Reponses to the Globalizing World, Decentralization and Korean Civil Society, Global Citizenship and Social Movement, Korean Civil Society in Globalizing Era, Governance in Korea, Democracy in Korea and Civil Society, State and Citizen, Korean Civil Society in Crisis, Citizens' Participation and Governance, Global Citizenship and Global Governance, Strategies and Issues of Democratic Civic Education, Global Civil Society and Korean NGOs, Decentralization and Reform, Korean Legislative Administration, Korean Legislative Politics, Korean Digital Legislature, Korean Legislative Reform, Korean Legislative Ethics, and Legislative Staff in Korea.

New Governance

Issues and Challenges

by *Park Jai-Chang*

Copyright©2015 by HANKUK UNIVERSITY OF FOREIGN STUDIES KNOWLEDGE PRESS
All rights reserved. No reproduction, copy or transmission of this publication may be made without written permission.

First published 10 March, 2015
Published by HANKUK UNIVERSITY OF FOREIGN STUDIES KNOWLEDGE PRESS
107, Imun-ro, Dongdaemun-gu, Seoul 130-791, Korea
Tel. 82-2-2173-2495, Fax. 82-2-2173-3363
E-mail press@hufs.ac.kr
Online http://press.hufs.ac.kr

Design EwhanD&B T. 82-2-2254-4301
Print Hyunmun T. 82-31-902-1424

ISBN 978-89-7464-964-7 93350
Price 16,000 Won